To Dorothy and Ned

This is a collection
of some of the
clippings we _might_
have sent you!

with love
from

Penny, Nick
and the boys.

Christmas 88

ALL
THINGS
CONSIDERED

ALL
THINGS
CONSIDERED

BERNARD LEVIN

JONATHAN CAPE
THIRTY-TWO BEDFORD SQUARE
LONDON

First published 1988
Copyright © 1988 by Bernard Levin
Jonathan Cape Ltd, 32 Bedford Square, London WC1B 3EL

A CIP catalogue record for this book
is available from the British Library

ISBN 0 224 02589 9

Photoset by Rowland Phototypesetting Ltd
Bury St Edmunds, Suffolk
Printed in Great Britain by
Mackays of Chatham PLC, Chatham, Kent

Contents

Acknowledgments

THE CAST OF helpers and supporters whom I have been happy and grateful to acknowledge for many books past has finally changed. My very dear friend Sally Chichester, my assistant and secretary for eleven years, left my office in 1987; she carried with her my profoundest gratitude, good wishes and regrets. She has been succeeded by Catherine Tye, who has already made herself indispensable; the writing and compiling of this book was therefore done under the aegis of both of them, and to both of them I offer my thanks. I thank also Bel Mooney, Brian Inglis and Margaret van Hattem, for reading the proofs, and Oula Jones, of the Society of Indexers, for creating – and it *is* an act of creation, at least in her hands – the index. (She read the proofs too.) My gratitude to her is all the greater for the fact that it was one of the first indexes she had done on a computer, and I speak as one who has only just begun to come to terms with a green glass screen all too prone to bark 'No such command' at me. I am also most grateful to His Grace the Archbishop of Canterbury for permission to include the interview I did with him in March 1987, and to Mr Tony Harrison for permission to include passages from his poem *v*.

Introduction

THIS IS THE fifth volume that I have culled from my journalism, following *Taking Sides*, *Speaking Up*, *The Way We Live Now* and *In These Times*.* In the Introduction to the first of them, I referred light-heartedly to the suggestion, first adumbrated by Juvenal, that writing is neither an art nor a science, but a disease, to which he gave the name *scribendi cacoethes*. Anyone who has read all four of the Introductions to these anthologies will, I think, have noticed that I have been unable entirely to shake off the possibility that Juvenal was right; well, I have finally come, very far from light-heartedly, to the conclusion that he was. I am now certain that journalism, at any rate the kind I practise, is an addiction, as powerful in its grip as any of the more familiar drugs of dependence, though fortunately not so destructive. On the other hand, I do not know of any rehabilitation centre or technique of detoxification which offers addicts the hope of being released from their thrall; for that matter, there is no study of the aetiology of the disease. But it is no joke to those who suffer from it. Let me explain.

I have never been, or wanted to be, exclusively a reporter, a specialist writer, a foreign correspondent, or any other variety of journalist with a defined 'beat' to cover. Though I have been a Parliamentary correspondent and a theatre critic, I have always made sure that my regular labours were matched by additional work of a wholly different kind elsewhere. I could rationalize this as a reluctance to be type-cast and thus stuck

---

* All published by Jonathan Cape.

with only one professional interest; it has also been handy in providing me with two incomes rather than the more usual one. But behind the explanations lies the truth. The only thing I have ever wanted to do with a pen, a typewriter or – now – a word-processor, is to say what I think about anything at all that takes my fancy. Odd.

At one time, I was regularly writing four long articles a week; how (and why) that ended I have described in *The Way We Live Now*. But not long ago, I astonished the Editor of *The Times* by telling him that throughout the years in which I fought all four blades of the windmill every seven days, the only professional problem I *never* experienced, not even on a single occasion, was a shortage of subjects to write about.

Nihil humanum . . . But it was more than that. I am, indeed, interested in a very wide range of things and ideas, and the list grows longer, not shorter, all the time. Yet the clue lies not in that fact, but buried deep in the addictive need for expression. That urge is, of course, what drives the artist; I am not an artist (no journalist is, and I have never met one who would argue otherwise), but the feeling that I must write or burst is presumably very similar to that which moves the true creators. (*Their* addiction comes presumably from a sense, however unarticulated, that they have a duty to create, a suspicion that that is why they were born. I recently read a huge volume of the letters of Richard Wagner;* I already knew a great deal about him and his music, to which I am addicted far more profoundly and helplessly than I am to writing for a living, but even so I was as astounded as I was repelled at the lengths, and depths, to which he would go, and the rebuffs, setbacks and failures he was willing to endure, in order to give an ungrateful world the fruits of his genius.)

Before I sum up the theory of my addiction, there is one more mechanistic explanation of it which, though it will be instantly recognized by any journalist reading these words,

* *Selected Letters of Richard Wagner* (edited and translated by Stewart Spencer and Barry Millington), Dent, 1987.

will be thought a contrived paradox by those outside the profession. Successful journalists are by nature lazy; certainly I am. We overwork because we know that if we don't, we shall rapidly fall into total sloth, leading to failure. The outward sign of this truth is the extraordinary lengths to which journalists will go to prevent themselves starting to write until the very last possible moment. I achieved my own record in this recondite practice when I was a theatre critic for a daily paper, and therefore writing my review immediately after the curtain came down. The time I had at my disposal when I arrived at the office was, of course, governed by how long the play had been, and also by the edition-time for the page my words were to appear in, both of which naturally varied from night to night. But I had an early run of evenings which, because of those two factors, allowed me only 25 minutes to write my notice. From then on, having discovered that I could manage the feat in that span, I would, whenever I had a longer span available, deliberately – or at any rate uncontrollably – waste anything up to half an hour in drinking coffee, eating digestive biscuits and distracting my colleagues, until the magic moment arrived, 25 minutes before deadline, when I would sit down and write. To stave off the conviction that I must be mad, I persuaded myself that the wasted time was not wasted at all, but that my article was gestating in my subconscious, ready to pour out in a single sustained flow as soon as I started. Lies, all lies.

After I returned to journalism following the immense sabbatical I took in the early 1980s, I deliberately cut my output to one regular column a week, together with an irregular series of book reviews, and felt extremely pleased with myself. Alas, the feeling proved to be no more than the refreshing and invigorating results of my 18 months off duty, and I soon began to itch for more words. I erected a line of defence in the form of a *weekly* book review feature (all novels), but I chafed under the inevitable restrictions of the review form, tied as it obviously had to be to the nature and quality of the book under consideration, and gradually I found that ideas for articles came crowding in, their number and variety far too great to be accommodated in a weekly column; the result was an agreement to write twice a week instead of once, and shortly before this book went to press, I embarked on the new regimen. Why?

Why does the heroin addict stick a needle in his arm? For the same reason, though thank God not with the same effect, that I, having read or heard or seen or thought something which interested me, would sit down and write about it. There is no logical connection between the two halves of that sentence, any more than between the two halves of the question. But a guess may be in order.

Middle age is a great provoker of thought, not all of it consisting of intimations of mortality. I am not so foolish – at least I *think* I am not – as to believe that if I write and publish enough words some of them will survive for the edification of future ages. (I found a permanent cure for that fond delusion some years ago, when I had a tour of the underworld, in the form of the British Library stacks. 'If you want anything looked up,' murmured the Virgil at my elbow, 'don't hesitate to ring – we've got eight million books here, you know.') But, as any journalist will confirm, it is impossible to compose in one's head; there must be paper (or, at the least, a green glass screen) to put the words on. I write, then, as an equivalent of thinking, and the increasing urgency to make sense of my thoughts is a reflection of my knowledge that time is, if not running out, at least not as ample as it used to be. I have said that the increasing hold which Mozart has on me is explained by my need to understand what he is telling me, lest I should die before I have understood, and thus render my death meaningless; in this volume there is my usual variety of themes, probably no fewer than in its four predecessors, but it is likely that regular readers will sense an extra ingredient in many of the items I have included, and if so, it must be derived from my growing inquisitiveness about life and what it means, if anything. But the only thing of which I am now absolutely certain is that it does mean something.

It is to me a never-ending source of amazement that so many people – educated, thoughtful, concerned – not only refuse to think about such matters, but think me very odd indeed for doing so. Read 'That dare not speak its name' (p. 217) for some of the implications of this extraordinary state of affairs and 'Jesus Christ Superstar' (p. 136) for a direct comment upon it. (But try also 'Applaud with the Lord' (p. 227) for a more encouraging view.) Some of the people I have in mind, who include some of my dearest friends, have an even odder approach; they think it is permissible, though eccentric, for me to think such things – *amicitia vincit omnia* – but quite beyond the bounds even of friendship for me to express them in print.

Now *I* think that if a man with a brief to write twice a week about anything he chooses decides to shut off discussion of the most important thing he thinks about, which is also the most important thing in the universe, he might as well retire, pausing only, like Faustus, to promise that he will burn his books. (And, incidentally, a fat lot of good his promise was to Faustus.) For there is surely no harm in looking, and much less in finding.

Enough of this autobiography; for a man who has repeatedly sworn never to write one, I seem to be hovering pretty close to a broken promise. Incidentally, I have frequently been asked, by friends, readers and publishers, why I have not written the story of my life and refuse to do so. Although the answer is extremely uninteresting, I may as well give it here and finish with the matter.

There are two reasons, each of which is independently conclusive. First, I haven't done anything. I have never been in prison or a war, I have never held any public office, I have never been anybody's *eminence grise* (*bête noire* is another matter), I have crossed neither the Sahara on roller-skates nor the Atlantic on water-skis, I have never found a cure for any otherwise fatal disease nor achieved by my eloquent pleading the acquittal of vast numbers of ruthless murderers; as far as I can recall, I have never even married Elizabeth Taylor. Even professionally, as I have just made clear, I have done nothing but sit on a comfortable chair and type; the exposure of scandal and the pursuit of revolutions have never tempted me.

The other reason is even more powerful a deterrent to autobiography. As a bachelor, I have found, not surprisingly, that the relationships with the women who have shared my life have been the most important element in that life, not merely in the happiness I have thereby found (albeit never permanently), but even more in the understanding and growth that I have garnered in that eternally sunlit meadow. I believe – and here I speak from knowledge – that the only experience greater than being loved is loving; certainly I have found it so. It follows – at least it quite certainly does with me – that in no conceivable circumstances would I expose to the public gaze my journeys through human love, and I am regularly appalled at the amount of kiss-and-tell in contemporary autobiography, when the former partner may still be alive and happily married to someone other than the autobiographer. Even friendship, which has been second only to love as the mainstay of my life, I have been willing to write about only in general terms. The consequence is that all the autobiography I shall ever write I have already written, in my book *Enthusiasms*, which records – though even that with very considerable discretion – some of the matter of my childhood and youth. And that is enough of that, and possibly too much.

The winnowing process involved in compiling these anthologies every other year always provides me with a remarkable aerial view of the state of the nation, though an inevitably foreshortened one; as I go through the sheaves of my articles, those which I do not select for preservation in volume form are just as useful for measuring progress or regress as the ones which I allow to survive. Taking both together, what do I now feel about the themes and variations I have played?

Cautious pessimism, I think. Take 'Gay go up and gay go down' (p. 26) and 'Who goes there?' (p. 204); each records a dismal tale of intolerance, respectively social and legal. Intolerance, to be sure, is an ineradicable weed in the garden of humanity, but in many respects it has shrunk over the years, and it is sad to see it, refreshed with the rain of a spurious necessity, growing again. The new campaign against homosexuals – and the word campaign is by no means too strong – may have started, as I suggest, with the truly dreadful Aids pandemic, but it has been strengthened and made more cruel by a growing revulsion from and contempt for homosexuals as such, after many years of increasing understanding and acceptance. The abolition of the peremptory challenge of a juror by a defendant on a criminal charge may be thought a trivial matter (though I do not think it so), but it typifies the growing harshness of the legal process (again, after years in which it had grown more humane) and, even more, the growing demand for even more harshness; hardly a week goes by without strident demands for longer prison sentences, despite the enormous quantity of evidence that longer sentences have no discernible effect on the crime rate. As I write this, the proposal to restore to the Court of Appeal the right to increase a sentence imposed in a lower court is still under discussion; by the time this book is published it may be law, and another advance will have been turned into a reverse.

My readers are familiar with accounts of injustice perpetrated in lands without the benefit of democracy; 'To be a pilgrim' (p. 162) is yet another such story, though a particularly poignant one. It has not come to that yet in Britain, and it is inconceivable that we could ever arrive at such a state of affairs. Yet injustice, in a country like ours, can be defined as a falling away from the highest standards, and even a slight decline is significant and ominous, quite apart from the fact that slight declines tend to become less slight. Thomas Mann said of himself once, 'I am a man of balance; when the boat threatens to capsize on the right I lean to the left, and when it looks like capsizing on the left I lean to the right.' Well, nobody could call me a man of balance; whatever may be thought about the opinions I express, they are unlikely to be classified as ambiguous. But Mann's metaphor is an apt one. For many years – I suppose up to the late 1960s and early

1970s – I leaned to the left in matters of liberty and authority, because it seemed to me that if the boat were to capsize it would do so on the right. Gradually, I began to feel that I was leaning the wrong way; the authoritarian streak on the left, now heavily reinforced by those for whom authoritarian attitudes were inadequate and only real totalitarianism would suffice, led to my crossing the boat. I would not go so far as to say that I am now tempted to cross back to the other side, even if only because the totalitarianism within the left has not been eradicated or even diminished; but if the boat shows no sign of turning over, it certainly seems to be rocking rather more than the choppiness of the sea would warrant.

I see no incompatibility in my unease at this trend and my continuing resistance to (I believe I coined the term) the Nanny State. 'People eating is wrong' (p. 35) seems to me to sum up the authoritarian tendencies of the left, which are invariably based on the conviction that some people, presumably gifted with special powers of observation and analysis, know better than the rest of us what is good for us – know better, that is, than we know ourselves. That attitude is so deeply ingrained on the left that it seems almost genetic in its origin, but the more recent stirrings on the right have, I believe, a more interesting provenance.

The present government, or at least its leader, came into office determined first to halt, and then to reverse, Britain's economic decline. Mrs Thatcher identified the cause of that decline (which by the time she came into office had been going on for something like a quarter of a century) as the desperate lack of competition, which, as she saw it, furnished not only the complacency which had led to the decline, and was constantly accelerating it, but a widespread belief, in every field from industrial production to welfare, that there must be no penalty for failure, and indeed no admission that there had been any failure, or even that such a thing existed.

I don't like the word 'corporatism', if only because it is almost impossible to define satisfactorily. But whatever it means, it was Mrs Thatcher's villain, just as her hero was independence. She set herself, with the enthusiastic support of some of her Ministers, the nervous and lukewarm support of others, and the silent hostility of still others, to make self-sufficient not just the country's economic endeavours but the people of the country as well. By the time she started on this extraordinary crusade, the habit of relying on others had become so deeply embedded in the national consciousness that even many who would have dearly loved her to succeed felt that it was impossible for her to do so. The strength of the attitude she was challenging may be gauged by 'Kindly take the blame' (p. 251) and 'The meat pie and the taxi' (p. 119), and remember that those articles were written when she had already been in office for seven or eight years. Her truly radical policies are, I believe, the only hope this country has of surviving economically and as individuals, but it cannot be denied that the terrain we have to cross to get to the promised land is a bleak and unwelcoming no man's land. You cannot have a revolution – and what she has set out to do deserves the word – without upsetting a lot of people who see no reason why the old ways cannot continue for ever. I cannot remember who stated it, but there is a socio-political law which runs: Any change will please some people and displease others, but the people who are pleased will be less pleased than the people who are displeased are displeased. And I believe that much of my disquiet at some of the present government's actions in the field of liberty is based on the fact that we do now live in a harsher world; it is true that the infinitely benevolent one we thought we were living in did not exist, but that only made the awakening more rude.

The increasingly lunatic actions of the government throughout 1987 (which as I write look like continuing all through 1988) in respect of what began as the *Spycatcher* affair, suggest that if there is any intention of making us less free, it is being carried out by people who have no idea at all of how to do the job. (The high point of the absurdity was reached when the British government declared that certain things said in Britain were false, but that when the same things were said in

Australia they were true.) I wrote little about the government's morbid and insatiable hunger for more secrecy, because I had little to add to what was being said on every hand; but it did, and does, increase my disquiet.

Two or three of these anthologies ago, I expressed a different kind of disquiet. There has always been violent crime, hooliganism and vandalism; there is a continuing debate as to whether our time is more violent than earlier ages. But I felt that there were certain *kinds* of violence in our society which, though they had precedents, were being seen at a level and frequency that was truly new. I listed some examples, one of which was as follows:

> . . . a youth, disturbed by the seventy-nine-year-old woman tenant of a house he has broken into, knocks her down and, before making his escape, pauses to stamp on her face; when she is found, his boot-print is clearly visible there.

I thought that that was as far as matters could be taken, but I was wrong; in the last couple of years there have been a substantial number of cases in which women in their seventies and eighties have been not only kicked and beaten, but raped. Another development which I could hardly have foreseen is the present practice of gangs of robbers, and sometimes gangs quite uninterested in robbery, of maiming their victims with knives, even when no resistance has been offered; for some reason (*what* reason neither I nor anybody else can even guess) this particular form of savagery seems to be the province of very young criminals, some of whom, not content with the hand-to-hand fighting they indulge in at football matches, make the slashing of rival supporters a regular custom. It does sometimes seem that mere anarchy *is* loosed upon the world.

Perhaps that is the inevitable fate of any country in a time of transition. Yet transition is itself the inevitable fate of any country at any time; there have been civilizations, such as the ancient Egyptian one, which did apparently remain static for many centuries, but no such stasis would be possible in a world as interdependent and dangerous to live in as ours. All the same, there are periods when the rate of change has itself accelerated, and in Britain, in the last few years, it has accelerated very sharply. Change tends to disturb; absolute change disturbs absolutely. It used to be fashionable to maintain that the violence and instability so marked in our society, and particularly among the young, was caused by a desperate uncertainty about the future, with the ever-present threat of nuclear annihilation; I have never believed it, and have always noticed that those who most loudly proclaim that they are unable to eat, let alone sleep, for worrying about the Bomb can be regularly seen tucking into a substantial meal with evident relish, and as regularly heard snoring a full and dreamless night away. I have returned to that theme in 'Bombs away' (p. 235), but critics of my view can legitimately challenge me to say, if it is not threat of the Bomb that eats away reason, what it is. I comfort myself with the knowledge that although I cannot answer the question, neither can anybody else.

There is, then, much to cause disquiet. And it is inevitable that one who, like me, chronicles our life and times, will tend to use more of the disquieting material which lies so copiously at hand than the more reassuring variety. This is not only a reflection of the fact that a headline reading 'Ten thousand aeroplanes land safely' will sell few copies of the newspaper. It is also, and more importantly, that the task of rebuking our political masters, when they deserve rebuke, is an essential one, whereas commending them is far less urgent, particularly since they spend an astonishing amount of time commending themselves. There are therefore few items in this collection designed to please any politician, let alone politicians in general, a partial exception being 'The price of everything' (p. 83); and that, after all, was published in the week of the General Election.

But anyone who reads this book will easily see where I turn for ultimate and unqualified solace. It is very difficult – at least I have always found it so – to write suitably in praise of a transcendent artistic experience; it is far too easy to gush, very difficult to convey to those who did not share the experience exactly what it consisted of. But 'See the conquering hero comes' (p. 190) and 'Man and music' (p. 258) attempt the feat. Neither of these essays simply gives an account of the film and the piano recitals, respectively, that it records; reviewers do that, and I have no need to. I find that what I instinctively do is to convey, or try to convey, what the experience was like apart from the contents of it. *Crocodile Dundee* and the music of Schubert played by Alfred Brendel have, on the face of it, little in common. But that is why I spend little time on the face of it. It is what they *mean* that matters, and what they mean is that beauty is truth, truth beauty. By that test, any work of art can be judged, or rather, anything that aspires to the condition of art can be tested for the true *stigmata*. For a work of art is, inevitably and for ever, more than the sum of its parts; that is how you know it.

In fact, that is the definition of art. But a man who claims that he has defined art, which is something that no one has been able to achieve in nearly thirty centuries of strenuous endeavour, had better shut up quickly before his less grandiose claims begin to come apart under scrutiny. With which cue I shall shut up, and let my pages speak for themselves.

March 1988   B.L.

Noises off

L AST WEEK, AN actor – an *actor* – was invited, on a public occasion, to express an opinion on a matter which involved political controversy, and refused to do so. Later, asked to explain his refusal, he said these memorable words: 'I have strong political views, but I like to keep them to myself.'

It can do no harm, and may do some good, to name this hero: he is Mr Paul Eddington, whose fame, as one of the two stars of 'Yes, Minister', should not be allowed to obscure the fact that he is a very good actor. It is not, however, for his talent that I come to praise him today, but for his reticence.

I do not know when, or how, the custom of regarding actors and actresses as political sages began; I suspect that it coincided with the rise of television to its now dominant place in entertainment. Before that, most stage actors were known to a minority only, and film ones were remote beings from another planet; when actors began to be found nightly in the homes of many *millions*, the line between illusion and reality began to blur, and for many it has now entirely vanished.

That does not in itself explain why, even if the public have come to believe that actors and actresses are real people, their political opinions should be eagerly canvassed and readily disseminated, let alone heeded. Mind, I have no objection to their views on political matters being *expressed*; an actor has as much right to sound off on site-value taxation, bond-washing, regional policy and South Atlantic fishing rights as anyone else. But no one is obliged to listen; how does it come about that so many apparently do?

Possibly it is an illusion, like the players themselves, and for all the attention paid by the journalists and broadcasters, nobody outside the ranks of Vanessa's Loonies and similar groups of groupies (see Macbeth's speech beginning 'Camorra, and camorra, and camorra') takes the slightest notice. I would like to think so, but presumably the attention paid to the mummers' opinions by the media must to some extent at least reflect the interests of the readers and viewers and listeners.

And it is worse than that; political parties, not all of them possessed by the belief that the world is flat and the moon made of green cheese, have taken to engaging performers for their party political broadcasts and election meetings, and these are expected not to sing or dance or juggle, or to speak the speech trippingly upon the tongue, but to express their political opinions and urge their audiences to adopt the same. Even the Tories, who would normally be expected to avoid such factitious shenanigans, once put up Jimmy Edwards for Parliament, as though there weren't enough clowns at Westminster already, and the Labour Party has for years been stuffing its electoral bandwagon full of Tuckets Without, Enter a Messenger and Third Citizen.

True, they came to grief recently, in the most delightful way, when Miss Anna Carteret (who is by no means the silliest actress in England, and one of the better, to boot) waxed fervent in support of Labour in a party political broadcast; the Labour Party's educational policy includes a promise to abolish all private schools, and the very next day Miss Carteret was found to be sending both her children to the very institutions her heroes would close down.

But the case of Miss Carteret and the other performers who extol the virtues of the Labour Party brings me to the heart of my objection. Forget about Vanessa; the Loonies are not in the business of endorsing somebody else's political product – they make their own. It is the actor or actress who is invited to speak on a recognized political platform who is the object of my curiosity.

For what is the hidden melody in a performer's political

performance? It is, surely, a massive *non sequitur*; the players are saying 'You like the way we act, or sing, or tell jokes, so kindly vote the way we tell you.' But their talent for acting, singing and joking, which is the only reason they have ever been heard of by the public, and thus the only reason they have been invited to play a political role, has nothing at all to do with an understanding of politics. Miss Carteret's longing for the Labour Party to govern the country (provided, perhaps, that she is excused actually having to suffer the effects of its rule) is obviously sincere; in that sense, she is not playing a part. But how does her acting talent qualify her to carry political conviction?

It doesn't. But it is not enough to say that although nobody is compelled to vote the way an actor tells them to, the actor is no *less* qualified to address the nation on the subject of his political views than a butcher, a baker or a candlestick-maker. If he were not a familiar figure on the screen he would never have received the invitation, as is clearly demonstrated by the fact that no such invitation goes to the butcher, the baker or the candlestick-maker.

But that brings me back to the first and most interesting question; how did we get to the point where the political opinions of actors and actresses began to be thought of in-trinsic interest? Practically all their expressions of political opinion, after all, whether on television talk-shows or in newspaper interviews, are of a stunning banality, couched in language so stale, weary and unprofitable that I would almost rather sit through a new play by David Hare. Yet they are deferred to, praised for the cogency and incisiveness of their views, and confidently – perhaps even rightly – expected to have influence. (So, as a matter of fact, is David Hare, and playwrights much worse than he, too. But that, though an even more grisly subject, cannot be dealt with today.)

I do not wish, though temptation is strong in me, to go back to the days when actors who got above themselves were liable to have their ears cut off and to be whipped through the streets at the cart's tail. (Mind you, I could name a few whose acting

would probably be improved by such treatment.) But I have
begun to despair of ever again finding an actor or actress
who has even read, let alone understood and committed to
memory, Hamlet's advice:

> And let those that play your clowns speak no more than is
> set down for them; for there be of them that will themselves
> laugh, to set on some quantity of barren spectators to laugh
> too, though in the mean time some necessary question of the
> play be then to be considered; that's villainous, and shows a
> most pitiful ambition in the fool that uses it.

So it does, too. But Mr Eddington has this day lit a candle
that shines like a good deed in a naughty world. For note: he
did not say, which would have been admirable enough, that he
had no political views to express; he insisted that he had such
views, and strong ones, too, but that he likes to keep them to
himself. Such an attitude, so boldly laid down, should be
properly commended; a knighthood for Mr Eddington would
not be too much, and for once the usual citation, 'for political
and public services', which normally means 'for being a servile
hack who supported anything his party did, however disgraceful, for more than 40 years', will be the literal truth. After
all, what more notable public service could a man do than to
refrain from talking about politics? Arise, Sir Paul; and the rest
of you, sit down.

The Times May 21st, 1986

Hard bargaining

A VERY SUCCESSFUL businessman of my acquaintance once told me that the only piece of advice ever given to him by his father (who had started and built up the business) was: 'Remember, there are no bargains.' My friend added that although that was the only counsel he had received from his father, he had never needed any other, and had based his approach to business upon the great principle enshrined in his father's words.

But you would be surprised (or not, depending on your view of human nature) how many people go through life, and often through the bankruptcy courts also, denying that immutable truth. The latest group to come a cropper from believing that in certain circumstances twice two, if spoken to nicely enough, will make five, are those who invested in buying what are called 'franchises', in this case from a company called La Mama, which found itself in the hands of the receiver. The buyer of a franchise buys the right to trade under someone else's trade name, normally in the form of a retail outlet; the financial burden and risk are assumed by the franchise purchaser, and he takes most of the profit, if any. In this case the if took precedence over the any, and the purchasers of La Mama franchises are bleakly contemplating the loss of large sums of money.

In a most sympathetic letter to this newspaper, Mr Robert Riding, who is the editor of *Franchise World*, a magazine devoted entirely to the practice of franchising, revealed that La Mama franchises were still being bought in the very month that saw the receiver installed, though by then, as Mr Riding said, 'the writing must have been clearly on the wall in the shops of the earlier franchisees'.

He also offered some practical advice to those contemplating the purchase of a franchise, advice which gave me goose-pimples to think that such elementary precautions as he was recommending ('Talk to existing franchisees – chosen by you, not the franchiser', and 'Those who buy in at the formative stage must realize that the risks are high', and 'Never take short-cuts in assessing a franchise') should have to be urged upon people thinking of parting with their life's savings, and be frequently, when urged, ignored.

I well remember the outbreak of a wheeze nicknamed 'pyramid selling'; over-simplifying, it could be described as a more elaborate form of franchising, but in this case it was obvious to even the greatest financial idiot in the land (me) that it not only *wouldn't* bring the predicted and longed-for riches, but that it *couldn't*.

Most of the pyramid-constructors were crooks; it is important to realize that most of the franchising companies, certainly including La Mama, are perfectly respectable firms, and that their business of selling franchises is entirely above board. *But there are no bargains.* In effect, franchise companies are shifting the risk inherent in any business from their own shoulders to those who buy their franchises. Should not that fact alone make a prospective purchaser realize that he is getting into water that may be too deep for him? Yes, it should; but it doesn't. And the reason it doesn't is the pathetic and ruinous belief that you *can* get something for nothing, that there *is* a crock of gold at the end of the rainbow, that if you give the stone another squeeze, just one more squeeze, it *will* drip blood.

Some years ago, there was a bearded sandwich-man who used to patrol Oxford Street with boards, fore and aft, bearing a legend which began with the striking claim, 'I won £163,000 on the football pools last year.' The sandwich-man was a very ragged, unkempt, heavily patched figure; without his boards, he would have been simply a tramp, and he occasioned much mirth as he went upon his errand, with its implausible announcement. Closer inspection of the message, however, revealed that it was not he who made the claim, but a man who had simply hired him to spread the word. And this man was selling his expert knowledge of how to win the pools to anyone who would stump up the fee for his regular weekly bulletin of advice.

And many did. Did *none* of them ask why, if he was such a dab hand with the Treble Chance, he should want to make a much more complicated living by selling his precious expertise to strangers? Why should he not simply win big every week, particularly since, in a *pari-mutuel* system like the pools, the more winners there are the less there is for each of them?

Christmas comes on the 25th of December, and *only* on the 25th of December. I am not going to turn strict moralist and talk about greed serving the greedy right; there are plenty of upright folk with a small nest-egg they would like to turn into a slightly bigger one, with which they could look forward to a slightly more comfortable old age. Invested wisely, the nest-egg might well steadily increase in size by a few per cent a year. What it will not do, however, merely by being invested in Consolidated South Sea Bubbles Ltd, is to increase overnight by 100 per cent, 200, 300, and those who allow themselves to think that it might, just this once (for the young man from Consolidated South Sea Bubbles was *so* confident, as well as charming), will end their old age with no nest egg at all, and probably not even any bubbles.

But that is not because the South Sea Bubbles man is a swindler, it is because there are no bargains. Many years ago, I came to the conclusion that I was not destined to earn any money, not so much as a bent *zloty*, except by writing words on pieces of paper, or speaking them aloud. The consequence is that I have no shares, no investments, no krugerrands, and oh my word, no franchises; even my surplus millions are accommodated in an ordinary bank, and I will not put myself to as much trouble as it would take to transfer some of them to a building society, though many experts, some of them knowing what they are talking about, insist that the building society would give me a better return.

The consequences are two; first, I must recognize that I cannot change my Rolls-Royce for a new one more than once every two or three years, or my yacht more than once every five; but second, I sleep soundly o'nights, with an innocent smile playing about my lips. And I willingly pay for the peace described in the second part of that syllogism with the grinding poverty implied by the first.

When the next wonder share gets into the headlines (whatever became of the Australian nickel-mine that turned out to be full of nothing but very rusty abandoned bicycles?) I shall not be found in the queue for it, and when those who buy it at £99 later sell it, looking bewildered, at fourpence a gross, I shall keep my own counsel, knowing that what brought them to their bewilderment was that they were not content to buy at 99 in the expectation of selling at 105, but must needs buy at 99 in the eager certainty that they would soon be selling at 877 on a still rising market. I am sorry for those who bought La Mama's franchises, but I must tell them that my friend's father was a wise man for telling his son that there are no bargains, and his son was a wise man for believing him.

The Times September 4th, 1986

All chiefs and no Indians

IN OFFERING MY view of the recent events in Fiji, I am embarrassed to admit that I was not at Sandhurst with Colonel Sitiveni Rabuka nor at Gray's Inn with Chief Justice Sir Timoci Quivanga. Clearly, it behoves me to be circumspect. Very well, circumspection it shall be; but it shall not be ambiguous circumspection. I therefore now state, with a conviction untouched by doubt, that if Colonel Rabuka succeeds in his aim of taking over Fiji, within three months he will have promoted himself general, and within six, field-marshal.*

You think I jest? Go read some history, anthropology or psychology; even geography would do at a pinch. For there is no reason to suppose that Colonel Rabuka is any different from the thousands of greedy brutes who, over the centuries, have decided that they would like to sit and feast at power's table – an item of furniture with a unique property, in that it has room for only one chair, which chair invariably stands at the table's head.

The Bisto Kids sniffed their enticing aroma with a passionate yearning, but the scent of power in the nostrils of the strong and unscrupulous is far headier, and those whose noses twitch at that rich scent are far more repulsive than any gourmand tucking his napkin into his collar before falling upon the roast sucking-pig, and far more dangerous, too.

We need not go back far to bag a couple of score. Without

---

* Shortly after this article appeared, he appointed himself Brigadier. Well, it's a start.

consulting a single reference-book, and leaving out Hitler, Stalin and Mao as *hors concours*, I can offer from our own time Castro and Tito and Ceausescu, Stroessner and Pinochet and Franco, Bokassa and Amin and Obote and Nkrumah and Machel and Doe and Sekou Touré and Gadaffi and Mobutu and indeed the rulers of practically every other state in Africa, and Kim Il Sung and the Ayatollahs and the Duvaliers and the Marcoses, and Perón and Pol Pot and Saddam Hussein and Assad, and – but the roll-call grows melancholy, and shows no sign of coming to a natural end.

You may have forgotten about the coup in Liberia which brought Master-Sergeant Doe (by all accounts a pretty thick one) to power. But anyone in Liberia who inspects Sarge's sleeve to see the insignia appropriate to his rank had better not smile when it cannot be found, because Sarge has gone up in the world and is now Commander-in-Chief, doubtless with a chest covered in medals cut out of a sardine-tin. For that matter, Bokassa appointed himself Emperor (it's a mercy he never appointed himself God), and I have always believed that much of Amin's bloodthirstiness derived from the frustration he felt at not being able to think of a military rank higher than field-marshal.

Not all of those who seize power and manage to hang on to their prize are murderous savages; Mobutu of Zaire, for instance, though his dictatorship is complete, spends much of his time in the comparatively harmless practice of transferring Zaire's national income to his Swiss bank accounts, and even the more brutal crimes of some of the others do not seem to be based on the paranoia inevitably attendant on an excess of power; Mr Mugabe, for instance, plainly murders the Matabele in thousands for reasons no more ideological than a desire to while away a dull afternoon in the rainy season. And some started out with genuinely good intentions; Marcos and Nkrumah for instance.

Yet much more often than not, those who seize power because they want it, and because they are strong and un-scrupulous enough to take it, are pursued in every waking hour and most sleeping ones by the terrible question 'Who shall usurp the usurpers?' All tyrants, from the least wicked to the bloodiest, devote – have to devote – unimaginable quantities of time and energy to watching their underlings, appointing spies to watch them further, appointing more spies to watch the spies (and still more to watch *them*), lest their own example should be emulated by their nearest and dearest, one night when there is no moon.

And I am convinced that the fancy titles they give themselves are meant for assurance; a sergeant does not feel as secure on his stolen throne as a Commander-in-Chief, though the throne is the same and the bum on it likewise. And remember that the present regime in Zaire was instituted by plain Colonel Joseph-Désiré Mobutu, but is now the fief of Marshal Mobutu Sésé Séko Kuku Ngbendu Wa Za Banga.

Most of us do not want power of this kind, and the sensible ones among us are very glad indeed that they don't. But for some men, who probably have the wrong number of chromosomes anyway, it is the only thing they want, and they want it so badly that they will commit the most terrible crimes to get it. Yet looking through the immense list of tyrants, ancient and modern, the student will inevitably be struck by the extraordinary paucity of any goal or purpose on the part of the usurpers. Hitler knew exactly what he wanted, which was to conquer the world and murder the Jews, and he had very considerable success in both ambitions, but in this he is exceptional; for most of the power-hungry the hunger is entirely self-contained.

Take the three most enduring personal dictatorships of modern times, those of Spain, Paraguay and Yugoslavia. Tito, as we learned on his death, had been for years looting his country for his own fortune; true, his vast riches were as nothing to the stuff Ceausescu and his relations have stolen in Romania, but in any case it is clear that becoming rich was incidental in his determination to keep absolute power. But what he wanted to keep absolute power *for* never became clear. And what is true of Tito is true of Franco and of Stroessner; for decades these three murderous thugs ruled – one of them still rules – millions of people, without showing any sign that their rule was intended to accomplish anything at all other than its continuance.

He who believes that Colonel Rabuka will be any different if he succeeds in establishing control over Fiji is probably still in the habit of staying awake on Christmas Eve in the hope of catching Father Christmas coming down the chimney. And he who, in addition, believes that the Colonel will long be content with that comparatively humble rank is also probably in the habit of looking under his pillow for the sixpence left by the tooth-fairy.

Blake knew:

> The strongest poison ever known
> Came from Caesar's laurel crown

But some, it seems, are immune to the poison, indeed demand huge bowls of it at breakfast every day. To be sure, they can spin excuses; Rabuka at present is playing the race card – there are too many Fijians of Indian descent. But if no Indian had ever set foot in Fiji, he would be announcing that only he can avert the frightful threat to the country's stability, prosperity and freedom posed by the crippling lack of Indians in the Fijian archipelago.

From what is known of Rabuka so far, his personal rule would probably be quite mild (at any rate to begin with). In any case, there is nothing that we in this country can do about it, and both the government and the Queen have made fools of themselves. Still, I hope that the Colonel is defeated. If not, expect a new Fijian general very soon; and one, moreover, who is driven about in a *very* large car.

The Times October 12th, 1987

Her name is legion

IT IS REPORTED from Nasa that evidence gathered by two Pioneer spacecraft powerfully suggests that the observed irregularities in the orbits of Uranus and Neptune can now be explained only by ꞏhe presence of a tenth, hitherto unknown, planet.

It was irregularities in the orbit of Neptune that first put astronomers on the track of Pluto. Its existence and orbit were worked out in 1930 by two American astronomers, and a third, studying a series of photographs of the part of the sky where the new planet was predicted, found it wandering about almost exactly where it was supposed to be.

'Wandering'; it wasn't wandering, of course, but following its allotted path. The ancients, who knew nothing of Pluto, or for that matter of Uranus, first seen in 1781, or Neptune, found in 1846, called the planets wanderers (that is what the word means) because they seemed to sail about the sky in a most scandalous manner, unlike the respectable 'fixed' stars. Yet by Shakespeare's day it was the exactitude of the planets' motions which was seen as the most striking thing about them. In the tremendous thunder of the 'order' speech in *Troilus and Cressida* (surely as close as Shakespeare ever got to an unambiguous statement of his credo) it is the planets that hold the universe together:

> The heavens themselves, the planets, and this centre
> Observe degree, priority and place,
> Insisture, course, proportion, season, form,
> Office and custom, in all line of order:

And therefore is the glorious planet Sol
In noble eminence enthron'd and spher'd
Amidst the other; whose med'cinable eye
Corrects the ill aspects of planets evil,
And posts, like the commandment of a king,
Sans check, to good and bad: but when the planets
In evil mixture to disorder wander,
What plagues, and what portents, what mutiny,
What raging of the sea, shaking of earth,
Commotion in the wind, frights, changes, horrors,
Divert and crack, rend and deracinate
The unity and married calm of states
Quite from their fixure . . .

Not only does Shakespeare here look to the planets for the
hoops of steel; he plainly accepts the heliocentric theory of the
universe ('. . . the glorious planet Sol/ In noble eminence
enthron'd and spher'd . . .'). Copernicus published his theory,
after many misgivings, in 1543, and there was no trouble;
indeed, he dedicated *De Revolutionibus* to Pope Paul III, who
was happy to accept it. The Copernican thesis was certainly
known in England, and so was the confirmatory work of
Kepler; it was only in 1616 that the theory was condemned
by Rome (though, ironically enough, it had been fiercely
denounced from the start by Luther). 1616 was when
Shakespeare died (he was, incidentally, born in the same year
as Galileo), but by then the Pope's writ had long since ceased
to run in England. There seems to be no book about
Shakespeare's cosmogony.

The ancients personified the planets, as they did the con-
stellations; some of the loveliest myths of the world relate to
the doings of the heavenly bodies. I do not find that at all surprising, but I am always astonished when I meet someone with
no interest in the stars, and positively astounded at dullards
who claim to feel no emotion when they look up at the night
sky; what *can* they be made of? (The dullards, not the stars.)

The poets know better; since poetry began, it has been used

to sing the glory of the heavens. Homer salutes Venus, and makes Ulysses steer by the Pleiades, Orion and the Great Bear; indeed, Calypso had warned him to keep the Bear on his left. Those unromantic Americans call the Bear the Big Dipper; well, we know it also as the Plough, but surely a plough is an object more suitable to mythology than a dipper, which is nothing but a tin ladle.

But a new planet! That is enough to stir the imagination of a door-knocker. Nor is the newcomer, it seems, only a grain or two of interstellar dust, like the asteroids (which are, strictly, planets); the Nasa scientists say that it has five times the mass of the Earth. Well, mass is not diameter, and if it is made out of that cosmic stuff of which the experts say that a teaspoonful would weigh uncountable millions of tons, it may prove a disappointment. But I am willing to bet on it; who would have thought that Saturn's rings were braided until Challenger passed by and saw? What would the ancients have given to know that wonderful and haunting fact? Have we no poet today to sing of Saturn's daughter and the beauty of her braided hair? (No, dear, Adrian Mitchell will *not* do.)

Those unromantic Americans are not as unromantic as it seems; just as the new planet swam into their ken, a Mr Jack Borden was propounding the very satisfying theory that star-gazing is good not only for the gazer but for the whole community. I am sure he is right, but he puts it in terms I would hardly dare to use: 'How many people who appreciate the beauty of the sky will ever mug a cashier?'

The heavens above us on a cloudless night make us catch our breath not only because of their beauty, but – even more – with the realization that there are more things in heaven and earth then are dreamt of in our philosophy. From wondering how the stars got there, and why, it is only a step to wondering how *we* got *here*, and again why.

But that brings me to the most important point. If there really is a tenth planet, and it is found, what shall we call it? There is a hideous danger that if it is left to Nasa it will be called CTD3194FH22G or, on the other hand, Ronnie.

I have nothing against either scientific precision or the president; but we can – we must – do better. First, we must insist that the new planet is female; *seven* of the present nine planets are male, and assuming that Earth is genderless, that leaves only Venus to uphold her sex. We can, of course, ransack mythology for an appropriate name, and indeed one springs immediately to mind: Proserpine was the wife of Pluto, and since Pluto is the planet most recently discovered, it might be fitting.

But I think we can be bolder; let us give the new orb a name of our own day. If we decide so to do, there is a name which conjures up beauty and tragedy together, as in all the greatest myths; it is a name which enshrines our age like a time-capsule buried beneath a new building, a name which in a real sense has entered into mythology. Her 36 years described a parabola, as she soared, loved by millions, to goddess-like heights, daring the sun to melt her wings, then plunged as steeply to earth, where there was now only darkness, failure, pain and a wretched death. Come; if there really is a new planet to grace the heavens, let it voyage among the stars to all eternity under the name of Marilyn.

The Times July 21st, 1987

Revenge is sour

THE GOVERNMENT RESHUFFLE has taken place, and nothing very astonishing has emerged from it. The least astonishing aspect of all is the continued exclusion from government or party office of Mr Cecil Parkinson; Miss Sarah Keays, with her fine sense of timing, has once again ensured that.

The ups and downs, ins and outs, rights and wrongs, truths and lies of the *affaire* Parkinson have been canvassed to extinction; I do not propose to go over the same well-tilled ground, though perhaps I may explain why not. As I said right at the start of the public side of the *affaire*, no one but the three people directly concerned, and possibly not even they, can really know what happened, what was meant to happen, what precise share of blame each of the parties should shoulder, what feelings were involved, what motives were at work. Miss Keays has had her say, and will no doubt continue to have it; Mr Parkinson has remained silent in public, and will no doubt continue to do so. The political consequences have been weighed and reweighed, and there is nothing more to be said about them until and unless they change.

I think, though, that there is one area which has, perhaps surprisingly, been almost entirely ignored, and it is that missing link which I want to discuss today. In order to clear the ground for it, I shall make some assumptions, which are not to be taken to represent my view but which are necessary if I am to be clearly understood. I assume, therefore, for the sake of the argument, that Miss Keays is *wholly* blameless and Mr Parkinson *wholly* at fault, that his behaviour was *entirely* conscious and callous, and that hers was *entirely* innocent and without artifice. What now?

Well, what *then* was that Miss Keays showed that she wanted her revenge, and that she took it; moreover, she is still taking it, and is apparently intent on continuing to take it indefinitely. Now from my premises, it follows that she is fully entitled to do so; she is an innocent betrayed, and her lover's conduct deserves the harshest available punishment, which in this case is the ruin of his political career. Serve him right.

The question I want to ask, however, is: though she may serve him right, should she? Should she extract from him the full toll of censure, ignominy and political extinction? Again, according to my assumptions she is doing no wrong in following such a course, and in any case she is entitled to argue that he is unfit for public office; but I want to tell her that it is possible to have the right to do harm to one who has caused harm, and indeed who may deserve to be harmed, yet to forgo that right, and that many centuries of accumulated wisdom suggest very strongly that that is the better course.

It does not lie in my mouth to remind Miss Keays of Christ's words on the subject of revenge, though I am tempted to quote them if only to draw attention to the wholly predictable silence of all the members of all the Christian hierarchies of Britain on any aspect of the Parkinson-Keays business, from the sternest comminations against adultery to the gentlest advocacy of forgiveness. But perhaps I may, without offending the Reverend Struckdumbs, offer her some Shakespeare, and urge her to consider joining that blessed company of 'they that have power to hurt, and will do none'.

The theme of mercy is extraordinarily strong in Shakespeare, and it is there almost invariably set in the framework I have laid out in my assumptions, taking the form of the renunciation of revenge even – indeed, mainly – on those who deserve vengeance. Shakespeare makes one of the reasons for this renunciation very explicit, in *The Merchant of Venice:*

Though justice be thy plea, consider this,
That in the course of justice none of us
Should see salvation. We do pray for mercy,
And that same prayer doth teach us all to render
The deeds of mercy.

If that will not serve, let me go on to *Measure for Measure* (the
only one of Shakespeare's plays, incidentally, with a title from
Christian scripture). The whole play culminates in a refusal to
exact vengeance, and the wronged Mariana (with whom Miss
Keays might well identify herself, pregnancy and all) has her
honour restored amid the general forgiveness. Scholars
have endlessly debated the meaning and symbolism of
that play, but there could hardly be a clearer statement
of Shakespeare's views on the subject of revenge than *The
Tempest*, which is both his swan-song and the play in which he
speaks more directly to the audience than ever before.
Shakespeare/Prospero, even as he prepares to renounce his
magic powers, renounces his revenge on those who trespassed
against him, and when Alonso speaks of pardon, he brushes it
aside:

There, sir, stop:
Let us not burden our remembrances
With a heaviness that's gone.

But it is in *Cymbeline* that he teaches most clearly the lesson
that Miss Keays has so far not learned. In all Shakespeare, there
is no man more grievously wronged than Posthumus, no man
more deserving of punishment at his victim's hands than
Iachimo. And when the knife is at the villain's throat, this is
what wronged innocence says:

Kneel not to me:
The power I have on you is to spare you;
The malice towards you to forgive you. Live,
And deal with others better.

None of that may impress Miss Keays; but it is only half of the argument, and the other half is more urgent even if less important. To forgive wrongdoing ennobles the forgiver, but she is entitled to reject nobility. What she cannot reject, whatever the case, based on his behaviour, against his return to office, are the inevitable consequences *for her* of continuing to thwart the man of whom she says that he is the only one she ever loved. If she does not learn now, she will learn far more terribly later that revenge is an acid, and that in the darkness of hate it eats away at the revenger, not at the revenger's enemy. I do not minimize the wrong she has suffered; indeed, my entire argument is based on recognition of that wrong. But to spend what is still, after all, a comparatively young life brooding over a wrong is the surest way to a terrible emptiness of spirit, and if she continues to clutch to her breast the dead past, she will lose both the living present and the unborn future.

If she cannot find it in her heart either to forgive Mr Parkinson or to forget him, she is moving inexorably to a hideously lonely old age, and long before she gets there she will discover that she can no longer turn back even if she wants to. She will also find that her vengeance ceases to give her even the shallow satisfaction which is all that vengeance *can* give, and she will then be left with nothing at all.

Suppose the worst; suppose that – perhaps after another election victory for the Conservatives – Mr Parkinson is restored to high office, that his career prospers, that his fall is forgotten, that everywhere he goes he is admired and applauded, which would she prefer then – to rock in her chair with misery when he appears on the television screen, successful, rich and handsome, or to smile at him strutting across his newly-restored political lands, and switch off?

At the moment, clearly, it is the first. If it remains so, she will be heaping the coals of fire on her own head, not on his. But she has it in her power to extinguish them altogether, for him and her alike. And while she is making up her mind whether to do so, let her know that those coals, though they burn, give off neither fructifying heat nor consoling warmth, and that those who ignite them are left in the end with nothing but dust and ashes.

The Times September 11th, 1986

Safety in numbers

N OW THAT THE writ-slinging in the Botham drugs affair
has officially stopped, I want to raise a related matter.
The man who first made the allegations against Botham tried
to minimize their effects by explaining that his sporting hero
did not use the 'hard' drugs; 'I am aware,' he said, 'that he
smokes dope, but doesn't everybody?'

I am in a position to give an absolutely authoritative answer
to that question: it is No.

To start with – and this is how I come to be such an
authority on the subject – *I* don't smoke dope. But that is not
what I rest the main weight of my denial on; the man who
asked what he doubtless thought was a rhetorical question
would be entitled to say that his 'everybody' was not to be
taken literally, and that what he meant was that *most* people
smoke dope.

Unfortunately for the gloss, I can give a similar assurance,
with a similar certainty, to the question 'Don't most people
smoke dope?' It is the same answer: No, most people do not
smoke dope.

Here we may imagine our questioner rephrasing his question again. No, of course *most* people don't smoke dope, but
you know what I mean – many millions of them do, don't
they?

I am sorry to go on so relentlessly in the negative, but the
question leaves me no choice. No, many millions of people do
not smoke dope.

Is there, then, no resting point for the accuser, nowhere to
stop the apparently inevitable slide towards a claim by me that

nobody smokes dope, no question that he could ask with hope
of my assent, however grudging? Yes, there is. If he were to
say 'Many of my friends, who are not in the least representative of the country as a whole and, I guess, a smaller number of
my more distant acquaintances, smoke dope, though of course
I realize that, considered as a proportion of the whole population, *all* dope smokers, not just the ones I know, form only a
very tiny percentage – three or four per cent, perhaps, possibly five or six – and even of these the claim that most of them
smoke dope regularly or often is plainly absurd, particularly
since many of them have had no more experience of the habit
than an occasional puff at school or university, and while we
are about it you must remember that I have no means of
verifying the claims of many others to be inveterate dope
smokers and strongly suspect that they have never touched it
in their lives and pretend to be constant users out of a rather
pathetic belief that otherwise they will be thought effete' –
why then, I think, he and I would find ourselves in complete accord. But then it wouldn't be a very interesting story, would it?

As I have pointed out before, a newspaper with the habit
of making its main headline of such unsensational matter
as '6,729 aircraft land safely' or 'Millions of Londoners
not mugged over weekend' would go out of business fairly
quickly. But the 'Most people smoke dope' claim, though it is
ridiculous in any form, is not just the equivalent of the bad
news that does sell papers. It is, subtly but significantly, in a
different category.

The reason why 'Practically nobody murdered last year' is
not interesting is that it corresponds to knowledge so deeply
embedded in us that it becomes an instinct, almost a biological
matter; the knowledge in question is of the rarity of the
occasions on which the smooth running of the universe is
disturbed. There are earthquakes, tidal waves and volcanic
eruptions, and some of these take many lives; but it is a curious
fact, well supported by evidence, that even people who live in
earthquake zones do not lie awake at night in anticipatory
terror of the shaking of the earth.

The claim that most people take drugs is different in one obvious sense: it inverts the headline rule and makes news out of the revelation that a dog has bitten a man. But that doesn't matter; what matters is that the small minority of which it is true is, in making the claim, clearly seeking the 'protection' of the majority. By mingling with the crowd, they can become anonymous and unrecognizable, part of the norm.

That could be useful legally, of course; if there is a general belief that dope smoking is practised by more or less everybody, it will in time come to be ignored, if it is not too flagrant, by the police, which is indeed exactly what has happened. But there is a far more important and interesting sense in which dope smokers seek to bind to themselves the majority who do not share their taste by insistently claiming that the majority do. It is that, for all the bravado, for all the assertions of the harmlessness of the habit, for all the forcefulness with which it is defended, there is a suppressed unease among the users, which strongly suggests that many of them are very far from sure that they are not doing anything wrong, and no nearer certainty that they are not doing anything damaging to themselves.

Not only do I not smoke dope; I have never done so, not even once. But I have found myself, in gatherings where the habit is customary, the subject of what can only be described as intense proselytising; more, I have in such circumstances been abused, and on one occasion offered physical violence, for saying, without heat, and without accusing anybody, that I do not and would not join in the habit, and not merely because it is against the law.

I do not know, or care, whether the accuser who said 'Doesn't everybody?' is himself included in the everybody. What interests me is why the myth has been allowed to take root.

And it has. I have nowhere seen it challenged, and almost everywhere seen it accepted without argument. Yet I will wager that tens of millions of people in Britain have never laid eyes on a joint, much less smoked one (it is, apart from anything else, a habit alien to British working-class culture), and if any of my readers would like to test my claim, let them go through their address book and make a tick against those of their acquaintance whom they *know* to be dope takers; I will wager even more that not one in ten who try the experiment will have ticked more than one in ten of the names.

Does this matter? Yes, it does. Not many years ago, it was fashionable among certain kinds of fool to talk about a 'drug culture', and to talk about it, moreover, admiringly. We do not hear such nonsense now, largely, I imagine, because the horrors that have followed from the use by a few of the hard drugs have been so well publicized. But it cannot be healthy for any society, particularly one as uncertain of itself as ours is at present, to talk itself into a belief that the entire population ('everybody') is constantly breaking the law and as constantly fuddled with dope. It may be too late to get that notion entirely out of our heads; but possibly we can persuade the sportsman's friend to pause in future before asking 'Doesn't everybody?' Failing that, we can at least start giving him the answer.

The Times July 25th, 1986

Gay go up and gay go down

I SAY, I'VE had a perfectly spiffing idea. Let's round up all the poofs, queers, homos and perverts, and cut their whatsits off. After all, whatsit–cutting has recently made a welcome return to the agenda after many centuries; Lord Denning and others want it for rapists, and if we play our cards skilfully, we might be able to convince Mr James Anderton. What larks!

Some people will feel that my suggestion goes too far; others may not. Some, indeed, may think it does not go quite far enough; from these, I shall be happy to receive suggestions for improving on my own plan – disembowelling, perhaps, or impaling, or burning at the stake.

You think I jest? I do, I do; but the laughter is hollow. For this country seems to be in the grip of a galloping frenzy of hate, where homosexuals are concerned, that will soon, if it is not checked, lead to something like a pogrom. I have not sensed such a tide sweeping away tolerance, reason and decency since long before the 1967 Act decriminalized homosexual relations between consenting adults in private; indeed, I believe that the present rush to judgement is actually worse than in the old days. Then, the main tone was set by anti-homosexual jokes, most of them contemptuous and many cruel, but which acted as a safety catch.

I would go so far as to say that many of those who joked knew instinctively what they were doing, and a spirit of live and let live reigned for long periods, broken when some zealous Home Secretary such as the dreadful Maxwell Fyfe instigated a hunt, or a local police force wanted a few more convictions or bribes. (Maxwell Fyfe once said, in Randolph Churchill's hearing, that he personally didn't know any homosexuals. 'Good God,' shouted Randolph, 'you've been sitting in the bloody Cabinet with one for the last five years!')

But today's nastiness and ugliness surpass all that. I suppose it started with the Aids pandemic; since almost all of the earliest victims were homosexual, the peculiar horror of the disease led to a widespread general horror of homosexuals, and when Aids began to seep into the heterosexual world the horror was reinforced by the feeling that the 'gays' were giving it to the 'straights'.

Which, it has to be said, they generally were. One of the most extraordinary facts to come to light when Aids began to spread was the level of promiscuity reached by a small minority of homosexuals who, in an ordinary lifetime, might have sexual relations with more than a thousand partners. (Britain, as far as I know, never had the notorious 'bath-houses' of the United States, where an individual might have a score or more sexual encounters in an evening, though one such venue was portrayed here in an American play, *Torch Song Trilogy*, before largely uncomprehending audiences.) Most heterosexuals were, of course, in no danger of catching Aids from anybody, but vicarious resentment was, and is, a powerful feeling, and a belief that homosexuals were poisoning the wells began to spread.

It also has to be said that a minority of homosexuals – again, a small minority – abused the new freedom that the Act offered by flaunting themselves in an extravagantly *outré* homosexual mode of behaviour, well calculated to disgust heterosexuals, including many who were sympathetic. And, perhaps more significant than any other cause of resentment, there was the aggressive tone adopted by many homosexuals campaigning for their 'rights', abetted by hard-left local councils promoting 'positive discrimination', in the most crass and bullying manner.

But all this put together, plus the debate on homosexuality in the Church of England Synod, does not justify what is happening now. On all sides, the baying of hounds can be heard, with eager voices urging them on. Homosexuals are being portrayed – portrayed literally as well as metaphorically – as creatures scarcely human; they are being abused not just in the old mocking way but in the foulest terms, meant with deadly seriousness; they are experiencing an increase in discrimination over a wide range of situations; already voices have been raised to demand the 'cleansing' of schools, as they have been for the purging of the church.

There was a fine array of these horrible and harmful attitudes on display when the House of Commons, a couple of weeks ago, debated a clause, hastily added to the Local Government Bill, to prohibit the 'promotion' of homosexuality. A year ago, the same proposal had been put forward as a private member's bill, and the government had opposed it, on the grounds that it was not needed and that it was impossible to draw the necessary definitions. Now, without any attempt either to maintain that the situation has changed, or to deal with the problem of the definitions, the government is supporting it.

One of those specially supple-spined ministers, always ready to argue that black is white, and indeed blue, green and purple, too, was in charge of the bill; challenged directly to say why the government had changed its mind, he said: 'I shall deal with that point in due course.' He then continued to the end of the debate without saying another word on the subject. He will go far.

The sound of the avalanche has been clearly heard. The Labour Party ran away from challenging the new clause as prejudicial, unnecessary, discriminatory and liable to arouse hatred (all of which it is), because they were afraid of being attacked as favouring the 'promotion' of homosexuality; that left the full attack on the measure largely to such discredited Labour MPs as Messrs Livingstone and Corbyn, together with Mr Christopher Smith, who is, after all, *parti pris*.

But the legislation is not the worst or the most important

item in the rising temperature of hate, except in so far as it will inevitably turn up the flame. And the tragedy of it all is that, after the 1967 Act, there had been a slow but real advance in understanding – which, in these matters, is much more important than an Act of Parliament. More and more people had come to see that homosexuality is not evil in itself, nor a threat to heterosexuals, nor disgusting, nor a chosen way of life, nor more likely than heterosexuality to include paedophiliac tendencies, nor necessarily accompanied by a lisp, a flapping of limp hands or the wearing of women's underclothes.

We are in danger of losing all that, and more. It has been wisely said that the test of any country wishing to be thought of as civilized is the way it treats its minorities. On the whole, Britain has scored well by this test. Are we really going to throw it away because the yahoos have scented blood? Are we really going to return to the days – there are plenty of people who would like us to – when a man like Alan Turing is publicly branded as both criminal and sub-human?

> Oh who is that young sinner with the handcuffs on his
>   wrists?
> And what has he been after that they groan and shake their
>   fists?
> And wherefore is he wearing such a conscience-stricken
>   air?
> Oh they're taking him to prison for the colour of his
>   hair . . .
> Now 'tis oakum for his fingers and the treadmill for his
>   feet
> And the quarry-gang on Portland in the cold and in the
>   heat
> And between his spells of labour in the time he has to spare
> He can curse the God that made him for the colour of his
>   hair.

Thus wrote A. E. Housman; but when he wrote it, he felt obliged to write in code. Are we really to go back to a time when homosexuals were not simply embarrassed or reluctant to disclose their sexual nature, but *afraid* to? Well, if we are not to return to such conditions, we had better start speaking up; if the price of liberty is eternal vigilance, the price of tolerance is enough voices saying No all at once.

I have just been informed on the highest legal authority that my initial suggestion of solving the homosexual problem with the knife is probably against the law. Bother. But I have an alternative proposal. Let homosexuals be compelled to wear, at all times, a six-pointed yellow star, sewn to their clothing in a prominently visible place.

The Times December 28th, 1987

The jewel in the crown

The Accompanist by Nina Berberova*

THERE ARE CERTAIN books – most of them short, though I don't know why that should have anything to do with it – which on first reading (generally somewhat further than half-way through) induce in the reader a kind of terror. This feeling can be so powerful that it leads to all the stigmata of real fear: clammy hands, a dry mouth, a rapid heartbeat.

What are we afraid of? Of a terrible, unassuageable *disappointment*. For the books in question have got that far without flaw or falter; they promise something very close to perfection, and since every reader knows how unlikely that is, a shadow falls on the remaining pages, a shadow within which there may be lurking a descent to bathos, a wholly implausible dénouement, a petering-out, a last-minute failure of imagination or taste.

The Turn of the Screw is such a book: *A Portrait of the Artist* is another; the archetype of them all is *First Love*. Each of these arouses our fear, and then belies it, and the pleasure with which we come, unbetrayed, to the end, is seasoned with relief.

Just such a book, arousing just such feelings, is *The Accompanist*, a tiny jewel (not even 25,000 words) without so much as a hairline crack, an irregular facet, or a cloudy patch. From the singularly meagre and maddening scraps of information which Collins provide (it may be time to start hanging a few

* Collins, 1987.

publishers from lamp-posts, *pour encourager les autres*) we learn
that the author was born in Russia in 1901, that she lived long
in France, that she was a professor of Russian literature in the
United States for 13 years, and retired from academe in 1971.
We are also told that she wrote the book in Russian, though we
are not allowed to know when (unless the '1936' which
follows the final words of the book is supposed to be the date
of the writing rather than the date when the book's 'diarist'
stopped, though there is no evidence either way); whether
there was a prior American edition is also concealed from us,
as is any indication of whether, and if so to what extent, the
book is autobiographical. It is not even entirely clear whether
Nina Berberova is still alive.★

The story is simple, wholly convincing, beautiful and poignant; the comparison with *First Love* is inescapable, and
Turgenev might well consider it a compliment. The book
purports to be a kind of diary, kept by a young Russian girl, a
pianist with talent but without genius, looks or personality,
and with the stigma of illegitimacy doubly hard to bear;
doubly because social disapproval (the book begins in the
years just before the October Revolution) is matched by her
own feelings of shame and resentment.

Sonetchka is taken up by a singer, Maria Nikolaevna
Travina, a hugely colourful and successfully-drawn figure, a
kind of Isadora Duncan with sense; she needs an accompanist
for her recitals, and Sonetchka gets the job, which becomes in
addition the role of confidante, assistant, part-time maid and
secretary. She clearly falls in love with the singer, though
never admits it to herself, indeed does not even realize that that
is what has happened; but even while she worships Maria, she
is tortured by her own unconsidered insignificance in the
shadow thrown by Maria's success, flamboyance and
selfishness.

She vows revenge; it is to take the form of betraying Maria's

★ It is only fair to record the fact that the publishers subsequently wrote to
me to explain that the meagreness of the biographical information was in
accord with the author's wishes.

infidelities to her husband. Soon that is not enough; a more dramatic curtain is required, though when it finally falls on an even more startling tableau it is not Sonetchka's hand that brings it down.

'She was unique and there were thousands like me'; that is the thought which torments Sonetchka like the lacerating anguish of love. It is described with the greatest delicacy, as though the author was engraving it on a goblet of the finest, thinnest glass, which will shatter if the stylus is pressed the merest fraction too hard:

> Another's fame, another's beauty, another's happiness were all around me, and the hardest part for me was knowing that they were deserved, that if I were not at the piano on the stage, if I were somewhere where no one noticed me, not somewhere behind Maria Nikolaevna in the dressing room but in the crowd clapping or running out after her into the passageway, I would have looked at Travina just as ecstatically, would have had the same longing to speak with her, touch her hand, catch a glimpse of her smile.

They flee from the privation and fear that the Bolsheviks bring in their victorious wake, and settle in Paris. The writing becomes even more spare:

> I remember, it was raining, it was evening. I was looking out of the window of the taxi at the street, at the passers-by . . . I remember my dreams in my room at the Hotel Regina, those first days . . . as if it were yesterday. Life . . . was starting all over again, tempestuous, colourful, and generous . . . there were evenings out, parties, restaurants. Summer came . . . I lounged around town, saw Napoleon's tomb, churches; I had money aplenty.

Mood and atmosphere; the book is little else, but they are conjured into vivid life, so real that I turned the pages imagining that they would shortly turn into pop-up pictures, physically three-dimensional as the author's are psychologically so. There is not a false note anywhere (apart from occasional lapses in the translation – 'he . . . kissed Maria Nikolaevna's hand two times', 'the junk dealer elaborated that he had purchased the notebook . . .'), nor a wasted word. And even as we hold our breath, with only a few more pages to go, the author banishes our fears, and brings her tiny giant of a book to a perfect end; not on the pistol-shot, but on the dying close of the mundane events which follow it, all passion spent. Magic.

Sunday Times June 21st, 1987

People eating is wrong

I T USED TO be the fashion, in shops selling trinkets, souvenirs and other rubbish, to include among their stock trays, beer glasses, tea-cloths and the like bearing the words 'Everything I like is illegal, immoral or fattening'. It was meant to be a joke, but has long since turned into grim reality. Those who have thus turned a jest to deadly earnest are the Single Issue Fanatics, who roam our society with their glittering-eyed claim that they have a right to force their beliefs on us whether we share them or not, and ultimately to give their beliefs the force of law, so that they may haul us before the courts for no greater crime than disagreeing with them.

The most extreme form which this pestilence has so far taken fortunately affects few of us; it is the legislation – I keep finding, when I tell people about it, that they do not believe me, being quite convinced that it is a joke – which makes it a serious criminal offence to annoy a bat. Not to *kill* one, you must understand, but even to remove it from your house, however gently, if it has nested there.

Just think how recently such legislation would have been unimaginable in Britain. Yet there it is, and the Single Issue Fanatics have chalked up another victory.

The most familiar of the enforcer's victims are, of course, the smokers, about whose persecution – the word is not too strong – I have frequently written. But there is now a new plague among us, which – mark these words, and date-stamp them, too, for I tell you that I speak sooth – will very soon now be as big as the harassment of smokers, and shortly after that, bigger. Yes, bigger; for no one, after all, is compelled to smoke, but we must all eat. And it is what we eat and how we eat it that is the next target for those who will not rest until they have compelled *us*, under the threat of prosecution, to do what *they* wish. Their impulse, as with all these people, is based on a conviction that they know what is good for us better than we do ourselves; that is, indeed, the definition of any fanatic, but if I tell them that their attitude is essentially totalitarian they will be either amused or indignant, or both, for their belief that they know what we want is perfectly genuine.

Only, it is mistaken. The undoubted leader of the new species of fanatic, hereinafter referred to as the Foodies, is Mr Geoffrey Cannon, who was Fooding away, not long since, in this very newspaper. I have no objection to that; but he can hardly complain, having had his say, if I disagree with him.

'Britain needs a food and health policy. The Government must do its duty.' Thus *The Lancet*, quoted with approval by Mr Cannon. Moreover, 'the present operation of the CAP in relation to dairy products and sugar is directly opposed to the dietary objectives that the United Kingdom should be aiming for.' Thus, the BMA, equally commended by Mr Cannon.

Most of what followed was designed to show that the Government and the food manufacturers are in cahoots; whenever he mentions nutrition scientists who disagree with him it turns out that they or their researches are funded by the evil capitalists (he weasels out of the innuendo by saying 'The question of their personal integrity does not arise'). It is delightfully significant that there is only one reference to the consumer, in the form of an aside, and it occurs exactly 83 per cent of the way through the article. (Mr Cannon, incidentally, exhibits another of the characteristic *stigmata* of the Single Issue Fanatic, an almost demented frenzy of acronyms; I waded through HEC, MAFF, JACNE, SNACMA, FAC and COMA, plus several Bulgarian ones such as FDF and BNF.)

The absence of the consumer from the argument is not surprising; remember that these people believe, most devoutly, in telling us what to do. Whence, of course, the 'need' for 'a national policy for food and health'; whence also the denunciation of the CAP for having the almighty gall to be 'opposed to the dietary objectives that the United Kingdom should be aiming for'. But I now leave Mr Cannon and turn to the broader principles involved.

I do not believe that free countries should have 'dietary objectives'; these are a matter for Jack Sprat and his wife, who had strikingly different dietary objectives, yet maintained their marital harmony by a process of give and take. The essence of a free society is that the citizens should examine such evidence and information as *they* think useful and appropriate, even if it comes from a source that the Foodies think unreliable, and then make up their minds. But I reject the claim that some people have the right to make up the minds of others.

I have been told that in the United States there are posters to be seen bearing the message 'Call a halt to salt'. It is useless, alas, to point out to Christian Foodies that both St Mark and St Luke said plainly 'Salt is good', and that the latter went so far as to insist that it should always be the fresh kind; it is equally vain to hope that Jewish Foodies will be impressed by the insistence of Leviticus that meat should always be accompanied by salt, because the Foodies would argue that meat is as bad for you as salt, if not worse. But the poster is yet one more item of evidence to show that the Nanny State is pushing out her frontiers.

Smoking is very likely to be bad for you; for all I know, or the Foodies know, so is salt, not to mention meat, butter, sugar, milk, cheese and bread (all of which are on the Foodies' hit-list). Since the experts' list of fatal foods changes every second Wednesday, it is very difficult for the average citizen to adjust his diet according to it, which is why most average citizens sensibly ignore the list. But I have to go one step further.

If a sign by the shore says 'Bathing here is dangerous because of fast currents', a man who plunges in does so at his own risk. You may call him a fool; I do. But I will not give anyone the power to chain him to a rock to stop him swimming into hazard. If he can't read, someone should tell him what the sign says; that is the equivalent of the reports on the hazards of smoking and of eating fatty foods. But when he is armed with the necessary information, the decision is his.

There is a reason for this. Free people in a free state can rarely know in advance which actions will be good for them and which bad. There is a gradation, not a gulf, between the two; even the show-off who dives into the racing current may come up with sunken treasure. And those who would insist that their fellow citizens must eat or smoke or travel or work or play or drink in a manner prescribed by those giving the advice, rather than those receiving it, are committing a double sin. First, they are denying the right we all have to pursue experience wherever it may lead us; second, they are, step by step, report by report, rule by rule, law by law, destroying our capacity to govern our own lives.

And it is the capacity to govern their own lives which sets off the free from the unfree. The Foodies and Smokies and Drinkies insist that they are hectoring us and bullying us and eventually punishing us only for our own good. Many of them undoubtedly believe it. But we, and we alone, must be the judges of our own good. We may judge wrongly; but that risk is the price we pay for being free. Were it ten times as high, I would pay it willingly.

Now comes the news that Haringey Council has rejected a useful sports project for the borough (which would have cost the ratepayers nothing) because it was to be sponsored by the manufacturers of Mars Bars. The Loonies' excuse? 'We feel too many are eating sweets . . .' Well, well; Nanny will put a stop to that.

The Times April 30th, 1987

Downstairs and upstairs

L OOK HERE, UPON these pictures, and on these. At the Hayward Gallery, on the South Bank in London, there are two exhibitions running simultaneously until January 10. They are both worth seeing; though for very different reasons and it is the difference in the reasons that supplies my theme for today.

The first exhibition, which occupies the ground floor and the mezzanine, is of the work of Diego Rivera, Mexico's greatest and best known artist. It is astonishing, and a matter of shame, that until now there has apparently been no substantial exhibition devoted to him in Britain; some of his work was included in an exhibition of Mexican art at the Tate in 1953, but the rest is silence.

Well, we have made handsome amends at last. The exhibition is enormous, comprehensive, handsomely hung, adequately lit and accompanied by a sumptuous and illuminating catalogue. It is also a glorious affirmation of life, struggle, beauty, compassion and a kind of holy rage on behalf of the poor and oppressed, a rage which has had the effect not of diluting or distorting his genius but of focusing it, so that, however overt the comment, it is art first and comment second. (There is no good art where the order is reversed, though you would be surprised how many technically talented artists have failed to discover that truth. Kindly bear the point in mind, and read on.)

Rivera was simultaneously fascinated and horrified by what the Labour Party calls the means of production, distribution and exchange; industrialization means machinery, and machinery, together with the architecture allied to it, provides a great part of the basis of his work. But he always saw the human being in the machine; his 'Proletarian art' had nothing in common with the sterilities of Soviet 'Socialist Realism', and his huge murals and other gigantic works, though they make the plainest of statements, none the less glow with his energy.

That energy was a burning fiery furnace, fuelled by the misery and brutality of his native land. He joined the Mexican Communist Party, but there was nothing at all in his political activities to compare with those of a Stalinist whore like Aragon, say; indeed, he rejected Stalinism, and was a friend of Trotsky, and it is also important to remember that he lived in great danger for many years in Mexico, where political murders were common.

He was in the middle of countless battles, artistic and political; some of his more outspoken attacks on Mexico's ruling class led to boycotts and threats, and although he was taken up early in the United States, he was dropped abruptly when the truly revolutionary nature of his work became apparent. (On one delightful occasion a large mural of his, hung in an exhibition, was hurriedly covered in a sheet painted to match the empty walls on either side, lest its uncompromising theme should disturb the visitors.)

But this protean genius cannot be classified according to the accepted canons. The range of his iconography, for a start, is immense; there are portraits (including some very revealing self-portraits), figure-studies, allegorical, historical and mythological subjects, pictures of the Mexican Indians, which include many of his finest works, a Cubist period astonishing in the way he transmutes the received techniques into his own language, Aztec themes, landscapes, some of which are executed in such intense close-up that they cover only a tiny patch of earth; all this in addition to the machinery and the buildings that so fascinated him. People, colour, flowers, masks, death, life, sun, roots, work – these are the subjects that fill the Hayward; if you stand still in the middle of the largest room you will begin to see the walls quiver in the heat and light he generates.

Invigorated and heartened by all the power and joy, the life and urgency, the indignation and hope, I wandered about the exhibition, drinking from the clear, scalding stream that was Diego Rivera and his art, and determined to blow a blast on the trumpet as soon as I could get to my typewriter.

And then I went to the top floor, where the other Hayward exhibition is being held. Everything that then happened was my own fault, and I shall not pretend otherwise; I failed to do more than glance at the catalogue, and thus did not discover until too late that it was written by Mr Richard Cork, in his most inflated politico-gaseous style, commending the nine huge pictures that the exhibition comprises as trenchant comments on Britain today. (That was the point; the show is called, apparently without irony, 'Art History', and the sub-title is 'Artists look at contemporary Britain'. Moreover, the monumental scale of the nine contributions is also meant to echo or parallel the work of Rivera downstairs.)

Mind; the pictures are what they are, and Mr Cork obviously makes them neither better nor worse. But if I had noticed his contribution in advance, I would at least have been prepared; when Diogenes was discovered begging for money from a statue, and was asked what was the purpose of doing so, he replied: 'I am practising disappointment.'

It is necessary to bear in mind that some at least of the nine artists represented are genuinely gifted; one, indeed – R. B. Kitaj – is a very distinguished painter (significantly, his contribution has practically no connection with the general tenor of the rest of this depressing experience), and among the others only one – Helen Chadwick – seems to have no talent at all that I can discern, at any rate to judge by this single item (I know nothing of her other work), while even Alain Miller and Keith Piper have a certain superficial facility, and Ken Currie and Peter de Francia real draughtsmanship.

But, as I have asked repeatedly, what is the point of being

able to say things if you have nothing of the smallest interest to say? It was, as I recall, the prolonged silence which greeted that question when I was a theatre critic that finally drove me to give up the job; there were a good many playwrights about who could write well, and construct a play with considerable skill, but the relentless negativity that they peddled – as false as it was otiose – persuaded me that I had better things to do of an evening.

Well, the nine pictures of 'Artists look at contemporary Britain' will not occupy an evening; say 15 minutes for Kitaj, 10 for Currie, five each for de Francia and Paul Graham, three for Michael Sandle (though only because there are a very large number of figures in it), two for Terry Setch (though only because you won't believe your first glance), 30 seconds each for Piper and Miller, and a blink for Chadwick, and you can be down the stairs and revelling in Diego Rivera till closing time.

Would you really believe, if I had not prepared the ground as I have, that, asked for a comment on contemporary Britain, Alain Miller and Keith Piper can offer nothing but huge pictures of Mrs Thatcher? Piper portrays her with a kind of halo made of missiles; ooh, the originality of it, the wit, the courage, the trenchancy! As for Miller, he does nothing but paint her twice, with an inset of the Mona Lisa (the Duchamp version) between the two images, which brings Mr Cork almost to his knees with the desperation he clearly feels in trying to say something about it; the result is too long to quote here, but should be included in any anthology of the Higher Bosh.

De Francia points out – nobody else ever having thought of it – that the authorities in South Africa often behave with the utmost brutality towards the blacks; this is included in 'Artists look at contemporary Britain' because the title proves, at least to Mr de Francia's satisfaction, that it is all Mrs Thatcher's fault. Paul Graham (undoubtedly a skilled photographer) has haunted McDonald's to find oppressed black employees, though they look singularly unoppressed.

Sandle shows us a kind of Gestapo cellar where the police (no doubt instructed by Mrs Thatcher) torture everybody in sight, and then has the wonderful cheek to say 'I'm exposing myself, I'm leading with my chin', as though he didn't know that he will have every poodlefaker in the business swooning, cheering and commissioning.

Currie, who can certainly handle paint, depicts a Glasgow bar as a Chamber of Horrors, culminating in a gang of thugs tattooing a Union Jack on their victim's arm; Mr Cork, curiously, deduces that they are 'Loyalists'. (Fourpence – no, Levin, be reckless – *ninepence* for the first contemporary painter, playwright or novelist to put the blame on the other side in Northern Ireland.)

Presumably, the contributors to the exhibition upstairs, or some of them, were in attendance when their pictures were being installed. They must therefore have passed through the Rivera exhibition. What I would like to know is this: did none of them, even for a moment, notice that although Rivera's left-wing credentials are impeccable, and his scorn for the ruling classes unbounded, and the political content in his work merciless, his work, like his life, is an affirmation, not a denial, and his expression of it a blazing trumpet, not a badly dented ocarina? And if they did notice, how is it that none of them thereupon instructed the people in charge to take their work off the walls, and burn it?

The Times November 16th, 1987

Your money or your life

AN ICE-SKATING star (neither Torvill nor Dean), who is at present working in the United States, is to stay away for some good while longer, the reason being that if he returns prematurely he will be liable for a massive tax demand, whereas if he remains out of his native country long enough he will not be similarly subject to the taxman's mulcting. I must stress that in choosing to stay out of the Inland Revenue's reach and thus relieving himself of a financial burden, he is doing nothing in any way illegal; he is indulging not in tax evasion but in tax avoidance.

That is a familiar tale. What caught my imagination was the headline (the words were repeated in the body of the story) over the item in the newspaper that reported the news. It was 'Ice star forced into tax exile.'

Well, dearie me. No doubt words change their meanings (see the *OED*, R. Burchfield prop.), but this use of 'forced' is a more than usually delightful one. The taxman does have a somewhat negative image; but 'force' suggests the midnight knock on the door, the waiting black maria, the handcuffs, the breakneck journey to the coast and the hurling of the victim into a leaky rowing-boat with no more than a week's food and water and a broken compass.

But the taxman does not behave like that. He demands his full due, and he is not above threatening (in capital letters) to seek court permission for DISTRAINT, but he doesn't force anybody into exile. The skater's waltz was an entirely voluntary act; he chose to go abroad and stay there to pay less tax than he would have done had he remained at home.

I do not intend to come over all sanctimonious in this matter; I pay my taxes only after claiming every proper allowance and deduction, and slithering through every lawful loophole, and I would consider myself, if I did not adopt that attitude, to be as big a fool as I would be a rogue if I went to the additional lengths of falsifying my returns.

I have no moral criticism of our *patineur* (it wasn't he, after all, who used the word 'forced'); it is just that I cannot encompass in my imagination the thought of leaving my native country for a year (I believe that that is the minimum term for saving substantial sums in tax), not because I want to travel or work elsewhere, not because I have grown disenchanted with Britain, not because the state of my health demands a warmer clime, not even *pour chercher la femme*, but because I can then thumb my nose at the Inland Revenue, and trouser another few hundred thousand quid.

In one scale put your love of your country, the country in which you have grown up, the country of which you know the physical lineaments and the endearing (and less endearing) qualities, the country in which you have made and kept most of your firmest friends, the country (it is not irrelevant) to which you owe allegiance. In the other scale put, of all things, *money*. Remember that I am talking only of people who do still love the country of their birth, and are not glad to be shaking its dust from their feet, and then tell me if you can understand those for whom the second scale outweights the first.

I'm damned if I can. Listen to this:

> The language I have learn'd these forty years
> My native English, now I must forgo;
> And now my tongue's use is to me no more
> Than an unstringed viol or a harp,
> Or like a cunning instrument cas'd up,
> Or, being open, put into his hands
> That knows no touch to tune the harmony:
> Within my mouth you have engaol'd my tongue,

Doubly portcullis'd with my teeth and lips:
And dull, unfeeling, barren ignorance
Is made my gaoler to attend on me.
I am too old to fawn upon a nurse,
Too far in years to be a pupil now . . .
Then, thus I turn me from my country's light,
To dwell in solemn shades of endless night.

Thomas Mowbray, Duke of Norfolk (for it is he), is there putting the case against being forced to leave his native country, but his objection wasn't to the Inland Revenue pursuing him with tax demands; his departure, and the sadness of it, were based on the fact that he had deduced that if he didn't go he would have his head cut off by Richard the Second. Even I would take the hint in that situation. But for money?

Some will no doubt sniff, and say that I have more money than the average man, and can thus afford such high and mighty attitudes. If they do, I think they have the boot on the wrong foot, and certainly the wallet in the wrong pocket. Only the very rich go into voluntary tax exile, those who, had they stayed, would anyway have kept x millions, and are leaving only because by doing so they will keep x plus y millions. But why isn't x millions enough, when to keep y millions as well involves the profound sadness entailed by any form of exile?

St Cyprian could hardly have been familiar with the British tax system, and there is no record of his haunting the ice rinks at Carthage, but he did contribute something rather shrewd to this discussion. Referring to the wealthy man, he said: 'He does not see, poor wretch, that his life is but a gilded torture, that he is bound fast by his wealth, and that his money owns him rather than he owns it.'

What better metaphor could there be for a tax exile? To be tugged out of one's own country by a golden chain is inevitably an ignominious procedure, for all the false glamour that surrounds great wealth. It can be argued, of course, that those who exile themselves for money can have had only a shallow feeling for their country. In some cases, it may be so; but I believe that in many more, they *thought* they didn't mind leaving Britain, and then found to their dismay that they minded very much.

For there is a sense in which exile is worse than imprisonment – whether it is the truly forced exile of the refugee from tyranny or the voluntary kind embarked upon in flight from taxation. I don't know if there are any British tax exiles in Calais (I wouldn't be surprised – they turn up in the oddest places), but their hunger for the forbidden native land they can see on a clear day cannot be much worse than those in, say, the United States who cannot see their own country but cannot, either, stop thinking about it.

Serve them right? Yes, I think so, though not because they are avoiding their due whack; rather because they have forgotten what money is actually for, or, more precisely, what it is not for. It is not, despite the impression given by many of those who have become enormously rich by howling, galumphing or skating, for worrying about, scheming about, seeing fleets of accountants about, and eventually leaving the country about.

I have no objection to money, and if any Croesus reading this would like to test my sincerity by tossing me a couple of million, fully taxable, I shall say thank you, very nicely, and stay at home. But St Paul will be glad to hear that I long ago decided he was right when he said, 'We brought nothing into this world, and it is certain that we carry nothing out.' Or, as the no less ancient proverb has it, 'There are no pockets in a shroud.' Nor in a foreign residence permit, come to think of it.

The Times October 5th, 1987

Missing the point

O N   A   R E C E N T   visit to America, I came across a story in the
New York Times which awakened memories for me, as it
must have done for many readers. But among those who read
it, I think I was one of the few, if not the only one, to have *two*
sets of memories recalled. The writer of the story was clearly
unaware of the circumstances giving rise to the second set, but
since the tail seemed to me to be more interesting than the dog,
I shall today tell both halves of the story; the moral of the
second half will, I think, be of particular interest to those who
relish irony, and especially in the realm of politics.

In 1951, there was a strike, in the American state of New
Mexico, at a mine where the workers were mainly Mexican-
Americans. The strike lasted for more than a year, the strikers'
wives played a leading part in it, and the strikers were successful in getting most of what they had struck for. A little later, a
film was made – fictional but based on the real events – called
The Salt of the Earth; the double meaning in the title was plainly
deliberate. The film was sponsored by a union (the Union of
Mine, Mill and Smelter Workers) which at that time was
under communist domination, a fact which had led to its
expulsion from the American equivalent of the TUC.

No doubt the film portrayed the workers as upright and
angelic souls and the mine owners as blackhearted villains, and
no doubt the political views of the sponsors were not rigor-
ously excluded from it. And indeed there *is* no doubt, for this
was the high tide of McCarthyism, and the director, producer
and scriptwriter (who took no money for their work on
the film) had all been called before the Committee on

Un-American Activities: the director was imprisoned, as one of 'the Hollywood Ten', for refusing to testify about his political connections; the others involved were blacklisted and found they could get regular film work only if they used pseudonyms. So *The Salt of the Earth* was also blacklisted, and very few cinemas dared to show it. (The actors, incidentally, were amateurs.)

Well, that was an ugly and shaming era in the United States, not to be extenuated or minimized, and gave America's real enemies a great and lasting advantage. But things have changed, for the point of the *New York Times* story was that a video-cassette of the film had just been released, and was apparently selling well. So it seems to be true that the whirligig of time brings in its revenges, though in this case rather too late for those involved in the film.

So much for the first half of my tale, the half that the *New York Times* knew about. Now for Part Two, the rest of the story, which neither the newspaper nor most of its readers were aware of.

At the time the film was made, a diplomat friend of mine was *en poste* in Prague. This was only a few years, remember, after the Soviet seizure of Czechoslovakia, and things were happening there far more terrible than the vileness of McCarthyism and the fate of his victims; Stalin's show trial, which wiped out almost the whole of the Czechoslovak Communist leadership, was fresh in many memories. *The Salt of the Earth* came, therefore, as a timely boon for the rulers of Czechoslovakia, who were in a pressing need of something to support their rule; a film which portrayed the iniquities of the United States was just the kind of weapon they needed.

The film was launched in a Prague cinema; it started sluggishly, but soon word of mouth did its work, and queues began to form at the box office. The authorities were doubtless well pleased with such a reinforcement, from America itself, for their own propaganda.

Then, abruptly, without warning or subsequent explanation, the film was withdrawn. For some time it was impossible for anyone to guess the reason, but my diplomat friend eventually heard it. It seemed that the Prague cinema-goers were indeed keen to see the film, and to learn from it a suitable political lesson. But the lesson they learned was not at all the one the authorities wanted to teach. The audiences were virtually unanimous in admiring the film because it showed the United States in so attractive a light.

Never mind the political message in the film; Czecho-slovaks had enough of that at home every day, and believed not a word of it. Never mind the meanness and cruelty of the capitalist mine owners; much worse meanness and cruelty constituted Czechoslovakia's lot. Never mind even the heroic stand of the workers. The Prague audiences noticed only three things in the film, all of them far beyond anything they could ever hope for themselves. First, the workers arrived at the mine for picket duty driving their own cars; second, they were allowed to go on strike; third, and most inconceivable, the workers *won* the strike. I have always maintained that whether a black cat crossing your path is lucky or unlucky depends on whether you are a man or a mouse. To the quislings of Czechoslovakia it seemed easy to portray America as a brutal enemy; to the people of Czechoslovakia, however, the only brutal enemy they could see on even the clearest of days was the one which had occupied and subjugated their country, which had extinguished every flickering lamp of freedom, and which was silencing, exiling, imprisoning or killing those who dared to resist. Any film shown by such people, with the clear intention of persuading its audiences to accept its political moral, would be instinctively and unanimously rejected. But in this case those who went to see it found something posi-tively to rejoice in: the twin facts that in the United States the workers were so prosperous that they could even afford their own cars, which showed how materially wealthy were even poor Americans by the standards the Czechoslovaks knew so well in their own lives, and that in the United States not only were strikes permitted but the government did not crush them by force and did not even support the bosses sufficiently to ensure that the workers lost the struggle.

The irony, as I suggested at the outset, is very enjoyable. But it is heartening, too, for it demonstrates something which should not need demonstrating, but manifestly does. It is that oppressive rulers may tell their subjects lies on almost any-thing and have at any rate *some* chance of being believed, except when the lies concern their people's own lives. Unless you take the precaution of hypnotizing him first, it is no use telling a hungry man that his belly is full, or a man in jail that he is free; he will always know better. What is more, it is not only a waste of breath, it leads to even worse consequences, because if the people know that their rulers are telling them lies on a subject they know about, they will assume that their rulers are also telling them lies on subjects which they cannot check for themselves.

And that is not just a theoretical construction. George Theiner, the editor of *Index*, once came back from a visit to Poland with shocking but understandable news; wherever he went, he found support and admiration for the South African government – not because the Poles had become devotees of apartheid, but on the perfectly logical ground that since they knew that everything their rulers said about Poland was a pack of lies, they assumed that everything their rulers said about other countries was equally mendacious. If their government said that South Africa was a country of cruelty, division and tyranny, it must be a land of happiness, harmony and democracy.

That, I agree, is going a trifle far. But who is to blame? The liars, or the lied to? As for *The Salt of the Earth*, who was it who said that the worst that can happen to us is for us to get what we asked for?

The Times August 9th, 1986

Arms and the Swiss

N ow that the echoes of the Hungerford massacre are ceasing to reverberate (and the next time something like that happens, could we perhaps be spared the dial-a-shrink comments of Dr Anthony Clare?), I want to raise an aspect of the matter that I think has not so far been discussed. And I shall begin with a simple exercise in extrapolation.

There has been much understandable disquiet about the number of guns lawfully held in this country. About 840,000 licences are held for shotguns (most, presumably, being for sport, game and pest control and the like), and certificates for some 160,000 more serious firearms, including handguns. It is argued, with considerable plausibility, that permission to hold a gun is far too easily obtained, and that the enormous number of permissions granted makes inevitably for more violent crime, up to and including such events as we have so recently witnessed; the Chief Constable of the Thames Valley police force has added, most pertinently, that in his view 'It does seem incredible that a man is allowed to keep ammunition in his own home'.

Now for the extrapolation. Let us suppose – this is not a trick or a game – that there are in Britain, lawfully held, not 160,000 unquestionably dangerous weapons, but *five and a half million*. Let us suppose further that these are all modern, effective, automatic rifles, with a lethal firepower comparable to the weapon used at Hungerford.

Bear with me a little longer, please. Suppose that the five and a half million guns are kept in working condition, regularly dismantled and cleaned. Suppose that each holder of a gun – I am reckoning one gun per owner – is, in addition, trained in its use and proficient in marksmanship. Finally, suppose that every gun is accompanied by a packet of live ammunition.

If that state of affairs prevailed, most people, I imagine, would conclude that Britain would be a Gehenna of robbery and murder, revenge and massacre, gang warfare and shoot-outs, where no one would be safe in the streets or the home, and where burglary and rape at gunpoint would be as common as parking offences are today.

You will tell me that the picture I paint is, of course, a grotesque fantasy; no such insane laxity in gun control could possibly be permitted to come to pass. And yet, in the teeth of your revolted incredulity, I tell you that the state of affairs with which I have been making your flesh creep is an *exact* description of Switzerland at this moment; the only extrapolation has been the one needed to match the proportion of guns to people. There are 650,000 such rifles in Swiss homes; the population of Switzerland is roughly 6.5 million, so there is one such gun and packet of ammunition for every 10 citizens. Britain's population is roughly 55 million, so my figures are correct: 5.5 million British guns.

The reason for the astounding total of weapons in Swiss hands is provided by the Swiss form of national defence. Every Swiss male is subject to conscription; he has a short period of basic training, followed by an annual recall to the colours for a refresher, and he remains on the reserve, doing his regular fortnight in uniform, for 30 years. He keeps his rifle and ammunition at home, and in perfect condition; he is obliged to maintain his proficiency as a marksman, and must undertake extra military service to bring him up to standard if his sharpshooting becomes rusty.

Spot the difference. Switzerland, so far from being the hideous graveyard that you just agreed Britain would become if five and a half million guns were available (together with ammunition and proficiency in using them), is well down the international table for violent crime, below not only Britain but also many countries with stricter gun control than ours.

There is only one possible conclusion, and only one possible question arising from it. The conclusion is that the number of guns in private hands in Britain and Switzerland respectively has no bearing on their respective crime rates. The question is, of course: what have the Swiss got 'that we haven't?

There are few direct answers to that question, and not a lot of tentative ones. Many of the indirect answers can be found in an extraordinary and fascinating book called *La Place de la Concorde Suisse*, by John McPhee (published in America by Farrar Straus Giroux); some of my own conclusions, inevitably more cocksure, will be found in my forthcoming book and television series, both called *To the End of the Rhine*. Whichever you choose, you will find many facts about Switzerland far more astonishing than the one about the guns.

However difficult it may be to discover why gun-strewn Switzerland is so much less violence-ridden than Britain, the attempt must be made, at any rate if we are serious about wishing to reduce our own domestic violence to more modest proportions. Some would say that restoring conscription would be the answer, but there is no reason to believe that it would; there are other countries which have compulsory military service and very high crime rates. Another voice would insist that the widespread loss of religious faith is to blame, and seek a renewal of it; well, as far as I know, there is nothing to choose for godliness between the Swiss and the English, and the Northern Irish have a hell of a lot more of it than either. The 'We are all guilty' school says that we are responsible because we have not taken enough trouble to understand criminals, whose crimes are only a 'cry for help', and a sub-division of this strain of thinking is the belief that it is all the fault of Mrs Thatcher. (Arsy-varsy, it's the blacks.)

I think it is something to do with self-sufficiency.

Switzerland's neutrality is based – indeed, is coterminous with – her determination to defend herself by her own exertions. Her state of military preparedness is almost unbelievably complete and extensive (see the works cited, *supra*), and no Swiss is in any doubt that it is for use rather than ornament.

Switzerland learned the lesson during the Second World War when, under the Churchillian leadership of Henri Guisan, she resolved to remain unsubjugated and democratic, and by heroic efforts, did. Since then, she has taken a huge yet quiet pride in the way that that resolution has been maintained and strengthened: 'We don't *have* an army,' the Swiss say, 'we *are* an army.' (An army, incidentally, that can be fully mobilized in 48 hours.)

Yet there is nothing militaristic about Switzerland; on the contrary, she is the most peaceful and unobtrusive nation in Europe. That unhubristic pride may be rooted in her military determination, but it has been transformed, as it has trickled down through Swiss society, into a pride that encompasses such concepts as cleanliness, efficiency, effort, and, above all, a quality of *civilitas* that makes the misuse of the citizen-soldier's rifle an act of shame as well as of crime.

Well, bully for the Swiss; but I am more interested in Britain. How do *we* start to build up our form of pride in self-sufficiency, in a common identity and common ideals, in a self-respect that can be learnt and in time no longer needs to be taught, in a sense of purpose beyond the concerns of living from day to day, in the belief that the old proverb is right, and if each man sweeps before his door, the village will be clean?

Now for the anti-climax; I don't know. But I know that if we don't start trying to find out it will be too late to put the answers into practice when we finally discover what they are. Dorothy Parker made a remark about Switzerland that has achieved world-wide *réclame*: she called the country 'beautiful but dumb', and we have laughed at it as long and as loudly as

her fellow Americans. Contemplating those five and a half
million automatic rifles, all of a sudden I don't think it's funny
any more.

The Times September 7th, 1987

Four women and Mr Clifford

L AST SATURDAY WAS January 30, and 'On This Day' [in *The Times*] selected a passage from the same date in 1928: a review of a performance in the Aeolian Hall by Ruth Draper. I am aware that, as they read those last words, two-thirds of my readers wavered in their normally iron-clad resolve to continue; I am consoled by my certainty that the rest instantly took the phone off the hook.

Ruth Draper died in 1956, at the age of 72. Either you know what I am talking about or you don't; if you don't, it is no use your seeking tangible evidence of what she was and did. Great musicians and actors have had their works recorded or filmed for many decades now, and writers have left their books, painters their canvases, inventors their inventions, philosophers· their influence. But 'some there be, which have no memorial; Who are perished as though they had not been born'. Ruth Draper's texts have been collected and edited; there are a few useless scraps of film of her; but the magic of her genius can never be reconstructed for those who did not see her, and will never be forgotten, until they die, by those who did. I am one of that fortunate second category, who by now can number few, if any, members under the age of 50. I saw her at least a dozen times, and I shall now reminisce about her; *und, wer's nie gekonnt, der stehle weinend sich aus diesem Bund*.

Ruth Draper was an American *diseuse* – a silly and almost meaningless word, but one which we are stuck with, since there is none better. She took a stage, and on it performed sketches (another miserably inadequate word) and monologues of her own devising. (Henry James wrote a playlet for her, though she never performed it.) She always portrayed all the characters herself, using no scenery other than black curtains, hardly any props except – in one item – a wooden chair (I'll come to the chair in a moment), no changes of costume (I'll also come to the triple use of a shawl in another), no noises off and no special lighting. Her portrayals of the various roles in a multi-character sketch were so meticulously differentiated – by her voice, by the very slightest change of physical stance, by an almost imperceptible gesture – that it had a truly hallucinatory effect; there was only one woman on the stage, but we were convinced, despite the evidence of our eyes, that there were two or more. Much more frightening – I do assure you that that word is not too strong – was her performance in the sketches in which she portrayed only one character, understood to be surrounded by a group of silent ones; before the curtain came down, real hallucination had set in, and we could see on the stage a crowd of people *who were not there*.

Let us take *Three Women and Mr Clifford*. Mr Clifford is a businessman, and the three women in his life are his wife, his mistress and his secretary. I can see 'them' now; the wife – old, crabbed, tight-mouthed, the secretary – smooth, convincing, loyal, the girlfriend – vital, sexy, comforting. Ruth Draper not only conjured all three into three-dimensional, separate life – she threw in the limousine that Mr Clifford and his wife travelled in; the imaginary motor car was as real as the three women.

Another three-hander – I have forgotten its title – took the form of a hearing before a family court. She was three generations; grandmother, mother, young girl. The girl wants to go west and live her own life, but that would mean that the mother and grandmother would have to go into a home. Each addresses the court, and that's where the shawl came in. A flick, and it was over the old lady's head; a twitch, and it was round the mother's shoulders; a ripple, and the girl was playing with it behind her back. With nano-second timing the voice changed with the shawl, but the point is that all three characters had their backs to the audience; only the invisible judge faced us from his bench.

Anyone who saw her will remember the item called *Showing the Garden*; I believe she included it in every performance. She was taking a visitor round, and the joke was that everything she was proudest of had either finished last week or would not be ready till next week; there were some roses, as I recall, the 'Mrs Huntley Buncums', which were always either late or early. To this day I cannot enter a florist's without a vague urge to demand a dozen Mrs Huntley Buncums.

Reading the 'On This Day' notice of that 1928 performance, I was struck by the account of one particular item, in which a young Frenchwoman, baby boy in arms, seeks her husband among the returning soldiers, and, on learning that he will never return, holds her baby high and cries '*Vive la France!*'

Now the returning soldiers of that item were returning, of course, from the Great War; well, I saw her, when I was a student, immediately after World War Two, and she had plainly not forgotten the old sketch and its effect. The new one portrayed a woman on a beach in Occupied France; her husband is about to slip away, across the Channel, to join the Free French in Britain. Her husband's aged mother, realizing she will not live to see her son again, is reluctant to let him go; the wife's pride flashes forth (the whole sketch was done in French, with no concessions to the audience) in scorn: '*Veux-tu que mes enfants soient des Boches?*' The boat pushes off; wife and mother embrace in grief; then, first faintly, then louder, we hear (but we *didn't* hear) the roar of aircraft. '*Ce sont des Anglais!*' she cries, '*c'est la Raf, la Raf! Des bombardiers volant vers l'est!*' Then, radiant, she turns her face to the sky and shouts: '*Allez-y, mes gars, allez-y! Bonne chance!*' And down came the curtain, with the same cry from an earlier war, '*Vive la France!*'

There were certainly no dry eyes in the house at that point, and I found my own distinctly damp just now, as, more than

40 years on, I remembered the words and Ruth Draper speaking them.

The *diseuse*, at any rate in the old sense, has almost died out. I never found Beatrice Lillie funny, not even the double-damask dinner-napkins, and Cornelia Otis Skinner was dreadful. There was our beloved Joyce Grenfell, of course, and I still miss her, but she did not have the genius of Draper; nobody did. But if you never saw her, I think you will have realized why I said it is useless to try to conjure her up, and understand her art and its perfection.

I suppose, then, that I owe an apology to the two-thirds of my readers who could not have seen Ruth Draper, for tantalizing them with what they missed. I comfort myself with the knowledge that I have made happy the other third, who did see her, and have been reminded, by my memories, of their own.

Ah, yes, I have omitted something that I promised you; the chair. It was a rocking-chair, and she used it in a sketch called *On a porch in Maine*. She was an old lady, looking back on her youth and her life; the monologue lasted some 10 minutes, and throughout it she rocked, in an absolutely even rhythm, back and forth, back and forth, the chair never deviating an inch from the arc it described in her rocking. And what was so special about that? Well, what was so special about Ruth Draper? The answer to both questions is: it *wasn't* a rocking-chair. She used a perfectly ordinary kitchen chair, and rocked it on its back legs, to and fro, to and fro, throughout the sketch. You remember? No, not you; *you*.

The Times February 4th, 1988

In the sweat of his brow

The Wrench by Primo Levi*

THIS IS NOT a book for journalists, or at any rate sensitive ones like me. Civil servants, too, will feel uneasy while reading it, and as for lawyers, they will never sleep again. For it is about man in his capacity as *homo faber*, a maker of things with his hands, and what has any of us ever made but words?

I say it is 'about' the man who makes; truly, it is more a hymn of praise than a description, and not only because the toiler who is the hero of the book is a hero indeed – a figure, in his humanity, simplicity, understanding and strength, worthy of inclusion in the catalogue of mythical giants alongside Hercules, Atlas, Gargantua and Orion.

He is Faussone, a rigger who specialises in putting up mighty mechanical structures – bridges, derricks, cranes, cooling-towers, hydraulic jacks. The book consists of a series of stories, told with immense relish to an almost invisible first-person narrator (who is clearly Levi himself); each of the chapters recounts one of Faussone's jobs, which are also his adventures. Sometimes, things go wrong; sometimes he puts right what others have allowed to go wrong; in many of the episodes there is a physical mystery to be pursued like a clue in a detective story – Why did the porcelain rings in the filter break? What caused the bridge to collapse? How could the crane be made to operate where there was no room for it? Faussone solves the problems by a combination of wisdom,

* Michael Joseph, 1987.

experience, improvisation and humility, and so satisfying are his solutions that Levi, at the end of the book, steps out of the shadows, takes over the story-telling from his friend, and gives an account of just such an inexplicable puzzle in his own work as a chemist, a puzzle which he solved in a spirit much the same as Faussone's.

In a word, Faussone is a philosopher, and he sums up his philosophy in a magnificent passage:

> If we except those miraculous and isolated moments fate can bestow on a man, loving your work (unfortunately the privilege of a few) represents the best, most concrete approximation of happiness on earth. But this is a truth not many know . . . To exalt labour, in official ceremonies, an insidious rhetoric is displayed, based on the consideration that a eulogy or a medal costs much less than a pay raise . . . There also exists a rhetoric on the opposite side, however, not cynical but profoundly stupid, which tends to denigrate labour, to depict it as base . . . as if anyone who knows how to work were, by definition, a servant, and as if . . . someone who doesn't know how to work . . . were for that reason a free man. It is sadly true that many jobs are not loveable, but it is harmful to come on to the field charged with preconceived hatred. He who does this sentences himself, for life, to hating not only work, but also himself and the world.

There can hardly be a better test of a book than the inclusion in it of technical information quite incomprehensible to the inexpert reader; this book contains a great deal of such matter, but so far from making me want to skip, it made me read the passage several times. Because it is so real to Faussone, we ache to enter into its, and his, reality; there is a two-page description of how copper pans are made that I defy anyone to read without yearning to get the ingredients and try it.

Faussone has a robust contempt for those who design the things he has to make. I daresay Ludwig of Bavaria's architect felt much the same thing for his royal master when Ludwig

sketched a castle with the aid of a stage designer, then told him
to build it; but there Neuschwanstein stands – though God
knows how – to this day. The architect, however, probably
did not confide thoughts like these even to his diary:

> There is the elephant-designer, the kind that is always on
> the safe side . . . he just doesn't want trouble, and where one
> would be enough, he books four . . . Then there's the stingy
> type . . . you'd think he had to pay for every bolt out of his
> own pocket. There's the parrot, who doesn't work out the
> plans himself, but copies them . . . There's also the snail . . .
> the minute you touch him he draws back and hides in his
> shell, which is the rule book . . . And, finally, there's the
> butterfly . . . all they think about is making something
> new and beautiful, never considering that when a work is
> planned carefully it comes out beautiful automatically.

Those last words are the essence of Faussone, and, I am sure,
of Primo Levi, too. And Keats, for that matter: 'Beauty is
truth, truth beauty.'

But Faussone is full of proverbial wisdom: 'The boss's bread
has seven crusts'; 'when things of iron become things of paper,
it ends wrong'; and – an enchantingly original and perceptive
insight, which I immediately tested and to which I can find no
exception:

> We had finished our coffee, which was loathsome, as in all
> countries (Faussone had told me this) where the accent on
> the word for coffee falls on the first syllable . . .

There is more to Faussone; his problems with women, for
instance, and the two aunts who bully him for his own good.
But he is defined, as he was shaped, by his skill with his hands
and his joy in that skill. The book was published in the original
Italian in 1978 (William Weaver's translation, incidentally, is
generally excellent, though there are a few false notes, such as
'loony bin', 'on the ball' and 'up the creek'); it is therefore
possible that there are other books by Levi still to come. But
the heart aches at the thought that when we have read any such

posthumous works, there will be nothing more from him. It is not clear how Levi died, a few weeks ago, though the circumstances strongly suggest suicide. *The Periodic Table* and (even more) this book are full of a serenity indicating that he had found peace at last. But perhaps he could find it only in the grave.

Sunday Times May 17th, 1987

Bring back the ratcatcher

B RITISH RAIL HAS announced that second-class travel is shortly to be abolished. Or rather: British Rail has announced that second-class travel is *not* shortly to be abolished. The trick lies in the words, not the travel; everything will remain exactly the same, except that second-class will be renamed 'standard'. The trains will still be dirty, uncomfortable and late, the food will still be disgusting and the fares will continue to go up; but second-class will be called standard, so all is well.

Shakespeare had something to say on the subject:

> Second-class, second-class! Wherefore art thou
>   second-class? . . .
> What's in a name? that which we call a rose
> By any other name would smell as sweet;
> So second-class would, were it not second-class call'd,
> Retain that dear perfection which he owes
> Without that title. Second-class, doff thy name;
> And for that name, which is no part of thee,
>   Take all my standard.

Or words to that effect. The poison of euphemism has worked through our language into our national consciousness; I have not the smallest doubt that the man who thought this one up genuinely believes that BR travellers will think they are getting better service by riding in a standard carriage instead of a second-class one. What is more, he may be right. But even if he isn't, he will think he has done a good job.

There are many sights and sounds and ideas and events in the world that disturb us, that offend us, that we would rather not think about. There are many ways to deal with such phenomena; we can try to understand them, and thereby lessen the offence they give, or we can take steps to destroy or remove them, or we can conquer our fear or distaste of them. But what, again and again, we do in practice is none of these things; we change the name of what we dislike, and by doing so persuade ourselves that we have changed the thing itself.

Let us start with something simple; sad, but simple. We all have to die; most of us grow old before we do so. In growing old, we cannot help knowing what it is that is coming closer; yet we have a desperate need to banish the thought of it. So we first call ourselves elderly instead of old, and then, when that medicine proves not strong enough, we call ourselves Senior Citizens.

But we die nevertheless. I suspect that we die harder, in more fear, than if we learned to contemplate, calmly, the fact of death in general and our own in particular. The world we live in, though, decrees otherwise; no one shall need to face anything disagreeable, even if it is as inevitable as death.

Let us go on to something stronger. Once, we referred to people whose bodies were deformed or incomplete, whether by injury or genetics, as cripples. At some point, the word became, or was decreed to be, socially unacceptable, and such unfortunates were renamed handicapped. Further dilution was demanded, and they became disabled. More time went by, and even that proved too strong for those who decide these matters (who, incidentally, are almost never the sufferers themselves); now we must get used to the word 'disadvantaged'. And it is not only people, but nations: for backward begat under-developed, and under-developed begat developing, and developing begat Third World.

It is offices, too. It was a long time ago (so long that people were still permitted to laugh at such foolishness) that the ratcatcher became a rodent officer; today, I doubt if any council employee in Brent goes by a title that would be recognized without a glossary. As for the moneys given to those who are unemployed or unable to afford lodging or food, we must use no word other than 'benefit'. Nay, those who receive the benefits may not even call themselves poor; they are all underprivileged.

But does a man with no legs leap up and walk when he is called disadvantaged? Is there less drought and famine in the Third World than in the backward nations? Has the underprivileged man more money in his pocket than his neighbour who is poor?

All euphemisms are lies. They are lies told for a particular purpose, and that purpose is to change reality. But no man can change reality, particularly by doing no more than wave a word at it. Then why the pretence? Because reality is very often painful, and it is the very bedrock and foundation of our world that no one should be obliged to suffer pain. Nor, the rule continues, shall anyone be obliged to suffer poverty, ill-health, disappointment, loss, bad luck, failure or an ugly face; since there is no way of avoiding all these, or for that matter any of them, we change their names, and think we have abolished them.

Naturam expellas fur – oh, all right, not again. But just as death, I believe, is very fearful for those who have refused to face it before it touches them on the shoulder, whereas it might come as a gentle visitor, or even as a friend, if they had earlier learned the wisdom of understanding it, I am not convinced that poverty is more easily borne because it is called by a prettier name; indeed I suspect that the instinctive measuring of the reality against the euphemism makes the poverty more bitter; not less.

It runs throughout our world. When it is said that the IRA has 'claimed responsibility' for another murder, should we not strip the lying euphemism from what has happened, and say 'admitted guilt'? The reason we should prefer the truth to the euphemism is exactly the same as the reason I have given for my other examples; the false word makes matters worse, not better, the IRA less evil, not more.

Poor British Rail, to be belaboured with such a sledge-hammer when it was only offering a perfectly ordinary nut! And yet there is a principle at stake, and an important one. It is not necessary to call a spade a bloody shovel, though it does no harm to do so. But if you call it a manually-operated earth-turning agricultural implement, you have damaged more than the language.

'Things and actions are what they are, and the consequences of them will be what they will be: why then should we desire to be deceived?' Bishop Butler is not known to have been given any sensible answer to his question; but then, it was really a rhetorical question. Human beings, I have suggested, cannot bear much reality. Perhaps not; but reality can bear any number of human beings, and will do so, come what may. It was Marghanita Laski who translated 'Simple inexpensive gowns for the mature fuller figure' as 'Nasty cheap dresses for old fat women'. No doubt the old fat women, as they donned their nasty cheap dresses, would have preferred the wording of the advertisement; but the translation told the truth, for all that, while the advertisment lied. Probably the British Rail spokesman who dreamed up 'standard' for 'second-class' thought he was being frightfully clever. But the standard carriages will not get us to our destinations a moment sooner than the second-class ones used to; not even, I may say, if he calls himself a spokesperson.

PS: I have just learned that the Post Office is now to call postmen 'delivery officers'. Have they told the dogs?

The Times March 17th, 1987

Cuban heels

REMEMBER THE VIETNAM war? While it was going on I used to address a question, about once every three weeks, to those who, in this country, were working so hard, and without hope of reward, to bring the delights of communism to those parts of the Vietnamese peninsula that the Vietcong had not already refreshed.

The question was this: why was it that whenever refugees fled, as well they might, from their villages, amid the horrors of the bombing and fighting, they *always* (I never heard of a single exception) fled southwards, to the embrace of the wicked Americans and the oppressive South Vietnam regime, instead of making their way towards the heroic liberation forces of North Vietnam, to settle eventually in the liberty, equality and fraternity of Hanoi?

I never got an answer. Truth to tell, I didn't expect one, which was why I asked the question. But in the last few days I have been sharply reminded of that time, because a very similar situation has arisen, which demands a very similar question, and which will similarly meet with the unbroken silence of those whose responsibility it would be to answer it, were it not for the dreadful epidemic of laryngitis that has struck them one and all.

A very substantial number of Cuban-born prisoners in American jails have been rioting, seizing control of their prisons, taking and threatening hostages (by the time these words appear they may have taken lives), resisting the authorities, risking death at the hands of the forces which have been standing by in preparation for storming the affected prisons.

(Again, when you read this such an assault may have taken place, possibly with the loss of lives on both sides.)

Some of these prisoners are among the hardest of the hard, villains involved in violent crime, with appalling records. The high-security prisons they are kept in are among the most bleak and harshly run in America; the walls should bear the legend *homo homini lupus*, which would cover the attitude of the criminals to each other and the mutual relations between them and the guards.

No wonder, anyone might think, that they are taking such desperate measures. Yet here we must pause for bewilderment. It transpires that the criminals are not seeking less grim conditions, or the removal of particularly brutal guards, or more prompt parole hearings. Above all, they are not trying to escape. In fact, their only demand – and remember they are clearly willing to kill or be killed in the pursuit of it – is to be kept where they are, behind the high walls and the iron bars. Any attempt to remove them, they have made plain, will be prolonged and bloody; desperate men will take desperate measures.

How can we explain this extraordinary paradox? How did I explain, in the rapt silence which followed my question to the admirers of Ho Chi Minh and his delightful smile, why peasants with nothing to lose did not flock to his banner, but rather flocked away from it whenever they had the chance?

Well, the prisoners in the American hoosegows have been told that they are to be sent back to Cuba, with its manifold delights, its heady air of true freedom, its benevolent and democratic system of government, its wise, kindly, far-seeing Father of his People, Fidel Castro. And they would rather kill, or die, or both, rather than accept such an assisted passage to their homeland.

Many of these men, perhaps most of them, were among those whom Castro shipped to the United States in 1980. At that time, he had made the rash promise that anyone in Cuba who wanted to leave would be allowed to do so; astounded and appalled by the numbers who promptly took him at his word (the most extraordinary thing I know about dictators is that they come to believe their own propaganda), he designed a chilling but neat revenge on the Americans who had promised to accept the refugees. Among the 125,000 who got out before the gates closed again, he inserted some 2,000 hardened criminals, who landed in the US and promptly went into American crime, many of them flourishing mightily because of their experience at home.

It is mostly these men who are involved in the prison risings, and who will go to any lengths to avoid being sent back. Now consider: the choice is living in Cuba out of prison, or living in America in prison (many of them, incidentally, are serving life sentences, and others have been told that even when their fixed sentences expire they will still have to live in detention camps).

And here comes my question, addressed to those who for so long have extolled Cuba as a land of milk, honey, brotherly love and freedom (remember the picture of Castro and Kinnock roaring with laughter together?): why do men wish to pace a cell in the dark degradation of an American prison rather than walk the streets of Havana (and remember that Cuba is their native land, which they have not seen for seven years) and breathe good Cuban air – now made all the better by the fact that Castro has given up smoking?

What, you may ask, can political freedom mean to men who will nevermore taste even the freedom to eat a hamburger in an Atlanta shopping mall? You may indeed ask it, but it would not be appropriate to ask it of me; send instead to the besieged prisons, and ask the frantic Cuban hardliners who man the walls.

I do not know the personal reading tastes of violent Cuban criminals in American jails. Possibly they pore over Mrs Thatcher's speeches, look forward eagerly to my *Times* columns, read and re-read the books of Alun Chalfont and Hugh Thomas. Or possibly not. Perhaps their feelings are even more refined, and they read nothing but Locke and Jefferson, Montaigne and Erasmus, Orwell and Solzhenitsyn. Or – very slightly more likely, I suppose – they read the books of those former political colleagues and associates of Castro who spent years of imprisonment and torture in Fidel's political prisons for disagreeing with him, and have come to the conclusion that to be *out* of such prisons would be a worse fate than to be *in* those that hold them at present.

Perhaps – it is what I have always believed – there is in people, even the most brutal and remorseless criminals, that spark of freedom that, however low it burns, never quite goes out. I have said before that Vladimir Bukovsky is an even more remarkable man than he appears. For he is of the generation of Russians who grew up in a sealed country, with no access to *samizdat*, let alone foreign books, and who heard nothing but the clichés of Soviet orthodoxy at school, at home and at the university. Where, then, did their knowledge of freedom come from? Where did they learn that what they were being told was lies? Where did they stumble across the amazing fact that there was truth to be had elsewhere?

Again, I must refuse to tell you, though I know; again, I must refer you to the Cuban prisoners in America; again, I must draw attention to the lack of any answer from those who have extolled Castro's regime for years; again, I must ask you to think of those who, in the last half century, have flitted from one communist tyranny to another, extolling each in turn as the only true repository of absolute freedom, absolute brotherhood, absolute peacefulness, absolute justice and even absolute prosperity.

I am too experienced in these matters, and too hardened against impudence, to suppose that Castro's admirers will even pause in their admiring to wonder why men would rather rot in an American prison than flower in Castro's garden of delights. But if you meet one of them – a Castro admirer, I mean, not a prisoner – you might try asking him. You will find that the ensuing silence is so prolonged that you can whistle the whole of the last act of *Götterdämmerung* while it is going on.

The Times November 30th, 1987

The spell of Richard Klingsor

T HE NEW COVENT GARDEN production of *Parsifal* illus-
trates with dreadful exactitude the phenomenon, often
remarked upon, of the man who divorces his wife and then
marries another woman who looks and behaves exactly like
her. I am sorry to re-awaken ancient grief but, high as is my
admiration for Mr Terry Hands, I have to say that his production of *Parsifal* in 1979 was a catastrophe registering about 470
on the Monsterflop Scale.

At that time, Mr Hands had directed only one opera –
Otello, in Paris – and although I wished him well, I foresaw
disaster. I foresaw it, however, not because I didn't believe him
talented enough for the task, but because directing opera is *not*
the same as directing plays, and a lifetime on the dramatic stage
will not guarantee success upon the lyric; a wholly new
approach (and, of course, technique) must first be understood
and assimilated. Moreover, Wagner demands an approach and
a technique different not only from the theatre but from other
composers, and a long course of immersion in his work and
thought, and assiduous attendance backstage throughout the
production of more than one of his operas, is essential to
success (which is not, even then, by any means assured).

Time passes; the Hands *Parsifal* is buried, and none so poor
to do it reverence; Bernard Haitink is appointed Musical
Director; and the question of a new *Parsifal* is raised. And then
somebody suggests Bill Bryden as director, and a lot of other
people, by no means all indisputably deranged, think it a good
idea. Bryden, who is also a very talented stage director – he
gave us *The Mysteries*, after all – had never directed any opera

at all, let alone Wagner; heigh-ho, up went the curtain, and five minutes later Mr Monster's useful invention was registering 396.

Let's get it over quickly; the idea of the production is that *Parsifal* is the end-of-term play at a minor public school in the 1930s, put on in the ruined church next door, with the doting parents of the performers scattered round the stage – handbags, hats, three-piece suits and all (Gurnemanz is the headmaster, incidentally); from time to time the parents are called upon to do things, such as light candles and hold them in their laps. I truly believe that it was only by the direct intervention of Almighty God – who, after all, has a substantial interest in the matter – that the Grail was not inscribed 'The Mrs Featheringay-Fawcett Cup for Outstanding Prowess in the Gymnasium'. (Perhaps it was; my sight is not of the keenest.)

You will doubtless suppose from that gloomy introduction that I had a bad time. Your supposition, though understandable, is baseless. Musically, it was without exception the finest *Parsifal* of my life; I have never before been so entirely overwhelmed by its force and meaning. And if you demand a context for my claim, I can offer some 30 performances in half a dozen countries; I never saw the legendary 1951 Knappertsbusch performance, though I treasure the recording, but I was at Bayreuth in 1962 for what was almost Kna's last revival of it, and some who heard both live swore that the latter was the better one. (Gundula Janowitz was one of the Flower Maidens – fancy! Mind you, Kiri Herself started as a Flower Maiden at Covent Garden.)

Over the years, the Wagner operas have rearranged themselves again and again in my mind in order of priority. *The Ring* (its constituent parts also go up and down in my ordering) stayed at the top of the charts for many years, but has slipped a little, while *Mastersingers* grows and grows; to *Tristan* I go resisting all the way, only to be drowned full fathom five the moment the Prelude starts; *Tannhäuser* I wouldn't much mind if I never heard again, and I have never really warmed to

Lohengrin (though I hope to hear Domingo sing it here in June even if I have to be carried in in a chair, like Amfortas, or indeed in a coffin, like Titurel).

But *Parsifal*, which I took a good many years to understand (it is not a work for youth), and have not yet finished understanding, and never shall, now stands at the very head of the page, beckoning me at one and the same time into Klingsor's Magic Garden, which is death, and the Temple of the Grail, which is eternal life.

The contrast between Wagner's prodigious genius and his horrible personal nature has been discussed endlessly and fruitlessly; there's no art to find the mind's construction in the music. Some great artists have been of the most beautiful and loving nature, and some have been anything from dishonest to the most frightful swine. (Caravaggio murdered a man in the course of a quarrel on the tennis-court; even McEnroe has never done that.) Wagner, to be sure, takes the dichotomy to lengths unparalleled in all history (Georg Solti calls him 'det old gengster') but there is nothing to be done about it, and surely *Parsifal* is the greatest testimony in all art to the terrible truth that so enraged Shaffer's Salieri: that any channel, even an unworthy one, will serve as an aqueduct through which the pure water of art can flow from Heaven to earth, and not be tainted by the corrupted vessel that serves it.

There is a moment, some two-thirds of the way through Act Two, when this lesson is driven home in the most violent possible way. Consider: the raging tempest of sensuality which the central act consists of is constructed out of musical materials very different from those of the two outer acts. This is reflected in the *leitmotivs* which Wagner uses throughout the act; naturally, Kundry's dominates the list, together with those closely associated with her and her past.

When Parsifal enters, he adds strains from the other world, and for a long time Herzeleide, the Wound, the Spear, Kundry's Wildness, Torment of Sin, Longing, Fool, and of course Klingsor, weave in and out of the heaving, flooding orchestral and vocal texture. Suddenly, without warning, we hear, for the first time in three-quarters of an hour's music, the Grail. It is like a blow in the face, so enmeshed are we in the struggle between good and evil; but I *never* remember that it is approaching, with its glorious news that the battle is almost over, and light has triumphed over darkness.

Well, this time, when it rose from the orchestra like Excalibur, I thought it would stop my heart, so far had I been drawn into the furnace of the struggle. Surely this is what the shepherds who were tending their flocks must have experienced when the angel appeared to them with glad tidings of great joy.

The tidings in *Parsifal* are brought in Act Three, when the Spear which pierced Christ's side heals the wound of Amfortas's guilt; even the poor production could not spoil that moment, so powerful and so complete was the spell of the conducting, playing and singing. But the spell of the performance was as strong as it was because it served, with the utmost fidelity, the spell of the opera – its drama, its meaning and its consummate ability to steep the whole evening in the balm of hope.

And when you come to think of it, what is the Christian message but hope? Of course it is an oversimplification to read *Parsifal* as orthodox Christian witness; Wagner wove much besides Christianity into his final work. But if we generalize a little, we can demonstrate that the redemption of Amfortas is indeed the symbol of the redemption of the world; remember that we hear, as Parsifal moves with the healing instrument towards the stricken man, the Grail, not Parsifal's own theme, and as the spearpoint closes the wound, it is not the weapon that sounds, but Amfortas himself. Surely Wagner is saying that Parsifal is neither Christ nor John the Baptist, but the Paraclete of St John's Gospel, who is sent to comfort the world: 'Peace I leave with you, my peace I give unto you.' And it is man, sinful but capable of redemption, who receives the divine gift from the hands of 'the innocent fool, made wise by pity'.

It is possible that Richard Wagner is cackling in hell as he reads these words in the Asbestos Edition, having caught yet another sucker with his hokum. But I doubt it; I heard the closing bars of the Covent Garden performance, and I saw the Dove flutter across the stage in the radiance of the Grail, and remembered how St John goes on: 'Let not your heart be troubled, neither let it be afraid.'

The Times February 18th, 1988

Four legs better

O F ALL THE Single Issue Fanatics who increasingly infest our society, with their conviction that nothing matters beside their particular cause and that any action, however violent, dangerous or criminal, is justified in their pursuit of it, the most extreme and monomaniacal are those who claim to defend 'animal rights'. Of course, reputable organizations such as the RSPCA also operate, legally and without violence, in this work; I am discussing only those which act outside the law, in particular the groups calling themselves the Animal Liberation Front and the Hunt Retribution Squad.

I have pointed out repeatedly that any study of the actions of these people, and of the words they use to justify themselves, makes it appallingly clear that what motivates them is not a love of animals but a hatred of human beings. Let me immediately quell any doubts arising out of that claim by quoting verbatim some passages from an interview with one of the leaders of the Hunt Retribution Squad, published in the bulletin of the Animal Liberation Front:

> We have quite a number of different ways to attack hunting. One way is to actually go to a hunt, pull a hunter off his horse, strip him, handcuff him to a tree and paint him red . . . another way is to go into their houses at night and rough the hunters up, with the aim of actually putting them in hospital. We will also use weapons such as petrol bombs and shotguns . . . We feel it is important to escalate slowly – so at first we will just inflict injuries, which will increase in severity. When a hunter ends up in hospital with very severe

injuries, the next stage then would be to actually take a hunter out completely . . .

Let's look at the last few months. In October (1984) we spread broken glass on the pitch where Jackie Charlton and Jimmy Hill's (both notorious hunters) team were due to play. In December we desecrated the Duke of Beaufort's grave. In the last few months we have steadily built up an armoury of weapons including knives, knuckle-dusters, club hammers, crowbars, axes, sledge hammers, chain saws and shotguns.

It is not enough to say that whoever spoke those words is deranged, and that he (or she – the women in these move-ments are no less violent in word and deed than the men) is living in a world of fantasy where the 'chain saws and shot-guns' are a dream of blood rather than actual weapons. In the first place, they *did* desecrate the Duke of Beaufort's grave, and in the second, the very fact that such seething, mad anthro-pophobia is at large in our society should be a matter of profound concern. Besides, even if the Hunt Retribution Squad only dream of violence, their allies, sympathizers and cousins in the Animal Liberation Front, though they claim to take care *not* to injure or kill human beings, have undoubtedly been responsible (on their own admission) for a list of violent crimes so extensive and horrible that it is already possible to make a prophecy that is virtually certain to come true: sooner or later, they will do murder.

Exaggerating, am I? Not so to judge by the account, in the bulletin of the ALF Supporters Group, of one of the ALF's more spectacular coups – the attack by two 'activists' on a Merseyside meat processing factory on March 23. It tells how they broke in through a ground floor window and then – in meticulous and loving detail, which I forbear from repeating since the fewer who know such things the better – the steps they took to contrive an explosion that destroyed the entire building, causing damage estimated at £20,000. The only part of the report I quote verbatim is the following: 'While a number of people have expressed concern about the jobs lost in a high unemployment area they are, needless to say, local political lobbyists.'

Do you still wish to deny my premise, that these people hate their own kind and will one day take to killing them? For remember, the building destroyed was not a place where experiments were performed on animals, or even an abattoir; it was a meat-processing factory. Furthermore, on the front cover of the ALF bulletin in which the words above appeared, the headline is: 'Factories don't burn down by themselves . . . they need help from you, Learn to Burn'.

And in case anyone thinks that that, however outrageous, does not really sum up the attitude and ethos of these people, I shall give a few examples (a truly tiny selection) of actions the ALF or Hunt Retribution Squad boast that their members have taken; I am trying to illustrate not just the violence, but, even more important, the totalitarian impulse behind it: the theme is that they can do *anything* to *anyone* in the cause they have selected.

In Sheffield, they smashed the windows of at least 15 shops which were doing no more than display posters for a circus. In Bedworth, Warwicks, they caused £10,000 worth of damage in an arson attack on an abbatoir. In Derby they smashed the windows of a fur shop. In Edinburgh they smashed the windows of five butchers' shops. In Cheadle, they smashed the windows of a house belonging to 'a man who shoots and snares animals.' At Stoke-on-Trent they smashed the windows of a 'vivisector's' house. At Beckenham they threw petrol bombs at the garages of officials of the Wellcome Foundation. In Carshalton they smashed the windows of a restaurant which served frogs' legs. In Devon they stretched piano wire, at neck height, in woodland through which hunters were riding. In the Peak District they destroyed some 250 shooting butts, with estimated damage of £200,000. In Yorkshire and Lancashire they caused thousands of pounds of damage in attacks on gun shops. At Oxford they beat up beaglers. In Warwickshire they scarred for life a follower of the hunt by pushing a broken bottle in his face. And finally, one of their more bizarre actions, bizarre not so much because of the action itself but because of its consequences, was to break into the research establishment of the Royal College of Surgeons, where they terrified girl assistants, caused £20,000 of damage and stole records. On the basis of these, the Royal College was prosecuted rather than the terrorists, and had to spend £100,000 on the case and an appeal before it was cleared of all charges and awarded costs out of public funds.

What will our world become if we cannot disabuse these people and the other Single Issue Fanatics of their notion that there are literally no limits to what they may do in furtherance of their ends? What sort of righteousness is it that leads to evil, what protection of animals to destruction of livelihoods, what casting out of Satan to letting in Beelzebub? What horrible frenzy grips these people so that in order to destroy the humanity in themselves they must needs abuse and daub and smash and burn and injure and perhaps at last kill? Why, when you and I see a pork pie do they see the devil, when we see a fishmonger they see a cannibal, when we see hunting pink they see red human blood and long to spill it?

I do not know. But I do know that before this thing is stopped men will die, and badly. The Nazis showed that, in order to destroy human beings by the million, it was necessary only to convince enough people that the beings were not really human at all. The members of the Animal Liberation Front and similar organizations show by the words they write and speak that they have already convinced themselves that a man who eats a lamb chop or uses a mouse to seek a cure for cancer is not a man but a sub-man, fit only for bloody vengeance. I am unable to believe that that vengeance can be much longer delayed.

The Times July 3rd, 1986

The price of everything

THERE IS A widespread belief in some political circles that
manifest nonsense will somehow turn into profound
wisdom if it has enough capital letters sprinkled over it. The
most familiar example of this tendency (apart, perhaps, from
the Militant Tendency itself) is Harold Wilson's Social Contract, but there are plenty more to match the customer's
sample, such as Caring Society, Racism Awareness, Fight The
Cuts, Outreach, Campaign for Nuclear Disarmament (often
abbreviated to Ban the Bomb), and for that matter Cultural
Revolution, Great Leap Forward and Five Year Plan.

Now there is a new one; we are promised that the socialist
dawn will be ushered in with a National Economic Assessment. It seems that representatives of government, the Trades
Union Congress (there's another!) and industry will be invited
to take part in that ancient British game (said to be older even
than morris dancing) called gettingroundthetable. The rules of
the game are very complicated but, as I understand them, the
object is to decide which manufacturing companies, not yet in
existence, will be most profitable ten years later, what hitherto
undiscovered scientific and technological inventions will
come into being in the same decade, which of the years up to
1997 will have fine summers leading to ample harvests, and
which will have much rain and cold with a consequent short-
fall in crop yields, what the pound will be worth against the
dollar after the next American presidential election but two,
and at what figure should the participants set the annual rate of
inflation, the balance of payments, and the pre-tax profits of
British Rail, from now to the end of the century.

I begin thus with the National Economic Assessment because the idea encapsulates an entire way of political life, and simultaneously distinguishes it from the other, opposite, political philosophy. The question at the heart of this divide, which no Drusus, no Brunel, no Bailey could ever bridge, turns upon what view is taken of the role of the state in a nation's life. A National Economic Assessment is nonsense because it is designed to do something that is impossible – to predict the economic future – and at the same time to do something it is incapable of doing – to take over the chief function of economic and business enterprise, with its tens of thousands of decisions being made every hour, decisions which may individually lead to success and advance or failure and bankruptcy, but which in the aggregate will invariably and fruitfully reward success, and briskly and impassionately dispose of failure.

I have long thought that the most damning example of the perversion of political and cultural thought that has taken place in this country in the past half century is the transformation of the world 'elite', which once meant everything that is best and most worthy of striving for, and has now become a term of contempt. But there is a worse example still; it is the similar transformation of 'the profit motive', which, though it is the sole engine which has dragged every advanced society – most emphatically including ours – out of poverty towards affluence, is now condemned as evil.

There are places in the world in which it has already been destroyed; in these, all personal and political freedoms have also been abolished. I, of course, would argue that the one destruction leads inevitably to the other, but it is not necessary to accept the causal connection; where individual economic enterprise is unknown, prohibited or restrained, all the people, other than the ruling class, will be poor.

The reason is obvious; systems without choice are based on the greatest of all the world's fallacies; that *you* know what is good for *me* better than I do myself. You don't; and even if you did, the state (which in this context can only mean a civil servant or a politician dressed in a little brief authority) certainly doesn't.

It will be argued – it *is* argued – that there are services which only the state can provide. Those who pursue that argument, if asked for a representative example, would most probably give the National Health Service. Well, the claim is obviously untrue, as Bupa and other private health services demonstrate, but there is no need to rest our case against statism solely on the fact that it is not indispensable. Let us look at one central, crucial fact about the NHS.

Let us look at it through the eyes of Drs Max Gammon and Miguel Nadal. In a study for the St Michael's Organization (a research body founded in 1973 with Professor Sir Ernst Chain – of antibiotics fame – as its first president), these two intrepid seekers after medical truth have returned from their search with some startling evidence. Their argument is complex, their statistics exhaustive and their conclusions cautious, but the report makes unnecessary practically all the current discussion of the NHS and its condition, together with the rival theories of how it got into its present state and how that state may be changed.

Gammon and Nadal demonstrate that in England alone, between 1974 and 1985, annual expenditure on the NHS had increased from £4 billion to £17 billion, the staff from 674,000 to 817,000 – within which, clerical and administrative staff had increased from 79,000 to 106,000 and nursing staff from 273,000 to 344,000 – *while the number of beds available had fallen from 406,000 to 345,000*.

You will see from the dates of the survey (1974–1985) that governments of both political complexions were in power while this was happening; the two doctors have, as it happens, extended their survey back to the inception of the NHS in 1948, and found that exactly the same process had been at work from the beginning. I have brutally summarized a long and detailed survey, but the conclusion is clear; whatever government is in power, more money, more administrators and more nurses are provided for the NHS, yet its services are available for fewer and fewer people.

Why? The answer is as complete as it is damning. The authors call the disease 'bureaucratic displacement', and define it thus: 'the growth of non-productive bureaucratic activity progressively displaces productive activity'; there is an extra poison at the heart of this development in the fact that the huge increase in the number of nurses is in effect fraudulent, since in addition to the greater numbers of non-medical staff, the nurses have found themselves doing less and less nursing, and devoting more and more of their time to administrative and clerical duties.

Gammon and Nadal do not draw the obvious conclusion; I shall. The reason for the scandal is that nobody in the NHS, from the highest management to the lowest general purpose employee, will suffer economically from this prodigious waste of money. If the NHS was a private business, it would by now either have put its finances, staffing and administrative structure on a sound and cost-effective footing, or gone out of business. It is only because everybody knows that the NHS will not be allowed to go out of business that no attempt is made, by government or by those who actually run it, to take the dramatic decisions which would turn it into an institution giving twice the service with half the employees at a third of the price.

Perhaps worse still, though, is the condition of so much of our local government. What clown invented rate-capping? The finger points at Mr Patrick Jenkin; but he plainly did not realize that however snugly the cap fits, those wearing it will never dismantle their giant bureaucracies, much less sack themselves and their colleagues, but will always instead do less of what the rates are supposed to be for, so that in time there will be an infinitely large local government staff giving an infinitely small service to the public.

But the NHS and local government, dropsical monsters though they have both become, are still only illustrations of what is wrong with the statist argument. The statists' belief that other people's money doesn't count, and therefore does not have to be accounted for, lies at the heart of their philosophy; but it, too, is not itself the philosophy, only what it leads to. And it leads, I believe, to a great crime disguised as a great kindness. The statist insists that failure must not be permitted, because it may, and generally does, cause pain to those who have failed. He thus poses as a philanthropist; but what he really is is a dictator. For you cannot, obviously, abolish failure, least of all by Act of Parliament; but what you can do is to make success almost impossible.

It wouldn't be difficult. Raise taxes, particularly Corporation Tax; give union power back to the union *capi*; legislate for a minimum wage; allow inflation to rise, leaving unharmed by its rise only the thriftless who have no savings to be eroded; crush competition wherever it can be crushed, and in particular when it is facing a state monopoly; let local government go back to untendered 'direct labour'; ban the private provision of non-medical facilities in the NHS; insist on 'positive discrimination' in employment; attack unemployment by compelling British Rail, British Steel and the Coal Board to hire tens of thousands of men for whom they have no need, and restore (with a good bit over) all the reductions in the numbers of the Civil Service achieved in the past few years.

Above all, abolish private education, abolish private health care, abolish private enterprise, abolish national wealth itself, on the pretext that these are depriving the poor of their share; and when there is no national wealth for anybody, proclaim that the revolution has succeeded.

And so it will have done, in a sense. Because a people who are willing to depend upon the state for everything they need are the state's slaves, and those who offer such a people such largesse are the enslavers. We have marched far down that road in the years since the Second World War, and it has not been governments only of the left who have led the march. For the first time, in the decade moving towards its end, we have had a real choice, and it lies before us at this moment more starkly than ever before.

We can have a society in which the power and extent of the state is progressively dismantled, leaving a safety net for those who cannot make their own way to a sufficiency, but for the rest offering the prizes that successful endeavour can bring, as well as the penalties that failure entails.

What I am talking about is a kind of personal privatization, in which half the nation no longer dies of shock and outrage if it is suggested that in return for lower taxes the said half might possibly have to pay to enter the V & A, or even to stump up a reasonable sum, no doubt means-tested, for a visit to the doctor. When the state is no longer casting its shadow over us all, we shall begin to think it rather odd that we used to depend so much upon it, and so little upon ourselves. Beside that realization, the fact that, with enterprise given its head for good or ill, we shall all be better off anyway, will be of little consequence. For what I am talking about is not how many cars we have in the garage, but what sort of people we are. By an extraordinary coincidence, we shall all have the opportunity to answer that question on Thursday.*

The Times June 8th, 1987

---

* Thursday was Polling Day.

Kiss and make up

THAT VERY GIFTED and intelligent actress, Janet Suzman, was born in South Africa, and she is at present running, and directing at, the Market Theatre in Johannesburg, which is one of the country's leading playhouses. It is a brave venture, and recently it became, abruptly, considerably braver. Miss Suzman decided to put on *Othello*.

Being a logical woman, and no doubt having read the play, she cast an African as Othello and a white actress as Desdemona. But, as must have been obvious to her, *Othello* in her native country is not like *Othello* anywhere else. *Hamlet* would have passed muster, for the dynastic problems of Denmark are remote from South Africa; *King Lear* is hard on ungrateful daughters, but there is no reason to suppose that these are more common in South Africa than elsewhere; *Macbeth* is brutal and violent, but everybody knows that the Scots are all mad.

The fourth of the great tragedies, however, impinges, to say the least. And some of the language in the very first scene must have raised – undoubtedly did raise – hackles in the audience. Here is Iago, awakening Brabantio:

> Even now, now, very now, an old black ram
> Is tupping your white ewe

And Brabantio launches into a torrent of rage mixed with incredulity, in words which echo a strain of thought still current in many parts of the world, and in South Africa most of all:

O thou foul thief! Where hast thou stow'd my daughter?
Damn'd as thou art, thou has enchanted her;
For I'll refer me to all things of sense,
If she in chains of magic were not bound,
Whether a maid so tender, fair, and happy,
So opposite to marriage that she shunn'd
The wealthy curled darlings of our nation,
Would ever have, to incur a general mock,
Run from her guardage to the sooty bosom
Of such a thing as thou; to fear, not to delight . . .
She is abus'd, stol'n from me, and corrupted
By spells and medicines bought of mountebanks;
For nature so preposterously to err,
Being not deficient, blind, or lame of sense,
Sans witchcraft could not.

Well, there it is; nearly four centuries ago the argument was laid out plainly and unambiguously: is it possible that black and white can mutually love and, if they maintain that they can, is there not something abnormal, something disgusting, about their claim and their behaviour?

Most civilized people will answer yes to the first question and no to the second. Yet the extraordinary thing about Brabantio's attitude, and the jeers of his tormentors, is that they are entirely recognizable today; indeed, today's versions are the very same ones, couched in modern speech. If the taboo is absurd, degrading and baseless (which is what I believe) it is taking the devil of a time a-dying.

I shall return to that aspect of the matter, but first, I must record the response to Miss Suzman's production. It was, I gather, an enormous hit, with massive advance bookings, packed houses, and critical acclaim. True, it was the first time such a great Shakespearean classic had been performed at the Market Theatre; true, also, that few members of the audience could be untouched by the special circumstances under which it was being played. Yet I learn that for the Johannesburg

Othello black and white alike flocked to the theatre and were enthralled by what they found.

With, that is, a few exceptions. The embracing of Desdemona by Othello, the kiss of black lips on white ones, was too much for some of the whites in the audience; they walked out. Shortly afterwards, hate mail began to arrive at the theatre. (Miss Suzman rejected the obvious solution to her problem; to insist that the play was about an Irishman, as white as any redneck, called O'Thello.)

It is no use trying to apply reason to these events; if the feelings that caused them were susceptible to reason they would have dissolved long ago. When a wound that has festered for hundreds of years bleeds afresh, it is not just pessimism that suspects it is incurable. And yet we have to cure it, or we shall one day all find ourselves in a *Kulturkampf*, the nature of which no one will be able to predict or control.

I do not believe there is any reality in Mr Enoch Powell's prophecy of inter-racial civil war in Britain; indeed, I see that he has recently felt obliged to freshen it, like all those prophets who announce the date on which the world will come to an end, and, when it doesn't, announce, not at all abashed, a new *Dies Irae*. But I do believe that unless we can become colour-blind we shall never find that nirvana of integration necessary to every individual, let alone the public integration that every society needs if it is to be healthy. But that brings me back to the ancient taboo that horrified Brabantio as much as it still horrifies those Johannesburg theatre-goers who walked out.

If there are areas where reason cannot penetrate, are we helpless to do anything but watch as the tide flows remorselessly on? Surely not. It used to be fashionable, among those who consciously or unconsciously felt hostility to those of another colour, to insist that legislation cannot make us love one another, and this was taken not as a truism, but as an excuse for inaction. We nevertheless passed a lot of legislation, and set up a lot of boards and bodies and commissions, all of which put together have achieved very little. *But they have not achieved nothing.*

You cannot stop a landlady hating Nigerians. But you can stop her slamming the door in the face of a Nigerian student with a cry of 'No niggers here'. I found very significant the recent story of the idiotic policeman who urged a community to watch out for 'coloureds' and note the number plates of their cars. The significance of the story lay not in the policeman's folly but in the reaction, first among the people he was exhorting to such monochrome vigilance, and then among general public comment; the reaction was decidedly unfavourable to Plod.

I have no doubt that there were people who read that story, and secretly supported the policeman. Secretly; they did not express their feelings. Some would say that that is because they are cowed by opinion around them; but so they damned well should be. Besides, I do not believe that that is the only thing that keeps them silent; I believe that over the years they have begun to feel shame at the attitudes and prejudices they cannot help.

Good; let us continue. In this country, of course, it is bedevilled by party; too many political spivs have battened on Britain's race relations, on both sides of the chasm. Yet who but Mr Powell could deny that our race relations have – slowly, haltingly and unevenly – got better over the years?

It is a desperately slow process; but within a framework of law there is a chance that the ancient nightmares which troubled Brabantio may begin to fade. Yet what chance is there of such a fading in South Africa, where the framework of law is designed to perpetuate the nightmares?

Only this chance: the great majority of the audiences there did watch the kiss that united black and white, and were not struck by lightning (or even by police truncheons) for their temerity. The Immorality Act has been repealed; its baleful influence will persist until the Group Areas Act follows it into history, but even now some South Africans must have noticed that the repeal has not led to the entire country being engulfed in earthquakes, tidal waves and the Ten Plagues of Egypt. If some have noticed, more will.

Whether South Africa's leaders have noticed, or are capable of noticing, I cannot say; if not, then a real and terrible war is sooner or later inevitable. But if they can awake, if that Eleventh Plague is avoided, a tiny part of this credit will go to Shakespeare and Miss Suzman.

The Times October 26th, 1987

Mrs Vanderbilt's moon

W E ARE AT a concert in a stately home built on a scale that Kubla Khan would have found daunting. To be precise, we are in the ballroom, which is three storeys high and has a *trompe-l'oeil* ceiling of blue sky and cotton-wool clouds, presumably – no, quite certainly – because the real weather cannot be trusted to meet the owners' exacting standards at all times.

At the end of the room there is a staircase, up (or down) which a cavalry regiment with a full complement of horses and artillery could proceed in line abreast; it forks a few hundred steps up, and the twin branches continue to climb until even the keenest eye can no longer see where they go; the general opinion is that they finish on Aldebaran.

When the interval comes, we wander out on to the terrace, which is roughly the size of Yorkshire. Dusk has fallen; the air is sweet and mild; the sea can be heard gently lapping on the shore just beyond the lawn, which in turn is roughly the size of Scotland. As we gaze upon the scene, a glass of Taittinger in hand, there sails up the sky, icily, haughtily, refusing to speak to anyone without a formal introduction, the silver orb of Mrs Vanderbilt's personal private moon.

This is Newport, Rhode Island, of which it may truly be said that if it did not exist it would now be quite impossible for anyone to invent it. *Now* impossible; but its modern fame *was* invented, virtually overnight, about a hundred years ago. For Newport was the place picked by the great American 'robber barons' of the 19th century to build their palaces and to fill them with their loot. Bellevue Avenue runs north–south for

four miles, from the centre of the town to Rhode Island
Sound, and along it, strung out like choice pearls on a necklace
(and no damned nonsense about cultured ones), are the giant
mansions of those giant rogues, paid for from their giant
profits, and built as giant, enduring monuments to their
giant pride.

Come with me down this amazing street, with its vistas of
amazing mansions. We start modestly, with Kingscote, patterned after a Greek temple, though actually made of wood;
then things rapidly get grander. Here, for instance, is The
Elms; it is a copy of the Château d'Agnès at Asnières, built for
Julius Berwind, who specialized in cornering America's entire
supply of coal. Where other houses have wall-paper – that is,
all over – The Elms has Louis Quatorze tapestries; it also has a
golden piano in working order, and a sunken garden that
could accommodate the Grand Canyon, with enough room
left over for the Tuscarora Deep. For that matter – and here I
stop exaggerating and present nothing but sober fact – the
main bedroom is 40ft across.

Next comes Château-sur-Mer, a copy of a Loire château,
only bigger. This was the William Wetmore pad; he made his
millions in the China trade, and a good few millions they must
have been, to judge by Château-sur-Mer, where the entrance
hall is 45ft high, and the staircase up it is lined on both sides
with 16th century stained glass.

And here is Rosecliff, built by the Oelrichs, whose fortune
was founded on silver-mines. No mere châteaux for them;
Rosecliff is a copy of the Grand Trianon at Versailles, and the
ballroom is 80ft by 40ft. Beyond Rosecliff is the bijou des. res.
of the Astors, where the term 'The Four Hundred', meaning
the 400 most fashionable folk in the United States was coined,
derived from the fact that the ballroom could comfortably
hold 400 dancers.

A little further, and we are at Marble House, the one where
the ballroom is entirely covered in gold leaf and the dining-
room (in pink marble), has bronze Louis Quatorze chairs so
massive that each diner was furnished with a servant who had

no other duty but to move the thing whenever the guest wanted to uncross his legs or sneeze. At Belcourt Castle, the owner, Oliver Belmont, went one better; well, several better, really. His dining room could – and did – seat 350 guests, lit by a pair of 17th century chandeliers, said to be the world's biggest (and looted from an Italian monastery); the stained glass in *his* ballroom was 13th century, and – presumably because the castle was for once not modelled on a French palace (it resembles the White House) – the ballroom fireplace was designed as a Loire château.

And here is the sea. But on the way back to town, we must make a diversion because the only one of these monsters not on Bellevue Avenue is The Breakers, Architectosaurus Rex itself, which is where the concert with which I started was taking place under Mrs Vanderbilt's moon. The Breakers, patterned after the Italian Renaissance, has 70 rooms, and it is said that 6,000 tons of marble were used for the interior alone; the ceilings are covered in gold and silver, and the outer gates, in wrought-iron, are 30ft high.

I forgot to mention that the hall door at Marble House is 25ft across and weighs 10 tons.

This is Gatsbyland; indeed, the film was shot here. But Newport is far older than the generations of newly-rich who built Bellevue Avenue. Away from the great house the town is an enclave, almost perfectly preserved or restored, of Colonial buildings. It is nearly as old as the Pilgrim Fathers, for it was founded by a group of freedom-loving families who rejected the iron theocracy of Massachusetts and fled it for somewhere they could breathe more freely. Presumably, the fame of Newport's tolerance spread rapidly, for the first Quakers to settle in America made for Newport, in 1657; more remarkable is the fact that in the following year the very first Jews to land in the New World made their homes in this lovely place, and Newport is proud to possess the oldest synagogue in North America. On the other hand, Newport's original prosperity was built on the slave trade, in a most ingenious form. Ships sailed from Newport to Africa with cargoes of rum; the rum was exchanged for slaves, and the ships then sailed with them to the West Indies and exchanged them for molasses, from which rum is made. A cut from each side of this equilateral triangle soon built up Newport, by the middle of the 18th century, into one of the richest cities in the East. In the War of Independence, however, the town was bitterly fought over and largely destroyed; it might have become a second Boston, but is now a community of only some 30,000 people (the numbers hugely swollen in the summer by armies of visitors), resigned to being – or rather delighted to be – a charming backwater. (Newport had one more flutter of history; during the Civil War the North's Naval Academy was sited here.)

It's a sportive town, in both senses of the word. The huge harbour is crammed with yachts, some of them sufficiently opulent to suggest that the Vanderbilts and their friends have returned in their original splendour, and although there is the usual round-the-bay-for-10-dollars trade, the sailing is taken seriously; after all, this is the home of the America's Cup race. There is serious tennis, too; the Tennis Hall of Fame is a building holding not only a museum of the sport, but the country's best-known grass courts, with tournaments to match.

At first sight, the wharfs look only quaint, full of tiny shops with achingly fashionable façades; look closer, though, and you will see that they are not selling junk. A miniature art gallery houses not Grandma Moses reproductions but fine Innuit sculptures; a shop selling costume jewellery proffers not the usual mass-produced rubbish but beautiful and imaginative designs; another, full of beach clothes, eschews not only T-shirts but Bermuda shorts; and in Le Bistro there is a quite startlingly good meal to be had.

The great mansions are now owned by the Preservation Society, and kept up meticulously as tourist attractions. But there is still a vast amount of money sloshing about in Newport, even if it is not flashed about so obtrusively as it was when Bellevue Avenue was young. Gatsby would certainly still feel at home at some of the parties; indeed, he would have given most of them, and would certainly have invited the Claus von Bulows.

But now I must tell what I was doing in Newport, for I am no yachtsman, and still less a tennis-player, and the mansions of the American rich are small beer compared to my memory of the weekend I stayed at the Moët et Chandon Château de Saran and drank the stuff in every great vintage from 1911 to modern times. The clue is that concert at The Breakers; Newport, for the last 19 years, has had an annual Music Festival for a fortnight in July (in addition to the Jazz Festival in August, though that lasts only a couple of days), and it is remarkable for two reasons. The first is that the concerts are held in the palaces of Bellevue Avenue; there are three a day, morning, afternoon and evening, and we scuttle from Rosecliff to Beechwood and from The Breakers to Marble House, and sit amid the gold leaf and the stained glass and the pink marble and the view of the terrace and the lawn and the sea beyond. What price the Queen Elizabeth Hall after that?

As for the second special quality of the Newport Festival, I must introduce you, if he will stand still long enough, to Mark Malkovich the Third, who looks like a particularly amiable bear, and is one of those glorious lunatics without whom the world would not go on, and wouldn't be worth living in even if it did. He is the Director of the Festival, and has been these 13 years past, and I have offered a prize of ten thousand dollars, advertised in the local newspaper, for anyone who can walk a quarter of a mile through Newport, arm in arm with Mr Malkovich, and not be stopped at least a dozen times by citizens wanting to shake his hand and pass the time of day with him. (The dynasty, incidentally, is assured; he and his wife kept introducing me to their immense collection of handsome sons, one of whom is called Mark after his father, grandfather and great-grandfather; there is also a daughter, who will soon be the cause of an epidemic of insomnia in Newport, spread by the incessant noise of young men shooting themselves on the Malkovich doorstep in the middle of the night for hopeless love of her.)

The Newport Festival cannot compete for the greatest international stars with the rest of the festival-strewn world (though it did manage to bag Shura Cherkassky this year). It is always short of money, like all small festivals, but now a fairy godmother has descended upon the place, out of the rising sun; Yamaha have not only guaranteed sponsorship, but scattered pianos through the town in astounding profusion.

Armed with such confidence, Mark Malkovich has repeated the extraordinary trick he has been playing for 13 years; short of the foremost names of music, he sets himself to devise programmes so extraordinary, so rich and so rare that they can and do (and should) draw music-lovers from thousands of miles away. He ransacks the lesser-known works of better-known composers and the unknown works of little-known ones, and comes up every time (and there were 38 concerts this year) with a vast array of discoveries, revelations and astonishments, exquisitely and unerringly juxtaposed; there was hardly a bar of it all that I wasn't delighted to hear, and quite four-fifths of it new to me. (He even found some Schubert – Schubert! – that I didn't know, and a piece of Rachmaninov that nobody knows, because he found it in manuscript, unpublished, in the Library of Congress.)

Newport has one more trick to play. It is called Cliff Walk, a sufficiently explicit name. But every visitor to the town must take it at least once, because the kings of Bellevue Avenue built their palaces, for the most part, facing the sea so that those walking down the Avenue see only the hindquarters of the mansions (imposing enough, to be sure), and for the greatest vistas they must have their backs to the water, and look across the lawns to the majestic facades.

No one builds like that any more; Forbes and Onassis and Khashoggi (and look what happened to *him*) and their like have neither the imagination nor the self-confidence to stare down a world in which these monsters built these monsters, and recked neither the cost nor the consequences. Like the brontosaurus and the mastodon, they have vanished utterly from the world, leaving no more than a heap of bones from which the experts deduce what they looked like. But in Newport, for a moment at dusk, they come to life, terrifying and ridiculous, unscrupulous and philanthropic, revolting and sublime. As I left, I paused for a final moment, and faintly, far off, there was borne on the breeze the sound of Oliver Belmont greeting his 350 dinner-guests, and Mrs Astor opening the ball. Half admiring, half appalled, I raised a hand in salute.

The Times July 25th, 1987

Just for a handful of silver

IT IS PROBABLE that the English-speaking world's most tenaciously held misapprehension is that Lord Acton said 'All power corrupts'. The runner-up must surely be the belief – no less mistaken for being as passionately maintained – that St Paul was of the opinion that money is the root of all evil.

What St Paul, that wise old bird, claimed was that the *love* of money could be thus described, which is another matter. (You can look up Acton for yourself.) And I think that recent events, to say nothing of imminently impending ones, would lead most reflective people to conclude that St Paul was right.

There is much talk, anent the Lester Piggott affair, of whether the word 'tragic' should be used to describe his fate. The harsher moralists declare that it should not, and are bandying words such as 'squalid', 'crook' and 'deserved'; others, perhaps more conscious of the frailties of humankind, are expressing something more like pity. I am decidedly in the pity camp; but I cannot help remembering the old definition of tragedy, into which the hero-jockey's fall fits with the utmost exactitude: a man brought down by that which made him great. But it is not his fall that I wish to discuss today; indeed, it is not really Mr Piggott at all. It is the extraordinary effect, on some individuals, that money has.

Let us begin at the pettier end of the spectrum. The Keith Best case is, as far as its important aspects of principle are concerned, more or less exhausted. But while it was going on, I spent a good deal of time trying to fathom the feelings and attitude of the now disgraced MP. Just come with me, tiptoeing lest we disturb him, into Mr Best's study, where he sits at his desk, a pen in his hand and a pile of British Telecom application-forms before him. He reaches out and pulls them towards him; he takes the cap off his pen.

What in the name of St Paul himself happens then? Consider: it was already obvious that the BT issue was going to be enormously over-subscribed. The allocations he had asked for were trivial, and the inevitable scaling-down would have reduced them – indeed did reduce them – even further. At every moment in the half hour or so it would have taken him to fill in the forms it must have been inescapably present in his mind that if what he was doing were ever to come to light his entire career and repute would be instantly destroyed. And yet he did not screw the top of his pen back on, tear up the forms and pour himself a stiff whisky and soda. He folded the forms, by now turned into lethal weapons, tucked them into the envelopes, licked the flaps, and sealed them. And somewhere in the universe, where such things are monitored, a gong boomed to signify that his fate was now decided.

Very well, those who break the law convince themselves that they will not be caught. Yet surely some kind of relativity principle must come in somewhere; if Mr Best had stood to gain tens of millions of pounds by his action, he might well have thought the risk worth it, damned silly notion though that would be. But to make a monkey of yourself for monkey-nuts?

> Men that hazard all
> Do it in hope of fair advantages:
> A golden mind stoops not to shows of dross.

Now slide with me across the spectrum, deftly averting our eyes from all those figures at present covered by the *sub judice* rule, to where Mr Piggott's life lies in ruins. The picture painted by his counsel, Mr John Mathew, QC, was doubtless heightened with some rich chiaroscuro – a plea in mitigation can hardly be too eloquent – but however high the discount rate the impression left is of a man whose legitimate millions had not touched, and could not touch, the isolation, emptiness and futility of every part of his life other than the hours spent in the company of the animals he loved, understood and rode to victory. If you open a window you will be able to hear clearly the sound of Swift turning in his grave, as he sees unfolded his tragic metaphor of a world in which man is utterly vile and only the horses are noble, pure and innocent.

Two men, then; one who broke the law to get a little money that he didn't need, the other who broke it to get a great deal that he didn't know what to do with. And that is no metaphor; Mr Piggott squirrelled away money in a score or so of bank accounts in most of the world's tax havens and in Britain as well, but as far as I can see he never took any of it out. Was he collecting it for his old age? No; his career as a trainer was obviously going to bring him in very large sums, even if not quite so large as he made as a jockey before his retirement. He did not live lavishly, he did not frequent casinos, he did not buy Van Goghs at twenty million quid a square yard.

The conclusion, for all the talk of the influence of his deprived childhood, is that he wanted the stuff because he wanted it. And, however different the circumstances, the same must apply, even if only obliquely, to Mr Best. And, of course, to millions more who have heaped up treasure on earth, legally or illegally, with no idea of why they were doing so, or what they would do when they had amassed a heap beyond the dreams of avarice.

I am not holier than thou. I don't break the law to get money, but I like to get as much as I can of the lawful kind. But I want it for what I can use it for, and I would think myself very foolish if I approached the getting of it in any other spirit. And I would think myself much more foolish still if I thought that any amount of it could provide anything other than pleasure, comfort and satisfaction.

What is wrong with pleasure, comfort and satisfaction? Nothing at all; but I chose that trio with great care, and if you think about them carefully for a moment you will see what they have in common: they are all shallow. Money cannot provide me (or Mr Best or Mr Piggott) with anything deep – serenity, peace, love, wisdom, fruitfulness, understanding. For that matter it cannot provide the slow movement of Schubert's D minor Quartet, and it will only demonstrate its impotence if it claims that it can provide the best seats in the concert hall to hear the music from. And least of all can it provide any of those inexplicable, unexpected, overwhelming microseconds of a bliss that is not of this world, yet stabs us to the heart as it transforms everything in it.

I am not an ascetic, nor do I believe that poverty ennobles. But neither can I understand what God put the dung-beetle on earth for, unless it was to teach a lesson about folly. If so, Mr Best and Mr Piggott have plainly failed to learn that lesson. But it is important to remember that if what they did had not been contrary to the law, they would have been every bit as pitiable, however much their careers and esteem might flourish.

The mystery remains. I cannot understand why men love money for its own sake, and will risk everything to get it. Chesterton couldn't understand, either; but he put his bewilderment neatly.

> Now he that runs can read it,
> The riddle that I write,
> Of why this poor old sinner,
> Should sin without delight.
> But I, I cannot read it
> (Although I run and run),
> Of them that do not have the faith,
> And will not have the fun.

The Times November 2nd, 1987

Black magic

A Sport of Nature by Nadine Gordimer*

THERE IS A strange paradox to be seen in the world of those writers whose creative imagination must feed off evil – the Soviet novelists and playwrights and poets who can publish only in *samizdat* and at the risk of their liberty, the South African ones who at any moment may be silenced by the techniques of house arrest and banning (or the even more effective technique of being thrown out of a tenth-floor window in Johannesburg police headquarters). The paradox lies in the way their work, though it is inevitably about the circumambient wickedness of communism or apartheid, rises, at its best, to a height at which the damnable facts loom small and are eventually subsumed in a greater theme which uses the base truth to tell a noble one.

Athol Fugard's *Boesman and Lena* is a haunting portrait of what apartheid does; but it is about love. Solzhenitsyn's *The First Circle* describes life in a Soviet concentration-camp; but, likewise, it is about the relation of man to his soul. And the less directly political such works are, the more effective and piercing is the political rage which, transmuted by art, overwhelms the evil.

What is so extraordinary about this book is that although, exactly half-way through, it ceases to put art before politics, it is plain that that is the author's deliberate intent, not a failure to sustain the indirect tone in which the first half is so effectively

* Jonathan Cape, 1987.

couched; she is saying, in effect, that art must wait (or even that it is useless) until the desperate and tragic struggle in her country is determined, and the majority of South Africa's people are free to decide their own destiny.

The 'sport' of her title is Hillela Capran, a Jewish girl whose mother has abandoned the family. Hillela shuttles between the homes of her two aunts and their husbands. Olga and Arthur are conformist and respectable, Pauline and Joe are liberals in the anti-apartheid struggle; Hillela, though she is wayward, defiant and indifferent to the conventions, adopts neither of the two opposite attitudes she is offered. Her character is built up with wonderfully patient slowness, as a sculptor adds tiny flakes of clay; the dense richness of the prose precludes skipping, but its quality precludes wanting to. Very gradually, with the faintest of hints, we realize that Hillela's story is being told in flashback, and that she has attained a position of considerable eminence, but the pace does not quicken; the reader gets the feeling that Miss Gordimer has hoarded everything she has ever seen or heard in case it might come in handy for a metaphor or a comment:

> He danced with her and stood in uproariously-laughing groups, an arm around her neck as a casual sexual claim understood in this circle, while jokes were told about copywriters, Afrikaners and Jews, who were present to laugh at themselves, and about blacks, who were not.

Hillela leaves both her homes early, drifts into a series of affairs, some casual, some not, both kinds easily terminated; this is a woman who does not look back, also one who is content to live on the surface of her feelings and of the reality of the world around her.

Suddenly, almost violently, she changes, and so does the book. She falls in love with a black South African revolutionary; from then on, Miss Gordimer thrusts in the reader's face, more and more brutally, the facts about her country's history and life of injustice. Hillela becomes as committed as Whaila

Kgomani (whom she marries), joins in the clandestine work, becomes a courier, emissary, fighter for the cause.

> Christianity against other gods, the indigenous against the foreign invader, the masses against the ruling class – where he and she come from all these become interpretative meanings of the differences seen, touched and felt, of skin and hair . . . The stinking fetish made of contrasting bits of skin and hair, the scalping of millions of lives, dangles on the cross in place of Christ. Skin and hair. It has mattered more than anything else in the world.

Real people pass across the stage: Tambo, Machel, Nkomo, Neto, Nyerere, Tutu. Miss Gordimer raises her voice: 'The necessity to deal in death, no way out of it, meeting death with death . . .' But in raising her voice, she lowers her humanity, and begins to make excuses for everything and anything done in the struggle, for any means to the end of a 'continent of black humans ruling themselves'.

If Miss Gordimer becomes political, so can a reviewer. There are precious few places in black Africa where 'black humans rule themselves', and a large number where black tyrants deny black humans any more say in their ruling than South Africa herself. 'The necessity to deal in death' can point in more than one direction, and it is not necessary to rely for illustration on mad savages like Amin and Bokassa, or sane ones like Obote; how much black rule is there in the Kenyan jails where Moi's prisoners are tortured, in Matabeleland where Mugabe's North Koreans pursue their ethnocidal course, in the townships of South Africa where the burning necklace ('Mistakes are made sometimes . . .') holds sway?

Towards the end, bathos is dangerously near. Kgomani is murdered, and Hillela eventually marries another African revolutionary, who becomes president of his country; he is chairman of the OAU the year South Africa attains majority rule, and he and Hillela are honoured guests at the ceremony in Cape Town. The scene is desperately unconvincing.

And yet there is more to Miss Gordimer's credit than the

first half of her book. There can be no acquittal for white South Africa, and if her second half is more tract than novel, it is a tract for the times. *A Sport of Nature* will have an honoured place in the National Library of black South Africa, and the fact that it is far more likely to perish in the flames of a racial holocaust does not invalidate its claim to stand on those shelves.

Sunday Times April 5th, 1987

The porn brokers

I THINK I HAD better explain (m'lud) what I am doing with a pile of American pornographic magazines. I brought them back for a friend (yes, m'lud, I know that's what they all say) who needed them as research material for a forthcoming book (yes, m'lud, I know that's what *they* all say), and if the friend in question is reading these words, let them be taken as a declaration of intent: in no circumstances whatever would I do such a thing again.

Mind; I was breaking no law (yes, m'lud . . .). The magazines are certainly pornographic, but similar things are available, unprosecuted, in any of our cities, and they are not prosecuted because the likelihood of conviction is so slight that the authorities ignore them; these, though I am assured that they are more extreme than the home-published ones, do not include scenes of sadism or bestiality (the rule-of-thumb test nowadays), and if the measure of what is legally permitted has now moved far enough to include such material, so be it: I do not propose to set myself up as a jobbing censor.

Only, you see, I felt it incumbent upon me (on the ground that all experience is valuable) to look through the magazines before handing them over, and I have to say that by the time I had finished doing so, my liberal views on matters of this kind had taken a relentless, powerful and unexpected battering.

First, let me get the most obvious point out of the way. I have never in my life had an experience so unerotic; these magazines seem to me so entirely anaphrodisiac that they might have been designed to foment an outbreak of fanatical celibacy. If they seem so to me, they must presumably seem so to others too, but here fallacy rears its head. I had no prior idea of what the magazines contained (I have never been interested in pornography, and cannot recall even leafing through such material), and have no intention of ever opening another, yet they are clearly sold in huge numbers, and if they are not sold to men like me, then there are men, and very many of them, who do find them arousing. And if that is so – and it must be, else how could they exist? – our world is in more trouble than I had known.

For throughout the magazines, photographs and text alike have one theme only, one attitude only, one lesson only, one invitation only. It is that women are *things, objects, receptacles, instruments*; that their nature is *passive, insensate, usable, empty*; that they exist to *comply, offer, submit, serve*.

There are, obviously, many pictures of coition, some of them in multiple form; in all, the women are portrayed as no more than an adjunct to the men's activity. Most faces are contorted; presumably the photographer and the models wanted to convey sexual pleasure, but to my eye they seem mostly to be registering boredom. Some of the faces are beautiful, some hideous; very few show any sign of feeling or thought, indeed of any capacity for either. More breasts are sagging than not.

The words that separate the photographs are of a monotony that is scarcely to be believed; however the theme is introduced, whatever the background, whichever form of sexuality is concerned, whether the article is entitled 'Confessions of a teenage lesbian' or 'Let's do it in the sand', the result is the same: a portrayal of a woman as nothing but a willing orifice, her world reduced to the filling of it.

Perhaps the most significant lines in all this collection are in a letter which purports to come from a man in prison awaiting execution. It reads: 'I want to say you've got the best mag I ever laid my eyes on and, to show my appreciation, I'm going to walk to the gas chamber with a copy of it and rule all the ladies in hell!'

Now: you will notice that I have not used any such words as

'dirty', 'filth', 'obscene'. Nor do I intend to; I am not in the same business as Lord Longford or Mrs Whitehouse, and I do not believe that what disgusts me should be abolished or banned, because I do not presume to believe that my response to such material is the only possible one, or for that matter that banning is of any use in this field. On the other hand, I have never been greatly impressed by the defence of pornography through the argument from catharsis, and I am very considerably less impressed by it now; the familiar – too familiar – claim that this material is nothing more than a masturbatory aid for men with problems about relationships cannot be disproved by my feeling that it is wholly repellent rather than inviting, because, as I have said, the existence of the magazines (and in such numbers, incidentally, I could have made half a dozen entirely different selections) shows that many men must be stimulated by it. But stimulation, like peace, is indivisible; the man on Death Row planned to die with a copy of *Hustler* in his hand, but he also planned to 'rule all the ladies in hell' afterwards.

I do not know, and nor does anybody else, whether, and if so to what extent, material of this kind tends to reinforce feelings or disperse them. The imitative effect, if any, can hardly be very straightforward; very few unhappy men in dirty macintoshes would be able to afford the settings in which the models are mostly portrayed (though a closer look makes clear that the lush surroundings are essentially cheapjack, and the level of sophistication pitifully low), and fewer still to match the physical agility demanded without running the risk of a slipped disc or a hernia. But that is, perhaps, the point. For if you take away the surface impression of the pictures, and the relentless throbbing and shoving of the words, you are left with a residue that, even if it has no lasting effect on the readers, is unmistakably composed of a deep, inevitably aggressive, desire to degrade woman. Not women, let alone beautiful women or ugly ones, ready ones or reluctant ones, feminine ones or feminist ones, but the very essence and nature of womankind. I do not believe it is possible for a man, whether a detached intellectual, an *homme moyen sensuel*, a lecher or a moron, to read through this material and not feel immersed in the hatred of the female sex that it exudes. A man may feel it, as I did, with horror, or with satisfaction, or with lust; but one who claims that it isn't there is deceiving himself.

The Labour Party's new Consumers' Charter includes a promise to restrict or even ban advertising which relies on the 'degrading' portrayal of women. You wouldn't think that even the Labour Party could get something as wrong as that; the whole point of the advertisements that are denounced is precisely that they do *not* degrade women, they falsely and impossibly glamorize them. Women in advertisements are always beautiful, and they are seen lying in luxury on sunny beaches, or reclining on the bonnets of very expensive motorcars, or sipping exciting drinks in the company of handsome and well-dressed men, or sweeping into stately homes in beautiful gowns. I don't know whether the Labour Party's promise is to be taken seriously (I imagine not), but if they suppose that advertisers could use Miss Frances Morrell to sell their products, they are greatly mistaken.

Now the Page Three girls are the same, *mutatis mutandis*, as the girls in the advertisements. So far from being portrayed as the degraded, infinitely exploitable, invariably available creatures of the pornographer, they are all romantic princesses, fairy creatures whom nobody has ever met in real life and who would crumble into powder at a touch. Of course, those Members of Parliament (almost all Tories) who sniggered and winked and licked their lips and belched when Mrs Clare Short introduced her Bill to ban Page Three are so many pigs, and displayed all the characteristic signs of the half-man who needs to convince himself of his sexual prowess because he fears that he cannot convince anybody else. But they did not prove that Mrs Short was right.

And yet I have to admit that I am not certain she was wrong. I *think* she was, because the distinction between the breasts on Page Three and those in *Penthouse* seems clear to me. There is a clue in the fact that the Page Three ones, and the ones in the advertisements, frequently raise a smile – a happy smile, not a contemptuous one – in the men who look at them, and the girls themselves are portrayed smiling almost without exception. But no one could raise any kind of smile in contemplating the pornographer's women, and in the 450 pages of the stuff that I have waded through, I could find only two or three smiling faces among many hundreds. Pornography, it seems, is no laughing matter.

But I do not know. I do not know what causes violence against women, contempt for women, indifference to the feelings or aspirations of women. I do know that the pornography I have so recently studied, whether it does harm or not, shames our world, not for the explicitness of its sexual matter but for its attitude to women. The need for such material betokens a desperate emptiness in the men who buy it, the provision of it a no less desperate deadness of feeling in those who sell. Such desperation, whatever it may issue in, cannot be healthy, cannot be on the side of life. Perhaps Blake was wrong; it is not the harlot's cry that will weave old England's winding-sheet, but the pornographer's. For my part, I can only conclude by saying that it will be a very long time before I can shake off the feeling that in examining those magazines I had peered into a sulphurous abyss, and it may be even longer before I can look at Page Three with the same eyes as before I did so.

The Times May 30th, 1986

Of human bondage

T HE OTHER DAY there was a striking headline in our dear sister, the *Sun*, reading 'I had kinky sex to become a film star'; a man was being prosecuted on charges of obtaining a wide variety of sexual favours by promises and threats. (He was convicted and imprisoned.) The practices described are not my concern; what caused me to start absent-mindedly buttering the coffee-pot instead of the toast was one particular detail of the claim that the *outré* activities were a quid pro quo for a career in the moving pictures. The claim itself, after all, is hardly new; I suppose that as long as there have been film stars there have been such offers made and accepted. The 'casting couch' may not have existed in physical reality, but the notion it embraced certainly does. No; the sign that tells me that the world may be coming to an end even more rapidly than I had supposed is the fact that the young lady making the accusation claimed that she had been promised a career not just as a movie star, but as a *blue* movie star.

Different people have different ambitions; you dream of becoming a leading brain surgeon, he of making millions through shrewd investment on the Stock Exchange, I of conducting the Chicago Symphony Orchestra in the Seventh Symphony of Beethoven. All sorts and conditions of men and women have their dreams of success and fame, and there are as many dreams as dreamers. And that has always been true, from the day that Adam and Eve dreamed of acquiring the knowledge of good and evil. But assuredly it is only in our world – and not because the cinema did not exist earlier – that a woman can apparently think of no aspiration higher than to be a blue movie star, and is willing to subject herself to a wide variety of degrading activities, many of which she finds (as was made clear in the case) repellent, in order to attain that state of grace.

'What do you do?' 'I'm a blue movie star.' As a conversational ice-breaker, that would probably fall short of complete success. But by the rules set out, the reply would have been given with pride rather than embarrassment, and for all I know the questioner would be despised for not knowing true glamour and achievement when he saw them.

Once upon a time, such a profession would be practised by stealth, and its practitioners blush to find it fame. It will be argued that today's greater openness is creditable rather than otherwise, and I have much sympathy for the view. But I am not arguing for the suppression of blue movies, nor indeed condemning the performers therein for taking part in them. I am merely pointing out that if a 25-year-old woman (that was the age of the one in the case) thinks that to become a leading lady in blue movies is the very best promise the world can hold out to her, then the limitations of her horizon must be so appalling that we really should stop and wonder how they got that way.

Pornography and allied trades have always existed, of course; Domina Albadomus was carrying on something frightful about Catullus fully 2,000 years ago, but the gigantic pornography industry that has grown up in the last two or three decades (certainly not longer) is without precedent. I am not, however, discussing those who want pornography; I am dealing with those who allow themselves to be pornographed.

There is an analogy to be pursued here. The old romantic belief that prostitutes went on the game because of poverty, hating every minute of what necessity had driven them to, has almost entirely died out, and been replaced by the theory that prostitution is a business like any other; on that supposition the practitioners presumably regard their trade as a personal service akin to hairdressing or cosmetic surgery. And it follows, *a fortiori*, that those who pose for the pictures in pornographic magazines or films take much the same attitude; there is no need to assume that they are prostitutes.

Now, however, we must move on one more step. Now it is neither shame nor indifference; it isn't even, apparently, money; it is an enticing and exciting way of life in itself. Pause for a moment to recall what 'it' actually is. It is submitting to film cameramen in a selection of explicit sexual poses and activities, together with everything else that ingenuity can devise, and technicians portray in colour, for the stimulation and delight of the customers.

In a remarkable and significant novel, *The Fourth of July*, by Bel Mooney,* there is an attempt, almost wholly successful, to define the nature of the world of pornography from both sides – that is, both those who manufacture it and those who take part in it. Whether the book is authentic I have no means of knowing; but it carries indisputable conviction. And it provides an important clue to the answer I have demanded.

For a very long time, the human race has had difficulty in coming to terms with its body. The uncleanness attributed to it since, roughly, the emergence of Christianity, has gone far to make it impossible for us to return to, or even to understand, the Greek ideal of the balance of mind and body; the mortification of the flesh must be one of the most dreadful and dangerous fallacies ever foisted on the world. For reasons I am too modest to remind you of, I am something of an expert on the 10th Satire of Juvenal, but I can still be enraged at the way his *Orandum est ut sit mens sana in corpore sano* has been appropriated by schoolmasters and turned into no more than a demand that their charges should take cold baths every morning and stop masturbating.

But there had to be a reaction, and there was. The glorification of the body, especially (but not exclusively) the female body, has in our time reached an intensity that no previous age could possibly have imagined; Rubens himself would blench if he

* Hamish Hamilton, 1988.

saw today's advertising hoardings, glossy magazines or Page Three Samanthas. But the new dispensation, though not as nasty as the old, has fallen into the same trap; it is as one-sided as the schoolmasters could wish, with the difference that it is displaying the other side.

Nobody would expect a blue movie star to have a *mens sana*, or indeed a *mens* of any kind, and as for telling her to worry about her soul, we would be in danger of provoking a very serious mis-hearing. The only thing she knows about in herself (though Miss Mooney's book does explore the extra-ordinary and touching earlier life of one of the girls) is her body and the way in which it can titillate or satisfy the lust of men.

It follows, or at least it has followed, that many women have come (been taught?) to regard their bodies not as part of an entity which comprises also a mind and a spirit, nor (as with the prostitute) as a commodity for sale in a straightforward transaction, but as a totem which, when displayed in appropriate poses, has a power and a character of its own, and which elevates the owner of the body into an empyrean where she can mingle with the gods on equal terms. I don't want to labour this point, but I do not believe that it is entirely coincidental that the word 'goddess' is now applied very freely to women, usually film stars, whose beautiful bodies are their only noticeable quality. Miss Mooney's book shows that she, at least, has taken the measure of this phenomenon; it is another sorry comment on our world that she seems to be about the only person who has done so. For her depiction of the pornographers is even more merciless to them in their role as makers of such dreams than in their character as glorified ponces.

And so the trail leads back to the lady who was willing to undergo sexual indignities in order to rise above the common ruck of people by becoming a blue movie star. It wasn't even, as far as I can see, a matter of going for the best deal she was likely to get in life; it was a belief that such a career constitutes not just glamour, but true glory.

Estimate, to three places of decimals, the extent of the

poverty of spirit and imagination that that fact implies. Then think about the nature of the world we have made, that has such poverty in it. Then reflect that no Band Aid, no Comic Relief, is likely to come forward to alleviate that kind of poverty. Then think of those women who deem that very poverty the greatest of riches. Then, if you have tears, prepare to shed them now.

The Times February 22nd, 1988

The meat pie and the taxi

I THINK I HAVE found a story which symbolizes to perfection both the condition of this country and the reason for it. A small but important union recently had an election for chairman; the holder of the office stood again, but was decisively beaten by the other candidate. (The new chairman is said to be much further to the left, but that is not what this tale turns upon.)

After his victory, his jubilant supporters expressed admiration for him, and it is the terms they used in expressing it that make my point. First, they applauded him for never having been promoted; he had remained throughout his working career in the same lowly grade. 'That means', said one of his followers, 'that he never sold out to management.' He also, it seems, scored bonus points for leaving school at 15, but this is not some septuagenarian remembering the Depression between the wars; he is in his early forties. Furthermore, his style of living was contrasted favourably with that of the man he had defeated; the loser, it was said, 'had become over-fond of restaurant meals', whereas the victor 'stuck to pints and meat pies'. Still worse, his ousted predecessor was married to a woman in the higher ranks of their profession; she could even be described as a member of management. And finally comes the item which, it seems, may have settled the election; at the union's annual conference last year the new champion had 'won the hearts of delegates by declining a taxi to his hotel during a downpour'. No wonder one of his supporters summed up expectations of the new regime by saying, 'It's a return to grassroots; John is one of the lads.'

No doubt; but is that, I ask myself, quite enough? In 1986, a man is elected to high union office by people who are *proud* to reveal that he is uneducated except at elementary level, that he was not considered suitable for advancement in his profession (or that if he was, he refused it), that he did not commit the grave solecism of marrying above himself, that he prefers bad food to good, and that he would rather get wet than ride in a taxi.

I have repeatedly said that the only real power this country's union leaders have is the power to keep their members poor. But I would not like it to be thought that by 'poor' I refer only to their wages. Poverty takes many forms, and I am by no means certain that a low income is the worst of them; there is poverty of the mind, of the spirit, of life, of surroundings, of desires, of needs, of expectations, and perhaps these impoverishments define the poor even more exactly than their pay packets. For, after all, there are millions who suffer from these limitations while having very satisfactorily plump pay packets.

Throughout the past 150 years or so there has been, among all the philanthropic and humanitarian reform movements, a strain of far-seeing thinkers who have realized this truth and striven to act on it. Shaw was one of the most notable of them; in our day Arnold Wesker has carried on the tradition (why do you think he called one of his plays *Chips with Everything*, and another *I'm Talking about Jerusalem*?). What such people saw, and see, is that the poor, even while they suffer from their material poverty, cling fiercely to their other impoverishments. There are even people who encourage them to do so, and applaud their unwillingness to rise, however slightly, in the world; Dennis Skinner, who *boasted* that he doesn't possess a passport, probably believes that Costa Brava is the Spanish for Sodom and Gomorrah and that the Midlands car workers who spend their holidays there are traitors to the working class for that reason alone.

And a newly elected union leader is praised for attitudes and qualities that the real reformers, the true friends of the poor, strove to remove because they knew that these were the ultimate barriers across the poor's road out of the real poverty trap. (Shaw said he hated the poor, by which he meant their contentment with their lot.)

It has long been said, in reference to the pitifully low salaries most of this country's union leaders receive, that 'if you pay peanuts, you get monkeys'. Most of our union leaders are honest and decent men. But along with the honesty and decency goes a desperate and tragic lack of vision and under-standing, which more often than not issues in a terrified reluctance to encourage in their members any yearnings beyond monetary ones – and, more often than not, even the monetary ones are frowned upon as unbecoming a member of the working classes if other members are earning less.

American trade unionism is far weaker than ours. Yet in the United States the leader of, say, the United Automobile Workers receives a salary, and working conditions, that would be the envy of a British cabinet minister. Well, of course, say those who applauded the union leader I started with, these false general secretaries have sold out to the bosses. So indeed they have; but in doing so, it has to be said, they have negotiated for their members wages (in real terms) some two and a half times those of their British equivalents. When will the members of the TGWU insist that their general secretary sells out to the bosses on similar terms?

That last question, it seems to me, is the really crucial one. When will the working classes of this country stop allowing themselves to be persuaded by their union leaders and the Labour Party that it is a matter for outrage and the downing of tools if the boss has a bigger Daimler every year, even if they have a bigger Ford? When will somebody teach them that, on even the crudest tests of self-interest, it is better to work for a firm which makes profits than one which does not? And above all, when will they understand that they have not betrayed their origins – or, if they have, the origins deserved to be betrayed, and not only betrayed but killed and buried – by raising their eyes from the trough to those areas of life which cannot be measured in terms of cash, but which constitute the reason for living?

When? Not, to be sure, while the Labour Party is led by men like Michael Foot and Neil Kinnock, nor while the TUC is represented by men like Norman Willis, nor while the individuals who run most of the unions derive their strength and their support from failing to qualify for promotion, refusing to take a taxi when it is raining, eating and drinking rubbish in a pub instead of food in a restaurant, avoiding marriage with a woman of the professional classes and resting for the remainder of their lives on the educational attainments they had reached when they were 15.

Pity the land without aspirations. But pity ten times more the land in which aspirations are energetically denounced by those whose task it should be to encourage them. And pity a hundred times more still the land where those who fail in their duty to widen their followers' horizons fail because they are too busy not being promoted, refusing to take taxis, being contented with the educational standards of a 15-year-old, and eating swill because they like it. Or, worst of all, because although they don't like it they feel they ought to.

The Times June 19th, 1986

Neck or nothing

Tomorrow, the House of Commons will debate a proposal for the restoration of capital punishment. I think it will be defeated, and that the defeat will mark the very last attempt to reknot the rope. At least, I hope so. The arguments have been ground to the finest dust and scattered to the winds; there is no point in my rehearsing yet again the statistics, the meaning of deterrence, the examples from other countries. I doubt if any MP will enter the chamber with one opinion and the division lobby with another; though arguments apparently rational will be deployed on both sides, this is not, and never has been, a subject susceptible to logic. Either you recoil in revulsion from the thought of capital punishment or you warm to the idea, and which of the two it is depends on you, not on the crime statistics.

Lord Denning thinks rapists should be castrated, and he is regarded as an eminently reasonable jurisconsult, so what hope have we of considering the ultimate crime and its ultimate punishment in the cold, severe light of reason? I remember Jonathan Guinness suggesting that convicted murderers should be supplied with razor-blades in their cells so that they could slit their wrists and thus obviate the necessity of strangling them, and if it comes to that, several hundred people apply, every time capital punishment is discussed, for the job of hangman. (I wouldn't be at all surprised to learn that Lord Denning's proposal has already provoked a flood of requests to be allowed to wield the secateurs, though it would be only fair to let the old boy have first refusal.)

Do not, therefore, imagine that argument will sway this

cause. Do not, indeed, expect me to be any more reasoned in my opposition to capital punishment than those who advocate it. A few lines ago, I used the word 'strangling' for what the executioner does; as it happens, I did so because it was the most offensive and emotive term I could think of, but it might just as well have been an unconscious choice on my part.

To tell the truth, there are an awful lot of people I would love to strangle. Why don't I do so? Not because I am afraid of being caught, though I am, but because I think murder is wrong; 'the deep damnation of his taking off' would remain as a moral sanction even if there were no legal bar to it. Indeed, practically all of us would refuse to commit murder even if it was extolled by both Oxfam and the Women's Advisory Council on Solid Fuel *and* rewarded with a bounty of a tenner a scalp. When you come to think of it, the number of murders committed in this country every year, even including the terrorist and intra-terrorist ones in Northern Ireland, is almost incredibly small. That is no consolation to the victims, but it does very strongly suggest that for most people the everlasting hath fixed his canon 'gainst it.

I believe it is much too facile to go on from that argument to the claim that the unique horror of killing which possesses most sane people leads them to feel that it is only right to match killing with killing; a unique punishment for a unique crime. The First Murderer (a fratricide, remember, which adds an extra layer of horror) paid for his crime not with his life, but with lifelong expiation; the mark upon him was his own. (And hands up all who had forgotten that the Lord forbade anyone to slay him, on pain of sevenfold vengeance. On the whole, I prefer the Lord to Sir Ian Percival.)

The murderer *is* a unique figure, arousing a unique shudder. Quick, quick, then; kill him, and we need shudder no more. Most people would not put it like that, or recognize them-selves in my putting, but they are there. Why do you suppose that most people do not know, and despite all the evidence implacably refuse to know, that most murders are committed within the family? Because that would demythologize the crime, indeed domesticate it, and overthrow the dark totem. It is not just that people *are* irrational on the subject; they *will* themselves to be.

That is why it is virtually useless to put forward the rational arguments against capital punishment, starting with the one about finding that a man is innocent after he has had his neck stretched, and finishing with the one about debasing our society with the beastly ritual and beastlier act that the ritual accompanies. Do think for a moment, I beg you, about what drew the crowds to a public hanging in the same spirit as they went to the fair; do you seriously suppose that the impulse in that dark fair-goer is absent from the advocate of hanging, just because he can't see it happen?

The name of Ruth Ellis still has power to dominate a discussion of this subject. She has the distinction of being the last woman we hanged, but there is a much better reason for us to remember her; the decision not to commute her sentence was probably the grossest single injustice done by the Home Office in modern times, which is quite a claim. But although they are forgotten, Peter Allen and Gwynne Evans, who were the last men to be hanged, died just as uselessly; nothing and nobody was better off for their death.

There was a man who saw capital punishment carried out; he had even helped instigate it. But he didn't like it a bit:

> . . . for Christ's sake pray for my wretched guilty soul . . . I am not a bad man . . . I meant no harm. I did not know what it would be like . . . I did not know what I was doing . . . You dont know; you havnt seen; it is so easy to talk when you dont know. You madden yourself with words; you damn yourself because it feels grand to throw oil on the flaming hell of your own temper. But when it is brought home to you; when you see the thing you have done, when it is blinding your eyes . . . tearing your heart, then . . . O God, take away this sight from me! O Christ, deliver me from this fire that is consuming me!

Do you think that Stogumber's feelings were caused only by his realization that St Joan was innocent? What if it had not been Joan but a common criminal – a murderer, no less? Would it then be 'easy to talk when you dont know'? Perhaps we should restore not only hanging, but the public kind, with the spectators obliged to pull on the rope; many – most, I think – would at last be brought up inescapably against the reality of what we do when we hang a man, for all that we delegate the doing of it to an offical appointed (from the throng of eager applicants) to do it for us. An accessory to murder is worse than an accessory to hanging, just as a murderer is worse than a hangman; but the greater evil does not extinguish the lesser. Nor is it the horrible barbarity of execution that is the worst thing about it; it is the calm, ordered, impersonal taking of a life, for the astoundingly irrelevant reason that the life in question has taken another.

Some countries have capital punishment and a very high murder rate – the United States, for instance. Some have no capital punishment and an almost negligible murder rate – Denmark, for instance. And vice versa twice over. Let us not waste time trying to extract a meaning from those facts. Let us just cleave to the great truth that the abhorrence of murder is deep within almost every one of us, and that it needs no gallows, no rope and no quicklime to keep that necessary and profound abhorrence alive. Or as Chesterton said:

> We whom great mercy holds in fear,
> Boast not the claim to cry,
> Stricken of any mortal wrong,
> 'Lord, let this live man die!'
> O mighty to arise and smite,
> O mightier to forgive,
> Sunburst that blinded Lazarus,
> Lord, let this dead man live!

The Times March 31st, 1987

Waking the dead . . .

IT WAS VOLTAIRE who said 'If I were accused of stealing the towers of Notre Dame I would make a bolt for it at once.' He thus dramatically encapsulated the terrible truth that there is nothing too obviously false for somebody, somewhere, to believe it. He might have added that there is also nothing too plainly inexcusable for somebody to excuse it.

These melancholy thoughts passed through my mind last weekend when I read an item in the *Sunday Times* about the circulation of a broadsheet, designed to look like a newspaper, called *Holocaust News*, the purpose of which is to maintain that the extermination of millions of Jews in the Final Solution never happened, and that the claim that it did is nothing more than the propaganda of a Jewish conspiracy.

I received a copy months ago; since my normal rule in these matters is to ignore such ravings, I did nothing. There is nothing new about *Holocaust News*; a few years ago a pamphlet appeared, with the title *Did Six Million ReallyDie?* This was published under a pseudonym, Richard Harwood, the author's real name being Verrall; this, too, argued that only a few thousand Jews died in the camps, mostly of natural causes. The editor of the new version, Richard Edmonds, a member of one of the Nazified *groupuscules* that split off from the National Front, does go a trifle further, claiming that the deaths that weren't from illness were of those 'executed for sabotaging the war effort'.

Charming folk, what? But though I am sorry to give offence in saying so, I cannot take even such pestilent vileness seriously. To be sure, it is widely rooted; there is Professor Faurisson in France, for instance, and the delightful Mr Butz in the United States, and in the Federal Republic there is the *Deutsche Nationalzeitung*, though those in charge of it have to be careful, because denying the Holocaust is an offence there.

Anti-semitism, like other irrationalities, will not be cured by reason; I must add that it will also not be cured by laws. (Copies of *Holocaust News* have been sent to the Director of Public Prosecutions.) It must be unnerving for these poor, crazed creatures to find Jews behind every door, plotting to take over the country, and meanwhile putting poison in the milk bottles on the doorsteps of clean-living Hitler-worshippers, but there is nothing to be done about it.

Before the Second World War there really was reason to be concerned about British anti-semitism; Mosley's riff-raff knocked out a good many Jewish teeth, and knocked in even more Jewish windows, and if their heroes and exemplars across the Rhine had won the war – but there is no need to finish that sentence.

I bet nobody but me now remembers Captain Ramsay. He was a Tory MP who was so devotedly pro-Hitler that he was imprisoned under the same emergency wartime regulations that netted Mosley and many of his followers, but he remained an MP. (The detainees were not charged with any criminal offence, so there were no grounds on which he could be expelled from the House.) He was let out, as was Mosley, in 1944, and the first thing he did was to bustle off to Parliament and introduce a Bill that would compel all Jews to wear a six-pointed yellow star on their clothing; I have to say, though I shall give even greater offence by saying it, that it is almost impossible to withhold admiration from a man so mono-maniacally consistent.

Ramsay wasn't the worst, either. There was a man called Arnold Leese who attacked Mosley for being *insufficiently* anti-semitic; indeed, he called the Leader 'the kosher Fascist'. Leese also put his mouth where his opinions were; he advocated the extermination of British Jews. (He was also the

leading authority on camel diseases. Well, I suppose somebody has to be.)

Then there was A. K. Chesterton, who was originally one
of Mosley's followers but broke with him and went on to set
up an outfit called the League of Empire Loyalists; he lived
long enough to gather together many *fascisant* splinters and
weld them into the National Front. A very rich South American lunatic, who kept his bath full of walnuts (of which he
feared a shortage), made a will leaving his considerable fortune
to Chesterton, but it was overturned. (No doubt Chesterton
blamed the Jews for cheating him out of his inheritance.)

You wouldn't think it to look at me, but I gave evidence in a
court case *on behalf of* Chesterton's Empire Loyalists; I was
there when some of them were beaten up by Winter Garden
attendants in Blackpool when they interrupted the Tory party
conference, and Aristides Levin, murmuring '*Fiat justitia, ruat
coelum*', described what he had seen. (It did no good; apparently they charged the wrong attendants.)

I am sorry (I seem to be spending this entire column
apologizing), but I really cannot get worked up about anti-
semitism in Britain today. The truth is that the Nazis demonstrated for all time just what that poison can lead to, and it
shocked almost all but the real swine into abandoning it. It
survives today only among the swine themselves, the ones
who are too mad even to talk to, and – very faintly – the last
heirs to the kind of genteel anti-semitism that was rife in
respectable 1930s drawing-rooms.

Leave *Holocaust News* alone; the dead can suffer no more,
and the living are in no danger, however much pain such
things awake in some of them. And if you want an illustration
of the eternal impossibility of getting any sense into the heads
of the maddest ones, those heads which seethe and boil with
their hate and terror of the peculiar people called Jews, let me
tell you a story of my own experience.

Some years ago I was asked to address a very respectable
Anglo-German body. After my speech, questions were invited, and it became clear that the organization had been

infiltrated by a group of diehard British Nazi supporters. As I was leaving the hall, a mad-looking little man plucked me by the sleeve.

'You're a Jew, aren't you?' he said. 'Why, yes,' I murmured. 'Ah,' said he, 'now the six-pointed Star of David is the Jewish symbol, isn't it?' Longing for a drink, but unable to get through the slow-moving crowd, I conceded his point. 'Well,' he said, his eyes now glittering, 'how can you deny that all the publishers and all the newspapers and magazines and books in this country are controlled by the Jews, when on every page they have put the Star of David?'

I patted him on the shoulder and said I hoped he would feel better in the morning. A few minutes later, with the drink before me, I described my encounter. 'What can he be seeing', I asked the company, 'to imagine that the Jews are everywhere he looks in any printed page?'

No one could even make a guess, so we agreed that madness is not explicable, and talked of happier things. A few minutes later there was a cry of 'I've got it!' from a girl from the German embassy. We turned to her: 'Look,' she said, opening a copy of a newspaper, '*asterisks*'.

It was true; wherever that poor devil saw an asterisk he saw the sign manual of the Jewish Beast, pursuing him every-where. Do you really want to try to reason with that, or to prosecute those who deny the gas chambers? One day, all people will be wise, enlightened, free of all prejudice, and rational. But while we are waiting for the day, we should remember that Nineveh, too, was a great city wherein were more than six score thousand persons who could not discern between their right hand and their left hand; and also much cattle.

The Times March 10th, 1988

. . . *to revile the living*

A ND NOW I think it is time that I had *my* say about *Perdition*, the play by Jim Allen that was withdrawn on the eve of its opening at the Royal Court.

I begin with my credentials. First, I have read the play, carefully, from beginning to end, and a copy of it lies beside me as I write. Second, I have maintained for something like thirty years that anti-semitism in Britain, however horrible in itself, is now a negligible phenomenon of no serious political or social account, and best ignored. For this attitude I have been frequently criticized by Jews and Jewish organizations. Most recently, it has been widely argued, against my view, that although the traditional anti-semitism of the Fascist Right is today largely silent and invisible (there is nothing at all to compare with Mosley's Jew-baiting), the anti-semitism of the aptly-named Fascist Left is of real significance, even if only because it is disguised as anti-Zionism and therefore likely to impress many people who would reject it at once if it was presented without its Israel-shaped figleaf.

I take the point, but remain of my opinion; because of it I am more unlikely than most to see anti-semitism where it does not exist. Moreover, I must be among the most completely assimilated of British Jews, and my sympathies for Israel have always been heavily qualified.

In that spirit I sat down to read the play; it is perhaps useful for me to say that I read it before the storm broke, so my reaction was not affected by any other comment.

The peculiar vileness of the work is difficult to convey without impossibly extensive quotation. As Orwell said of

Dali's memoirs, 'If it were possible for a book to give a physical stink off its pages, this one would.' But the precise nature of its vileness is exceptionally interesting.

Perdition is written in a state of what may be termed moral illiteracy. Let me explain.

The Holocaust is a fact that beggars the imagination; only in recent years has it been possible to step back from the thing itself and see it in a historical perspective, as something to understand and draw lessons from, beyond the appallingly obvious ones. Thousands of years of discussion of the quality of evil gained a new dimension; the very concept of teleology was brought into question; the famous exchange, 'Where was God at Auschwitz?' – 'Where was *man* at Auschwitz?', set off a debate that will go on forever; the nature of cowardice and heroism, the meaning of Europe and its culture, the identity of the Jew in the modern world, the role of the Christian churches throughout history and of Islam today, the idea of race and blood, the symbolism and archetype of the scapegoat, the still unsounded depths of the human psyche, even the music of Richard Wagner – mankind's attitude to all these things, and many more, was changed, and is still changing, in the darkness cast by that black sun.

And throughout the play there is nothing – *nothing* – to suggest that even one of these tremendous and inescapable themes has impinged even to the very slightest extent on the mind of the author.

Before I continue, please pause and contemplate that fact. A writer, not wholly untalented, takes a story which will continue to exercise the minds and feelings of men and women until, quite literally, the end of the world, and with it demonstrates that his mind is so limited, so confined, so worthless as an instrument of understanding, that every aspect and echo of that story escapes him entirely. Would you have thought that possible in any but the most ignorant, uneducated and brutish elements of our society?

Well, then, how *is* it possible? It is possible, indeed it is inevitable, because the author, incapable of recognizing unprompted anything of what I have listed, has a purpose which to him is plainly sufficient; if he reads this article, he will dismiss it without disturbing in any way the even banality of his mind, because his purpose fills his tiny horizon so completely that there is no room for anything else. And his purpose is to repeat the ancient rubric, *Delenda est Carthago*, in modern terms: Israel Must Go.

I do not want to go over ground already covered by others, but a few words of summary are, I think, necessary. Mr Allen is on the hard left, of the bit (one has to specify, because there are many, and their numbers multiply daily) that is happy to use Stalinist disinformation, which he reproduces, unashamed, in his play. We learn that Ben-Gurion, Weizmann and the other principal founders of Israel, together with their underlings in Europe (who happily co-operated with the Nazis in the Final Solution), smiled upon the Holocaust, and deliberately blocked attempts to save more Jews from the gas-chambers, so that the world would be shocked into setting up a Jewish state; the state in question is, of course, itself little better than the Nazis in its racism. Mr Allen's ignorance, and implacable unwillingness to have his ignorance dispelled, have left his play littered throughout with inexcusable errors and horrible lies; there is no evidence that Mr Max Stafford-Clark, artistic director of the Royal Court Theatre, was disturbed by this, and a good deal of evidence that he wasn't.*

The language of the play is as crude as its objective; whether it would seem dramatic in performance I cannot say. That the anti-semitism which oozes from it is the unconscious kind does not seem to me to go very far as an excuse, and oddly enough it is less of an excuse for one of Mr Allen's politics than for others, because it is the far left that insists on digging out such buried feelings so that the bearer of them can contemplate them by daylight; a course in Racism Awareness (I am sure Brent Council would find him a place on one) seems urgently

---

* Mr Stafford-Clark subsequently made a belated and inadequate attempt to feel ashamed of himself.

necessary if he is to understand what he has – at present unwittingly – done.

In this sorry tale there is one touch of consolation. So far, at any rate, the other Israel Is Guilty of Everything lobby has been silent; not a word about *Perdition* has escaped Messrs Michael Adams, Christopher Mayhew, Dennis Walters, Andrew Faulds and the rest. It is, alas, no use hoping that they have realized how much they have contributed over the years to making Jim Allen possible by whipping the dogs of hate.*

What follows? The play was withdrawn in circumstances that are still not clear; those in charge of the Royal Court seem to be anxious that there should be no full explanation. But that does not concern me greatly. What does concern me is what may now be the permanent suppression of the play. From what I have said about its character, it may be assumed that I believe suppression is the most condign fate it could suffer. I do not.

I reject suppression, however, on grounds other than the ones that have already been put forward; these are that if the play is never seen it will *increase* anti-semitism rather than diminishing it, because people will believe, or be persuaded, that a cabal of Jews extinguished it lest the wickedness of Israel should be exposed, and that it must have been an uncommonly fine and well-written play to have provoked such wrath in its opponents, and that a playwright is not to be tested by the same criteria as a historian.

No; the play should not have been withdrawn, in my opinion, because free speech is indivisible. As I have said so often in other contexts, I believe that anything which may *lawfully* be said may *actually* be said. I have defended the rights of the National Front and Socialist Workers Party, those mirror-image twins of totalitarianism, to propagate their doctrines freely, while they remain (the proviso is obviously crucial) within the law. I have pointed out that free speech is

---

* I spoke too soon. The moment this article appeared they were all squealing for their 'right of reply', which *The Times* gave them. Not a single word of contrition came from any of them.

for swine and liars as well as upright and honest men. I have insisted that any legally permissible view, however repugnant, is less dangerous promulgated than banned, and I would defend its promulgation even if the opposite were true. I have gloried in the central paradox of democracy, which is that it tolerates, and must continue to tolerate, the activities of those who wish to destroy it.

In all these beliefs I have lived, and I am minded to die in them; how then could I defend the suppression of this play? I cannot, which is not to say that if it had never been written it now should be. But it exists, and 'He that is unjust, let him be unjust still; and he which is filthy, let him be filthy still.' With heavy heart, I yet must say it: Let them have their play.

The Times February 2nd, 1987

Jesus Christ Superstar: I

'THERE IS NO comparison to be made,' said the Right Reverend the Bishop Suffragan of Warrington, 'between Christ and John Lennon.' Well, no. But the bishop must have had a reason for stating the obvious in such bald terms. As it happens, he had a very good reason; it is that just such a comparison has been made. A German artist has painted a portrait of Lennon as Christ, crown of thorns and all, and it now hangs in a Liverpool museum among other Beatleana (unless the bishop's words have caused the curator to take it down).

The bishop is evidently a gentle soul; instead of commination all round, he said 'there are surely other ways to represent the Beatles, who after all brought much joy to many'; and, as to the direct question, he added to what I have quoted above only a description of the incident as 'an unfortunate choice of image'.

Well, yes. Before going on to the substance of the matter, I must recall the fact that the painter's comparison of Christ and Lennon had been anticipated by Lennon himself, who insisted that the Beatles were as famous as Christ, and possibly more so. He also called upon Beethoven to roll over, though Beethoven took no notice; possibly he didn't hear the instructions.

Now if you want to be literal, the Beatles in their day *were* at least as famous as Christ; millions of people thought about them daily and hourly, in numbers possibly much greater than turned their minds on the other chap. As for Beethoven, Lennon, despite the somewhat brusque way he put it, was right again; I have no doubt that all the records of Beethoven's works ever sold do not approach the total racked up by the Beatles, and if you add their television appearances to their live ones, their concert audiences must have far outnumbered those who have gone to hear his music played, for all that he had 150 years start on them. (If it comes to that, Christ had getting on for 2,000.)

Nevertheless, I am on the bishop's side, as well as Christ's and Beethoven's. I must make my usual disclaimer; I am not a Christian, and any comments I may make that touch upon the theology of these matters must be taken as strictly *obiter*. In the context, I would like to be written down a fan, as – with less circumspection – I can say also of my attitude to Beethoven.

What John Lennon forgot, and the German painter forgets, is *time*, which, like an ever-rolling stream, bears all its sons away. My favourite image for the process is what I have called History's Sieve; down the years and down the days, it is being gently, unceasingly, shaken, and since the holes never vary in size, it follows that sooner or later that which is of enduring value will remain in the sieve, and that which is not will fall through. No one can cheat it, no one can arrest its action, no one can bribe the shaker; Christ and Lennon, the C sharp minor Quartet and 'I Wanna Hold Your Hand', you and me – the quiet, inexorable susurration of the sieve goes on.

It is, of course, notoriously difficult to see *at the time* which phenomena are eternal and which ephemeral; in art, those who laughed at the Impressionists cannot be blamed for being unable to break free of the conventions of their era; their eyes and feelings simply could not be restructured. As for the Roman Empire, it not only laughed at the Christians, but killed them. Where is the Roman Empire now?

It is true that our time is much more prone than earlier ages to blow up the bubble reputation until it fills the horizon, and the fact that every such bubble (as is the way of bubbles) is sooner or later stretched too far and bursts does not, apparently, deter those who blow the next one. But time doesn't care, for it has an infinite supply of soap, and be the bubble a mile across, yet it will go though the holes in the sieve as soon as it bursts, and leave not a wrack behind.

It is also true that in our time the mayfly reputations seem to have been built mostly around pop musicians and the sounds they make; this must be at least partly because it is young people to whom they most appeal, and this is the age of youth if ever there was one. But it is one of the inevitable consequences of being young that you gradually grow older. One of those odd people who prefer Christ to Lennon (to be fair to him, he never knew the latter) once enshrined this truth, rather memorably, in a letter:

> When I was a child, I spake as a child, I understood as a child, I thought as a child: but when I became a man, I put away childish things.
> For now we see through a glass, darkly; but then face to face: now I know in part; but then shall I know even as also I am known.

And that goes, if you think about it, for much more than the process of growing up. In a sense, life consists of learning what is true and lasting (they are the same thing, of course), and what is false and brief (likewise identical). Lennon, as the good pastor said, brought much joy to many; it was a rootless joy, quickly felt and as quickly lost, but it was joy none the less. Yet joy, too, will fail, if it is only the joy that is found in a house built upon sand. Beethoven himself must cede to Christ the title of chief joy-bringer, *and what is more, he did*, no matter that in many of his works even the least attentive listener can hear the voice of one that crieth in the wilderness, Prepare ye the way of the Lord, make straight in the desert a highway for our God.

The other mistake Lennon made was to believe that fame lies in the number of people who have heard of you. Practically everybody had heard of him, but even if his music had justified all the *réclame* and more, the comparison with Christ would still be invalid. Lennon seems to have been a gentle and loving figure with a head full of harmless nonsense, and his murder was a particularly senseless and horrible one; perhaps the German artist who started all this with his picture of Lennon as Christ may have been trying to make a point about the slaughter of the innocents. But it is still necessary to point out that Lennon did not die on the cross; to wear a crown of thorns you have to earn it.

I can easily see what has disturbed the bishop, and even more easily what has offended those of his flock who have protested at the picture and its hanging. But I urge them all to be of good cheer; Christ is a lot tougher and more enduring than any amount of implausible analogies, however absurd or even distasteful. His message has been derided, his followers persecuted, his teaching dismissed as the ravings of a madman, his very existence denied; we have even been told that he was a mushroom, and a hallucinogenic one, at that. And yet, each time the smoke and dust clear, there he is, impervious to it all, and beckoning still. For long after the last trace of Lennon and his music has vanished utterly, Christ's fame, which is the real kind, will still be challenging and comforting mankind. So, now I come to think of it, will Beethoven's. But then, he never told Mozart to roll over.

The Times July 13th, 1987

Jesus Christ Superstar: II

J ESUS CHRIST IS causing trouble again – certainly not for the first time and, alas, almost certainly not for the last. The truth of the matter is that the fellow simply won't lie down, or at least won't stay lying down, and considering some of the goings-on that he has been responsible for one way and another for the last couple of thousand years or so, not to mention the pickle that some of the more rash of his followers have found themselves in from time to time, the latest lark does indicate an astonishing lack of imagination.

It all began when a bookseller in Southend decided to fork out £50,000 (bookselling in Southend seems to be a remarkably successful trade) to have postmarks reading 'Jesus is alive' stamped on 50 million envelopes; it seems that the Post Office arranges such slogans or exhortations as a commercial service for anybody who wants to put a message across in this fashion. (Presumably, lines are drawn somewhere this side of impropriety; if they aren't, I now give notice that I intend to have every envelope in the land franked 'Would you buy a second-hand legal opinion from the Attorney-General?')

I take it that the Southend Jesus-freak has timed his campaign for the run-up to Easter, a festival specifically designed to support the opinion expressed in the postmark. Well, it's his money, and he can presumably spend it on whatever he pleases. At least, you and I might take such a relaxed view, but it seems that there is another opinion in the matter, expressed with all the gorgeous, uninhibited and desperately single-minded lack of a sense of humour that characterizes bodies like the British Humanist Association, whose 'Director of

Development' (there's posh you are, boy!), Mr Martin Horwood, has, on hearing about the proposed envelope wheeze, worked himself up into such a fury of indignation that if somebody doesn't play a hose on him soon he may suffer the final indignity of spontaneous combustion, made all the worse by the fact that he presumably doesn't believe in it.

In a letter to the *Guardian* he spluttered a mighty splutter last week: 'It is outrageous of the Post Office . . . those of us who believe that Jesus is dead – and have devoted some thought to the matter – do not wish to be told every day for six weeks that he isn't . . . this particular form of advertising is persistent and cannot be put down or turned off . . . find this quite offensive . . . worrying that the Post Office does not exercise more control . . . system seems open to much more harmful political and religious abuse . . . a peculiarly insensitive means of promoting one's faith . . . dangerous example . . . hope it will be withdrawn immediately . . .'

Now there goes a man with a well-developed sense of grievance, I must say. (It would be worse in the lands of the Orthodox churches, where believers greet each other on Easter Day with the words 'He is risen'.) First, though not most important, he has clearly joined the legions of those who make clear in writing to me that they don't know what a waste-paper basket, and/or the Off button on a television set, is for. The offensive franking is to be put, after all, only on the envelopes of Mr Horwood's correspondence; there is no suggestion that the words are going to be imprinted indelibly on, say, his wife's forehead. Surely he can survive the experience of opening such a poison-pen letter by the simple expedient of throwing the envelope away immediately and thus ensuring that his eyes will not rest for a second more than is necessary on the terrible words. Indeed, he could teach himself to open envelopes with his eyes shut (I have just tried the experiment, and found that it is very easy to get the hang of it).

But that is not the most remarkable problem for Mr Horwood and those who think like him (Miss Barbara

Smoker has inevitably given tongue); the really important
question is, obviously: what on earth, let alone in heaven, are
they so frightened of? And *so* is surely the right emphasis;
there is a sense of uncontrollable panic in Mr Horwood's
words, which might be justified if the Southend godman was
proposing to have him crucified, whereas even the most
ingenious Roman hit-squad would be hard put to it to do
him in with an envelope.

My late mum used to say, when comfort was required,
'Sticks and stones may break my bones, but names can never
hurt me', and I dare say that Mr Horwood had – has, I
hope – the same assurance from his own mother. But in
choosing such an example of a sense of proportion to recommend to him, I am actually understating the case, for the
Post Office frank is not going to say 'Horwood, you bastard,
Jesus is alive', or even 'Jesus is alive and anybody who
disagrees is a rotter'; it is to consist of the bald assertion alone,
and those who get the message can take it or leave it.

Let us think for a moment of those who prefer to leave it.
Most of them, when they receive a letter with the fateful
message beside the stamp, will shrug, or smile, or neither,
then throw the envelope away and get on with reading the
contents, giving the franked claim not another thought.
Others may pause, briefly or less briefly, to consider the
possibility that the claim might be true, only to conclude that it
is not, whereupon they will proceed in the same manner as the
others.

But a few, notable among them Mr Horwood, will have
seven and seventy fits; what is the difference between these
few and the much larger indifferent group who, though
rejecting the audacious claim, do not experience a severe and
abrupt rise in their blood-pressure?

There is no character in the modern world whom I dislike
more than the Chelsea dinner-party amateur psychiatrist, who
has read a pamphlet called *What Freud really meant* and forgotten most of it, and on that insubstantial basis proceeds to
analyse his fellow-guests. All the same, the hysterical

stridency of Mr Horwood's rejection of a surely harmless message, presented in an even more harmless form, requires explanation. (Sir Hermann Bondi's even more hysterical reaction in his letter to *The Times* – '. . . greatly perturbed . . . obscene . . . most offensive . . . trample underfoot the sensitivity of a minority . . .' – also requires explanation, but anyone who has read him on the subject of religion will understand quite how silly a really clever man can be.)

The obvious explanation suggests that what Mr Horwood is worrying about is not so much the claim itself as the thought that gave pause to my second category above: the thought that out of the mouths of babes and Southend booksellers hast thou ordained strength.

Here I must once again pause for my familiar disclaimer; I am not a Christian, and have no *locus standi* from which to pronounce on Christian beliefs. If I *had* to answer the question implied in the notorious envelope-frank, I think that on balance – a very fine balance, in which the scale turns so slightly as to be to all intents imperceptible – I would have to say yes, but nobody is obliged to take any account of that, even if I haven't misread the trembling scale. But I do have the right to ask even Mr Horwood another question altogether, in a strictly hypothetical mode, and it is this.

Suppose you were wrong – oh, surely you don't mind just *supposing*, if we all promise not to tell anybody – and that the bloke in Southend who is hooked on the pale Galilean (to such an extent that he proposes to shell out fifty thousand smackers on promoting him) is right in the supposition which started all the trouble, *what would be so terrible about it?*

I have asked this question up hill and down dale – indeed, I have asked it up the Mount of Olives and down the valley of dry bones – and I have never yet had an answer of any kind, let alone one that made sense, from anybody who starts with a rejection of the possibility that the supposition might be true. I don't expect an answer this time, either. Nevertheless, I shall wait with interest for my first envelope franked 'Jesus is alive', and next time I am in Southend I shall certainly buy something in the shop of the bookselling Holy Roller, as a tiny contribution towards his massive outlay. Who knows, if enough of us do the same he might make a profit on his gesture; then he can have a new frank reading 'Jesus is good for trade, too'. Though what that would do to Mr Horwood's pulse I dare not imagine.

The Times March 7th, 1988

Monumental mason

I HAVE BEEN TO the Alfred Gilbert exhibition at the Royal Academy, but I could hardly do so without pausing in Piccadilly Circus to inspect the only work of the sculptor which is instantly recognizable to everyone in this country and countless millions elsewhere. Eros looks splendid after his refurbishment, though it is unlikely that anyone will remember that the monument was meant to symbolize, in the overflowing fountain which Eros crowns, the overflowing goodness and philanthropy of the Earl of Shaftesbury, and indeed that the whole structure is his memorial.

Anyone who has read Richard Dorment's hugely entertaining biography of Gilbert will know, before he turns into Burlington House, that he has an exhilarating experience before him. Gilbert's high noon was also the pinnacle of Victorian confidence, and his genius (the word is fully justified) was so assertive, so original and so free that the comparison with Benvenuto Cellini, frequently made and as frequently denied, cannot fail to come to mind.

If, on entering, you want to know at once *why* it cannot, go straight to No. 53, an epergne, mostly in solid silver, so enormous (it's four feet high, and if it was ever used as a table centrepiece the table must have been reinforced) and so elaborate that I defy you not to think of the similarly gargantuan golden salt-cellar that Cellini made for Francis I, now in the Kunsthistorischesmuseum in Vienna; if you could have a bath in Cellini's creation, you could stage a swimming race in Gilbert's.

But it is not the size of the piece which leaves the lasting memory; it is the exuberance. You can see this in almost all Gilbert's *pièces d'occasion*, from the huge memorials, culminating in the one for Queen Alexandra, to the ewer and dish commissioned by the Brigade of Guards as a gift for the Duke of York (No. 56), and indeed in some of the least massive items in this show, such as the sets of ornamental silver spoons (No. 58). They are all so crammed with energy and excitement that they seem to be alive; the bowls of the spoons swirl before your eyes, the St George on the Duke of York's ewer drives his lance through the dragon as you watch, while as for the Preston mayoral chain, I swear that if you look at it long enough the shape of the mayor – the original one, not today's – will begin to swell with self-importance in its magic circumference.

Gilbert's life was one vast tragi-comedy, again reminding us of Cellini. True, he didn't murder quite so many people as the Florentine did (or, to be exact, as the Florentine claimed to have done), but in his business dealings he inclined more to the style of Falstaff than of the Governor of the Bank of England. He suffered, much of the time, from artist's block in an extreme form – perhaps the most extreme known to history – but that could cover only a few of his sins, and his record of taking money for commissions and not executing them, to say nothing of his habit of taking back finished works to improve them and not returning them, was too flagrant to be tolerated for ever, and he was successively expelled from the Royal Academy, made bankrupt and forced to live in exile.

But his life was melodramatic as well as tragi-comic, for he lived to return from exile, to be restored to all his honours, to be knighted (successive monarchs had repeatedly washed their hands of him for his impossible behaviour), and to be entrusted – it was his swansong – with the memorial to Queen Alexandra. It is possible that Shaw based Dubedat, in *The Doctor's Dilemma*, on him; certainly that portrait of a genius and rogue seems drawn from the life.

We cannot think ourselves back into the age in which Gilbert flourished, sank and resurfaced; we can more easily join hands with Shakespeare's England than that of the years between Queen Victoria's Golden Jubilee (there is a marble bust of Victoria, from Gilbert's earlier career, that is very far from flattering) and the death of Edward VII. Significantly, the catalogue includes a device I do not remember having seen before at an exhibition; a set of parallel chronological tables which tell us what was happening in Britain and elsewhere throughout the course of Gilbert's life and work.

Who, to take the most obvious question, commissions tombs today? Most of those who might want to are so afraid of death that they will have no reminder of its existence, and the rest think it would be ostentatious, or even likely to bring bad luck. (Where they would now go for a tomb designer even if they wanted one is another matter; Zeffirelli, I expect.) The Victorians may have been damned to a man, but they would not have known that in advance, and they marched into their marble and bronze mausoleums certain that they would be given advance intimation of the sounding of the Last Trump. Gilbert's greatest funerary work (he finished it 36 years after he started) fully accepts this attitude; it is the tomb of the Duke of Clarence, in Windsor Castle.

Talk about confidence; the Duke did nothing significant, partly because he seems to have been rather dim, and partly because he did not have time to – he died at 28 – but Gilbert's creation would still have been rather excessive if it had been designed to hold simultaneously the mortal remains of John the Baptist, Shakespeare, Pope Gregory the Great, Thomas Jefferson and Scipio Africanus. No fewer than 12 saints surround the royal resting place, each introduced by a pair of angels, while another angel crouches weeping at his feet, and the whole thing is enclosed in a massive bronze grill of extraordinarily elaborate complexity and richness.

Gilbert began work on the tomb in the year in which Gladstone become prime minister for the last time, Walt Whitman died and Shaw wrote his first play; he finished it in the year in which the Kellogg-Briand Pact was signed, John Logie Baird gave the first transatlantic demonstration of television and Mussolini published his autobiography. In that span of years, the world came to an end and began, unrecognizable, again; the *Titanic* went down almost exactly halfway through.

But in the end, mere history cannot confine art. Gilbert may have been the epitome of his age, but he was a great sculptor first. Leave the tombs and the presentation objects, the memorials and the medals, and look at the bust of his mother (he had the bizarre idea of calling it *The Mother of the Ninth Symphony*, in homage to Beethoven), or better still the head of a Capri fisherman, or best of all, perhaps, that of Sir George Grove (he of the *Dictionary*). They are not just obviously taken from the life; they *are* life, caught in plaster or bronze, with all the humanity and warmth that are necessarily excluded from the fantasticated *objects* and the classical subjects. For all Gilbert's shady dealings and prevarications, these portraits are the living truth. For all his moving in royal circles, the Queens and Dukes stirred only his genius, not his heart. But his mother, the fisherman who caught his eye and his friend Grove, awoke both. I am glad that he lived to be rehabilitated, and that this exhibition does him justice.

The Times June 7th, 1986

United nations

I T IS VERY unlikely indeed that Mr Gorbachov has ever read Chesterton's *The Napoleon of Notting Hill*. In that respect, therefore, I have the advantage of him; I have read it at least a dozen times, and I read it again last week, with him specifically in mind. Those of my readers who know it will at once see the connection; for the others, and for him, let me explain.

Chesterton's fantasy is of a London turned into a great league of city-states, at the whim of the whimsical King:

> All these boroughs where you were born, and hope to lay your bones, shall be reinstated in their ancient magnificence: Hammersmith, Kensington, Bayswater, Chelsea, Battersea, Clapham, Balham, and a hundred others. Each shall immediately build a city wall with gates to be closed at sunset. Each shall have a city guard, and, if convenient, a gathering cry . . . If, therefore, any of you happen to have such a thing as a halberd in the house, I should advise you to practise with it in the garden.

And so it comes to pass, to the great embarrassment of the prosaic and respectable rulers of the various boroughs. But one of them takes it seriously; he is Adam Wayne, the man of the book's title, Lord High Provost of Notting Hill, and he takes it so seriously that in standing firm for justice and honour in his tiny, absurd, magnificent fief, he brings about a bloody and terrible internecine war. In the book's dedication (to Hilaire Belloc), there is a verse which sums up the story and its meaning alike:

Likelier across these flats afar
These sulky levels smooth and free
The drums shall crash a waltz of war
And death shall dance with Liberty;
Likelier the barricades shall blare
Slaughter below and smoke above,
And death and hate and hell declare
That men have found a thing to love.

And now you know what this has got to do with Mr Gorbachov, if you didn't before. The events of the past few weeks in Soviet Armenia are not, of course, to be explained simply in terms of nationalism; the whole of the Soviet Union's southern marches is a seething stew of religion, race and bitter memories, as well as directly national feeling. The original *casus turbae*, it is true, was largely nationalist, consisting as it did of the Armenians' demand that the predominantly Armenian area of neighbouring Azerbaijan should be detached therefrom and incorporated in their own region; what is more, the gigantic Armenian demonstrations in furtherance of this cause were rapidly followed by rioting in Azerbaijan, clearly designed to resist any such transfer of territory. It is still an over-simplification, though, to believe that these portents are cut from the same cloth as the stirrings in the Baltic states and the even more tenacious sense of identity in the Ukraine.

An over-simplification; but not a fallacy. Stalin saw, very early in his rule, the threat to him posed by the multifarious nationalisms of his empire, and he set about destroying them with a genocidal ruthlessness; *eight* entire nations were deported from their homelands, their very identity obliterated; almost half of all of them died. (The dreadful story is told in detail by Professor Robert Conquest in *The Nation Killers*.) But he had a special and even more terrible fate in store for the Ukrainians; the deliberately engineered famine was designed to destroy a people's knowledge of themselves, and in the course of it to destroy more millions of human beings than

died, on all sides put together, in the First World War.
(Professor Conquest has told this story, too, in *The Harvest of
Sorrow*.) And the extermination in the Gulag of literally
uncountable thousands of Latvians, Lithuanians and Estonians
was similarly directed to destroying not just human beings but
the idea of being Latvian, Lithuanian or Estonian.

All Stalin's successors have recognized the same danger, and
although the rabid slaughter of men, women and children
ceased, the oppression did not; again, the Ukraine bore the
brunt. For well over half a century, then, the rulers of the
Soviet empire have set themselves, employing whatever
means they deemed efficacious, to root out of the hearts of the
Soviet people any feeling that their own historic nationality
takes precedence over their nationality as citizens of the USSR.

And they have failed. Indeed, they have done worse than fail;
all the decades of murder and repression have served only to
increase the nationalist feeling among the Soviet empire's
subject peoples, and however complex and individual are the
causes of the present unrest among them, that sense of a
separate and definable collective identity is somewhere in
there. Adversity, of course, is a powerfully cohesive force, and
persecution even more so, as the Jews have history's best
reason to know; the Soviet nationalities clung the more tightly
to their national memories the more the tyrants sought to
deprive them of any such recollections. For the rivers of
Babylon flow in every land, and there is no exile remote
enough for its victims to lose the knowledge that there is a
world elsewhere. 'If I forget thee, O Jerusalem, let my right
hand forget her cunning.'

It is easy to see this in the countries which the Soviet Union
has seized since the end of the Second World War. Nobody but
a fellow-traveller would deny that the feeling towards the
Soviet Union in, say, Poland and Czechoslovakia, is one of
unassuageable and virtually unanimous hatred, and nobody
but a fool would be surprised. Ruled by traitors, garrisoned by
the enemy, looted and abused, they wait in silent rage for the
night to end; I flatly refuse to die before I have received an

invitation, as an honoured guest of a free Poland, to attend upon the hanging of General Jaruzelski.

Why, then, should anybody suppose that the nations within the Soviet Union are any different from those outside? It is true that most of them have been part of the empire much longer than those sucked in by the gravitational pull of Stalin's conquests, but nationalist feeling is one of the very strongest forces in the world, and also one of the most enduring; there can be few Crimean Tartars left alive who were among those deported from their homelands in 1944, but the generations born since have rapidly acquired a sense of their original identity – whence their continuing demands for repatriation.

I have never believed that the end of the Soviet Union and her empire will come about by revolution, whether fuelled by a longing for freedom or resentment at material deprivation. But the most likely route to freedom for all the Soviet peoples is the one traced, over many decades or even centuries, by the explosive and uncontainable force of nationalism. The amazing demonstrations by Soviet Armenians, with hundreds of thousands of people taking part, have visibly shaken Mr Gorbachov, and extracted from him a promise, however false, to consider their case; but they have done something ultimately more important. They have, by their remarkable temerity, shown others in the same position that if they are equally brave, equally determined and equally united, they too can be heard. And that benign bacillus is spreading through the bloodstream of Soviet sham, where nations live together in perfect harmony and loyalty, conscious of their origins but never thinking them paramount, and passionately devoted to the Soviet state.

I back the bacillus to beat the sham. After the hanging of Jaruzelski, and the week-long celebrations that follow it, I propose to go on to the independent kingdom of the Ukraine (where, incidentally, half my own forebears come from) and then nip up to the equally independent republic of Lithuania (where the other half started), though I shall probably not visit the Armenian-Azerbaijanian border, since there will be a civil war raging there over who gets Nagorno-Karabakh. Well, well, revolutions are rarely tidy; I can wait. So can the Ukrainians.

The Times March 3rd, 1988

Tell us the old, old story

STRANGE NEWS FROM China; and the strangest thing about the news is that it is not at all strange.

The authorities there are worried about a rising crime-rate, two aspects of which worry them particularly. First, it seems that gangs of adolescent youths have been terrorizing the country; robbery with violence seems to be their speciality.

And as if that is not enough, there have been numerous executions among a somewhat older generation, the sons or grandsons of leading figures in the present Chinese leadership or of heroes of the revolution, the Long March and the conquest of all China for Communism; murder and rape seem to have been the leading crimes in this category.

I am tempted to say that those of my readers who are genuinely surprised at this news ought to be sent to a Chinese 're-education' camp; there would be plenty to choose from, though anyone eager to sign up should be warned that the experience will be not at all like a 1930s summer school at Dartington.

You see, if you were surprised at the news that in China there are violent criminals scarcely out of short trousers, and even more violent ones who believe that their illustrious ancestry is protection enough for them to do as they like without retribution, it can only be because you have come to believe, as so many have, that China, or to be precise, Communism in China, has literally changed the nature of man. That, after all, is what your fathers (if they were as silly as you) believed about Stalin's Russia, where . . . well, Malcolm

Muggeridge's great apostrophe to human folly will bear quoting once more:

> Wise old Shaw, high-minded old Barbusse, the venerable Webbs, Gide the pure in heart and Picasso the impure, down to poor little teachers, crazed clergymen and millionaires, drivelling dons and very special correspondents . . . all resolved, come what might, to believe anything, however preposterous, to overlook anything, however villainous, to approve anything, however obscurantist and brutally authoritarian, in order to be able to preserve intact the confident expectation that one of the most thoroughgoing, ruthless and bloody tyrannies ever to exist on earth could be relied on to champion human freedom, the brotherhood of man, and all the other good liberal causes to which they had dedicated their lives.

They even had a word for it, New Soviet Man, and the fact that at much the same time Hitler was instituting a New Order apparently gave no one pause. The central paradox of Stalin's Russia and those outside who worshipped it was that a system recommended as heaven on earth held, and holds unbroken to this day (by a very wide margin indeed), the record for the greatest number of innocent human beings deliberately done to death in the entire history of the world; but that monstrous and unforgivable misapprehension is so vast and bloodstained that it has understandably tended to obscure another fallacy, less murderous in its effects yet perhaps more subtly dangerous, if not to life then at least to reason.

Despite Stalin and Hitler, Mao and Pol Pot, Tito and Franco, Stroessner and Castro, the Duvaliers and the Dergue, and all the other mad and murderous brutes who have defiled this century and defile it still, it seems to me plain that mankind in general is better than it was in the earlier centuries. There is more altruism, more respect for the individual worth of others, more generosity, more resistance to state evil, more rejection of arbitrary discrimination, more acceptance of the limitations of human action, more understanding of our own ignorance, even more tolerance. We progress, it is true, by fits and starts, and for every four steps forward that we take, we slip three steps back, but slowly, inexorably, we move forward.

Human nature, then, can change. *But it cannot change quickly*, and, above all, it cannot *be* changed, least of all by political action.

I have said it two dozen times, and in any case Horace said it before me: *Thingummy expellas furca, whatsit whatsit recurret.* 'Grant that the old Adam in this Child may be buried', says the Anglican ceremony of baptism, 'that the new man shall be raised up in him'; what is more, it sometimes happens. But those who plan to sit around until it happens to all mankind had better bring a cushion and a very long book. In China, as in Britain, some people want what they haven't got, and some of these are willing to take it, if necessary using the greatest violence, from those who have it. In both countries, too, the children of the powerful are more inclined than the generality to believe that their family connections will give them immunity, and quite often, and for quite a long time, they are right in that belief. The same, on both counts, is true in Albania, Burundi, Chile, Denmark, Ethiopia, France, Guatemala, Haiti, Indonesia, Japan, Kuwait, Liechtenstein, Mexico, Nigeria, Oman, Portugal, Qatar, Romania, Sierra Leone, Thailand, Uruguay, Venezuela, the Windward Isles, Yemen and Zambia, and if there was a country beginning with X it would apply there, too.

It must be said that although the belief in the rapid perfectibility of man is wholly without foundation, and the belief that it has actually taken place through the workings of a particular political system not only baseless but very dangerous indeed, the belief is not *in itself* unworthy; on the contrary, the longing for perfection is one of the noblest and most persistent of all human dreams, and although those dreams have, again and again throughout history, turned to waking nightmares, mankind dreams them still.

Professor Paul Hollander's *Political Pilgrims*, now a permanent signpost in the country of the blind, has shown how, decade after decade, some of the world's worst (and, in some cases, most obvious) tyrannies have been visited and hymned, and that as disillusion sets in with one, the disillusioned have instantly, so deep and irresistible is their craving, adopted another. When, some 30 years after they took place, Stalin's show-trials were admitted (by some, anyway) to have been not quite according to the *Corpus Juris Civilis* of Justinian, and the Terror to have been aptly named, it occurred to few of those who were thus finally disabused to question the origin and basis of their so tragically misplaced belief; they, or their spiritual heirs, simply turned to Mao – second only to Stalin in the murder contest – and believed no less passionately that he had turned China into Paradise. When they began to feel, uneasily, that he might not have done so after all, there was no lack of alternative candidates: North Vietnam, Cuba, Mozambique, Ethiopia, even Cambodia . . . the dogs bark, but the caravan moves on. It has even moved on to Afghanistan, where Jonathan Steele, of the *Guardian*, found those *nice* Russians doing so *much* for the locals, who were naturally so *grateful*, and wished the Russians would *never* go away, particularly since they were the locals' only defence against those *wicked* rebels, who were not in the *least* grateful to the Russians and thoroughly *deserved* to have those *sweet* little Russian bombs dropped on them. (And the latest, of course, is Nicaragua.)

But that, you see, is why I took care to defend the dream as harmless only *in itself*. In the Garden of Eden there was a serpent, and careful reading of the story will reveal that the serpent must have been already in residence when Adam and Eve arrived, nor is there any suggestion that when they were driven out, he was expelled also. The revelation that China, too, has a crime wave, that it extends to children, and that the scions of leading families in the Communist hierarchy are foremost in the law-breaking, is indeed momentous news. But it is also the oldest news in the world.

The Times August 16th, 1986

Freedom of speechlessness

WITH THE POSSIBLE exception of a planarian worm that has been cut in half both across and lengthways, there can be no creature, animal, vegetable or mineral, so congenitally spineless as the administrative head of a British university. I suppose the filleting process began in the Sixties, but it has gone a great deal further since; by now, if anyone slams a door near a vice-chancellor, he is likely to put his hands up and start reciting the names and ages of his dependent relatives.

When, recently, the government introduced legislation, as an amendment to the Education Bill, which would oblige university authorities to ensure that the principle of free speech within the law was upheld on their premises (following many incidents in which it had been denied, with violence, to visiting speakers and even to the institutions' own teachers), passers-by were deafened by the resentful and indignant squealing of those whose job it would be to carry out the law, rather than, as they preferred, to let intimidation do its work while they looked the other way.

They said that a law was unnecessary, that it would be unenforceable, that boys will be boys, that the trouble had been much exaggerated, that a punch in the nose was good for catarrh, and that while they did not themselves believe that Mr John Carlisle, MP, practised cannibalism, at any rate regularly, reports that bones had been found in his dustbin could not be entirely discounted and that in any case a visit from him was undeniably something of a provocation.

The government ignored the squealing and pressed on with the legislation; how right they were to do so can be seen from recent events at the University College of Cardiff. For if university authorities are in general over-supple of spine, the conduct of those in charge at Cardiff must suggest that the Boneless Wonder has risen from the grave.

The Cardiff authorities have made a formal agreement with the students' union which enshrines the right to deny a hearing to any speaker deemed 'controversial'. If such a speaker is invited, the union will be officially allowed to stage an 'orderly' demonstration outside the hall. (In practice, of course, that means that the students will continue, as is the fashion, to bang and spit upon the speaker's car, to try to prevent him from getting into the hall, and to scream abuse at him.) When the meeting is about to start, the official demonstrators from outside are to officially enter the hall and take up official position. Should the speaker say something that displeases them, 'official heckling' will then begin, and if the speaker persists in saying things they do not approve of, they will then exercise their right, enshrined in the memorable words 'chanting will take place', to prevent him being heard.

This treaty, in the even more striking words of those who agreed upon it, is designed to ensure 'both freedom of speech within the law and the equally important freedom for students to express opposing views'.

A student spokesman, after the announcement of the details, expressed himself well pleased with them, since, as he engagingly declared, the agreement would enable the students to continue with their policy of denying a platform to speakers of whose views they disapproved. For good measure, incidentally, the college's ignominious surrender was made even more abject by a codicil to the agreement, under the terms of which the authorities agreed to drop the disciplinary proceedings they had initiated against ten students who had been among those who recently prevented Mr Enoch Powell from completing a speech.

Presumably the Cardiff authorities hope that their agreement will, when the legislation is finally made law, enable them to ignore it; I trust that they will be rapidly disillusioned.

But the grotesque nature of their surrender may have obscured the dishonesty that lies at its root. They claim that the agreement ensures a double freedom of speech; the right for a speaker to give his views and the 'equally important' right for those who disagree to express *their* views.

Now leave aside what will happen in practice, which is that no unapproved speaker will be heard over the 'official chanting'. In what way is there equality of free speech when a speaker is trying to give his views and a section of the audience is licensed to shout him down? The right of the students to 'express opposing views' suggests, and is plainly meant to suggest, that a debate or a discussion is envisaged; the 'controversial' speaker puts his case, and someone else puts the contrary argument. But that is not at all what has been agreed. 'To express opposing views' means, under the terms of the Cardiff agreement, the right of the students to shout abuse ('Racist! Racist! Sexist! Sexist!') in unison, until the speaker, wearying of the unequal struggle, abandons his speech.

That is what is liable to happen as things are; but what the Cardiff agreement does is to make certain that it *will* happen, with the approval and support of the authorities. We are accustomed, by now, to those who preach an equality between the fire brigade and the arsonist; Cardiff has gone a step further and now insists that the fire brigade's hoses should squirt petrol rather than water.

The tolerance of views we disagree with used to be the chief characteristic of civilized discourse. In a sense, it still is, though since civilized discourse has practically vanished, there is now little scope for its exercise. The rise of the *groupuscules* of the fascist left, with their unshakeable conviction that no opposite views may be expressed, did not at first matter very much; but when the fascist left began to capture local authorities, and put their intolerance into practice, anyone who cared for freedom had cause for alarm, and when, soon afterwards, the same enemies of freedom gained a bridgehead in Parliament (now certain to be hugely expanded after the next election, whoever wins it) the alarm was even more urgently justified.

Yet those who, like me, were brought up in a different tradition believed that some pillars of the open society would never fall, and that among these would be, second only to the law, our universities. We should have known better, and when the University of Oxford refused to give Mrs Thatcher the customary honorary degree (largely because she hadn't given it a big enough monetary bribe) we did know better, though in truth the evidence by then was extensive and undeniable.

That evidence showed that in any struggle which required courage the universities would be found to practise cowardice; that in any call to them to defend freedom they would bow to freedom's enemies; and that when there was a challenge to the very nature and essence of a university as a place where all views, all theories, all beliefs could meet and be heard, they would run away from the challenge.

But surely not even the most cynical observer of our universities believed that they would run as far as Cardiff now has. To ignore intolerance is one thing; to legislate it into the statutes is another. To ignore the cries for help uttered by freedom under assault is shameful; to rush to freedom's side and help to belabour her is more so. And to leave a bully to his bullying is bad enough; to proclaim the bully's 'equally important rights' is the very worst.

It is not yet clear exactly what form the forthcoming 'free speech' legislation will take. In particular, it is not laid down what means of enforcement the law will have against universities which fail in their new legal duty, and what penalties are envisaged. I can suggest an obvious remedy; let any university which is guilty under the proposed law lose its grant. For even Cardiff, I imagine, would be willing to defend free speech if failing to do so would entail a threat to its income.

The Times December 1st, 1986

To be a pilgrim

E VEN IN BRITAIN, I imagine, there must still be some
connection between Christmas, Christianity and Christ,
so perhaps this is an appropriate time of year (though Easter
might be even better) for me to write about a man who is
undergoing terrible persecution in the Soviet Union, probably
unto death, for professing the Christian faith, and for nothing
else at all.

His name is Alexander Ogorodnikov. He was born in 1950,
and at the age of 23, while a student at the Cinematography
Institute in Moscow, his interest in Christianity was awakened
for the first time by the Pasolini film *The Gospel According to St
Matthew*; soon afterwards he was received into the Russian
Orthodox Church. Shortly after that, he was expelled from
the Institute, and began on the *via crucis* that is the lot of any
Christian in his country who wants to proclaim, and live by,
his faith.

With a group of like-minded friends, he began a private and
informal discussion group called the Christian Seminar; they
did not take any kind of public action, though they kept in
touch with other such groups, and drew much inspiration
from Father Dudko, who had suffered years of persecution for
his Christian witness.

Soon the pressure began. Ogorodnikov was driven from
job after job, and from his home; he and his fellow Christians
were interrogated, threatened, beaten up; some were put into
the notorious Soviet madhouses-for-the-sane. (Ogorodnikov
wrote to the World Council of Churches for help, but got
none.)

In November 1978 he was arrested and charged with 'parasitism', the Catch-22 of the Soviet Union; the victims are prevented from getting a job, then prosecuted for not working. (As it happens, Ogorodnikov was arrested when he was actually on the way to be interviewed for a job; possibly the authorities were afraid he might get it.)

The 'trial' was of the usual kind; the public benches were filled in advance by the KGB, so that his friends could not get in (even his wife and mother were admitted only after long arguments and for only part of the trial), and he was not allowed to call his witnesses. He was sentenced to a year in a concentration camp in the far east; he was beaten with truncheons after being sentenced, and beaten again when, on the way to the camp, he asked to see a priest.

Some of his colleagues in the Christian Seminar suffered similarly; Vladimir Poresh, for instance, was sentenced to five years in a concentration camp, to be followed by three years 'internal exile'. Ogorodnikov was accused of further offences arising out of Poresh's trial, at which he had refused to testify; he was therefore not released at the expiry of his sentence but transferred to a prison in Kalinin where, in September 1980, he was charged with 'anti-Soviet agitation and propaganda'. The same procedure was followed, except that this time only his mother was allowed into the courtroom, and at first for only a few minutes; later in the trial, it seems that either he made an attempt at suicide or he was attacked and injured by those who were holding him – at any rate he was bandaged, and an ambulance stood by outside the courtroom throughout, while his mother was admitted again. This time Poresh was called as a witness, and in turn refused to testify against Ogorodnikov.

Ogorodnikov, who was badly weakened by the hunger strike he had embarked on three months before his trial, was sentenced to six years in a 'strict regime' concentration camp (it was the notorious and sinister Perm complex of the Gulag) to be followed by five years 'internal exile'. Meanwhile, other members of the Christian Seminar and their friends were being imprisoned in jails or madhouses.

In the camp, Ogorodnikov started another hunger strike, this time to force the authorities to let him have a Bible (they refused), and later on yet another hunger strike, in protest at not being allowed to see a priest. He was allowed no visitors.

He was subjected to specially inhuman treatment; he was often in a cell so cold that the walls were covered in ice, another cell was deliberately flooded with sewage, he was repeatedly put in the punishment cells for trivial reasons or for none, and letters were withheld from him. It is hardly surprising that, in a letter smuggled out of the camp and ultimately to the West, he wrote: 'Occasionally it seems to me that I should school myself to accept the idea that my welfare does not interest anyone but God.'

Towards the end of his sentence, the same trick was played; he was charged with further offences, re-tried, and sentenced, in April of this year, to a further three years in a strict-regime concentration camp. In May, he wrote the letter to which I have referred; it is worth quoting at some length:

> You must see that death appears to be the only way to end my agony, the only release. I have already committed the mortal sin of attempting to commit suicide. So I beg of you – please appeal to the Presidium of the Supreme Soviet to show me a measure of mercy by ordering my execution by firing squad in order to put an end to the prospect of a lifelong, painfully slow torture by deprivation of living conditions fit for a human being, deprivation of books and culture, torture by hunger and cold, by incarceration in punishment cells, humiliations, total lack of rights. They even forbid me to pray, and my cross has been torn from around my neck on numerous occasions. I have spent a total of 659 days on hunger strike, to protest against their refusal to let me have a Bible and prayer book . . .
>
> Only the full glare of publicity can alter my fate . . . Only this can restrain the hands of those who are otherwise free to wreak whatever atrocities they will . . . Only the incorruptible daylight can force lawlessness to pause . . . It seems to

me that the outside Christian world knows nothing about the protest fasts which I have conducted, *not* to secure my release from prison! No! The aim was to have a Bible at my disposal, a prayer-book and a cross to enable me to draw faith from the source of Divine Revelation . . . Will not the Universal Christian Church say at least a word in support of one of Her persecuted sons – errant and sinful, but still her son? What awaits me now? Only God knows.

No doubt; but at least a few more people now know what has previously awaited Alexander Ogorodnikov for the crime of being a Christian. But there are a few more who seem to need further instruction, and since the further instruction is now available, in the form of a document written by a group of Soviet Christians *in partibus infidelium* to their co-religionists in lands where Christianity is not a crime, I think it worth concluding with some excerpts from that document too:

Your Christian delegates are keen on visiting our country; your Christian preachers return home with a host of pleasant memories. But . . . we are not permitted to live by simple Christian feelings – to believe, to be merciful, to entreat, to defend, to love, to bring up children, to work and to teach. All these attempts are met by harsh persecution . . . Maybe our position will become clearer to you if we simply say that service to God is forbidden to us . . . Knowing this . . . please abstain from helping the persecutors to hammer yet another nail into the crucified body of Our Lord Jesus Christ, which you do every time one of you makes confident assertions that there is no persecution of believers in the USSR . . . We entreat you to raise your voice in defence of Alexander Ogorodnikov and, with all the means available to you in your free and democratic way of life, to try and secure his release.*

The Times December 15th, 1986

* Alexander Ogorodnikov was subsequently released.

To be a martyr

T HE FINAL PARAGRAPH of Solzhenitsyn's *The First Circle* records the complacent impression of a French journalist in Moscow when he sees a bread van go past him in the street; he records in his notebook a comment to the effect that the distribution of food is in good and efficient hands. The van, however, so clearly labelled 'Bread', is in fact full of prisoners on the first stage of their journey to the Gulag, and the irony symbolizes the folly, and worse than folly, of all the thousands – by now it must be hundreds of thousands – who, frequently even without any ill intent, have gone to the Soviet Union and other totalitarian states, and there written down in their notebooks whatever they were told, and believed it, and repeated it when they got home, though they had absolutely no means of knowing whether it was true or not. If they had heard the same claims from an official in South Africa, they would undoubtedly (and rightly) have treated them with a good deal of scepticism. But when the Moscow van says 'Bread', into their notebooks goes a favourable comment about food distribution.

Some of my readers may recall the BBC television series from the Soviet Union called *Comrades*. I took issue with it rather severely, I recall; the producer, Mr Richard Denton, had simply filmed what he saw as though it was reality, whereas he would never have believed that a Wild West street built in Hollywood for a film was any more than a series of façades. And façades is the right word, because the famous 'Potemkin Villages' that so impressed visitors to Tsarist Russia were indeed no more than that, and the innocent guests drove past them in their carriages quite persuaded that there was a whole house where there was nothing but a theatrical design. But what 'my useful idiots' (the phrase is attributed to Lenin) will never learn is that the whole of the Soviet Union is one giant Potemkin Village, and in addition that there are enormous numbers of officials whose job – for which they are carefully and assiduously trained – is to persuade the visitors that the village is real and the van is full of bread.

The behaviour of the adult 'useful idiots' on their own behalf is bad enough; but what can be said without profanity when children, who really cannot be expected to know better, are sent to Potemkinland, bringing back favourable impressions and never suspecting that their own openness and spontaneity are being reciprocated by well-rehearsed responses according to a carefully-shaped script?

That is what has happened to a group of British schoolgirls from Kent, who have just come back from an exchange visit to the Soviet Union; the Soviet girls will be arriving in Britain in July. The British girls had a wonderful time, and, as was reported in *The Times*, found that 'all their preconceptions were overturned', and that 'the Soviet Union was not the gloomy, forbidding place they had imagined'.

'My overall impression,' said the girl whose account of the visit was given in *The Times*, 'is that the Russian people are friendly and very generous.' They are indeed, young lady, and I am not surprised that they took you to their hearts, nor that you responded with all the honesty and gratitude of your youth. Much the same happened to the *Daily Mail*'s girl on the tour: '. . . I found friends . . . I don't think I have ever experienced such genuine kindness, or so many hugs and kisses . . .'.

I don't doubt that either. And who am I to spit in the loving cup, or to offer disillusion to innocence by telling the schoolgirls that the families they were billeted on were by no means ordinary or average, let alone picked at random, and that long before the British girls arrived, their hosts had been carefully rehearsed by the appropriate Comrade Potemkin, who would also have inspected the premises to ensure that they exhibited the proper level of simple comfort.

Let the girls dream; but as they are nodding off, let me introduce them to a man who would have liked nothing better than to be billeted on a comfortable and warm-hearted family in his native country – a man, indeed, who has been offered just such hospitality by just such Soviet hosts, but is not permitted to accept it. He is Vasili Shipilov, and before I recount some of the details of his strange life I shall give one tiny detail, specially directed to those young ladies who were so kindly and generously entertained in the Soviet Union, and who responded like the polite and thoughtful visitors they are. I do not know, of course, to what religion, if any, they adhere; may I assume, for the purpose of what follows, that they come of Christian homes? Actually, it doesn't matter if they are Buddhists or Jews or nothing at all, though the Christian ones among them are likely to get a slightly worse shock at what I am about to reveal. Remember that these girls have had all their preconceptions about the Soviet Union 'overturned', and – even more important – have discovered that 'the Soviet Union is not the gloomy, forbidding place they had imagined'.

Only, you see, it is a most frightfully gloomy and forbidding place for Vasili Shipilov, *who is regularly beaten, to the extent of a fractured skull, solely for crossing himself in the course of his Christian devotions.*

Vasili Shipilov is entitled to call himself the Father of the Gulag. He has been in concentration camps, prisons and penal psychiatric hospitals since he was 17 years old; he is now 65. (He had one year of freedom, in 1949–50.) His family was deported to Siberia in the 1920s and set to forced labour on a collective farm which formed part of the Gulag. His father was killed when he tried to get out in search of food for the family; his mother starved to death. Vasili became a Christian; he was arrested and imprisoned. In prison, he became a priest, ordained by fellow-prisoners who were already ministers. For baptising other prisoners who sought to be received into the

Church, he was sentenced to another 25 years on top of the sentence he was already serving. After his brief release in an amnesty, he was rearrested and imprisoned, for trying to bring food (berries he collected in the forest) to those still in the camp he had been released from, and for his religious ministrations. Soon, he was sentenced to incarceration in various Soviet madhouses-for-the-sane. In one of them, he was told: 'If you don't give up your faith you will stay here, unless they kill you.' One of the 'doctors' told him: 'No one knows about you. No one will ever find you.' He was tortured with drugs, including doses of insulin that led to coma; his skull fracture led to epilepsy. He remains steadfast in his faith, including in his prayers his jailers and torturers. As I said, there is a home waiting for him outside the walls; for that matter there is a home waiting for him in the West.

The Reverend Richard Rodgers has shut himself up voluntarily in a makeshift cage at St Martins in the Fields in London; the cage is as close to a replica of one of Vasili's cells as he can get. He did the same for Irina Ratushinskaya, the poet, a year or two ago, and again for Alexander Ogorodnikov, yet another Soviet Christian martyr; the daft bugger seems to take his religion seriously. He has shaved his head, and proposes to keep a vigil for Vasili for 46 days, one fewer than the 47 years of Vasili's *via crucis*; he will live on bread and water throughout. You can talk to him directly if you like; he has a phone in his cage, and the number is 01 930 1538. Perhaps – they seem thoughtful enough to do it – some of the girls who went on the trip to the Soviet Union might like to speak to him.

Of course, it would be a pity to make them feel sad at the realization that some of their preconceptions should not have been overturned quite so readily; but, after all, no blame attaches to them. All they were doing was responding gracefully to the kindness they were shown. The fact that it was to a large extent a false kindness should not alter their gratitude for it, any more than the fate of Vasili Shipilov should. But once, not many years ago, they believed in Father

Christmas. They lost a part of their innocence when they discovered the truth about the presents in their Christmas stockings, but they gained a greater measure of maturity and understanding when they did so. Perhaps it is time for them to lose a little more of their innocence, and gain yet more adult wisdom. Vasili Shipilov, come to think of it, lost his innocence about the Soviet Union at much the same age as the girls are now.

The Times March 14th, 1988

The mating game

THE BATTLE BETWEEN Kasparov and Karpov sways, like more lethal battles, back and forth; here a frontal assault by the infantry, there a long-range artillery duel, anon a surprise dash by the cavalry. The metaphors are inescapable, but the warlike ones are only a tiny handful of those images, parables, referents, moral lessons, symbols, dramas, figures of speech, legends, fables and quotations which have been given birth, over the centuries, by the greatest game the human race has ever created.

'Over the centuries'; we are at once in the heart of the first mystery. When? How? By whom? The arguments of the chess archaeologists continue, and will do so for ever; no sooner had general agreement been reached on India in the 6th century AD than somebody in Russia dug up some chess-looking figures from four centuries earlier. There are no written records before the Indian hypothesis, but that proves very little; my own favourite version is that it was invented by the watchmen on the walls of Troy, to while away the years.

The Vikings, they say, brought it to England; certainly it was familiar here by the 12th century. Elizabeth I was a keen player, and she is reputed to have been a good one, though since she presumably played mostly with her courtiers, there may have been an element of co-operation, on the part of her opponents, in her victories. Philip of Spain played, too. So did Canute; and what is more, he cheated.

The game developed gradually; the older forms are hardly recognizable as chess (some versions included an aleatoric element), but today's standard form has been long established.

Capablanca, one of the very greatest of world champions, got bored with beating everyone who came against him, and proposed a board enlarged by two squares each way and with two extra pieces, one of them called the Chancellor. He might have got the new version off the ground, too, had it not been for the fact that soon after he put it forward Alekhine took the championship away from him on an ordinary board with not a Chancellor in sight. Alekhine was perhaps the most self-destructive great player of this very dangerous game until Bobby Fischer went one worse. Ironically, if there is a 'greatest' chess player (an absurd concept anyway) it is surely one of those two.

It *is* dangerous; too many great players have been on the edge of madness, or over it, for it to be a coincidence. The mind of a grandmaster is something that cannot be properly understood, so extraordinary is its ability; and those of the handful of what may be called the supergrandmasters defy imagination. So, of course, do the great artists; how *did* Beethoven think of the second movement of the Eighth Symphony? But there is a difference, which will be immediately apparent if we contemplate that astonishing – indeed, alarming – chess phenomenon called blindfold.

The player is not, of course, blindfolded; he simply sits alone, without a board or pieces, and plays the game in his head, his opponents' moves being told to him as they are made elsewhere. And the apostrophe in 'opponents' is in the right place, in case you wondered; there are authenticated instances of chess masters playing more than *fifty* such games simultaneously. I sometimes think that the real wonder of the supergrandmasters is that a good many of them are perfectly sane.

Some, indeed, have been wonderfully full and rounded men. Not surprisingly, mathematics and music figure prominently among the leading chess players, and one world champion, Max Euwe of the Netherlands, was a lecturer in mathematics, mechanics and astronomy. Some have had odd sidelines; Lasker, for instance, tried a variety of business schemes, all of which came to nothing (or to bankruptcy), his record being a pigeon-breeding establishment which failed, not surprisingly, because he tried to mate two male pigeons to get the thing properly started.

In addition to those who went mad under the strain (Akiba Rubinstein, for instance), and those who were probably mad to start with, it is clear that the rules of the mind are suspended for much of the chess world. High intelligence, for instance, though many leading players have had it, is plainly not needed; Fischer is not known to have done, said or thought anything at all other than about matters pertaining to chess, and once, when he gave up chess temporarily, he did nothing but play billiards for a couple of years.

It is widely believed that the history of chess is as thickly strewn with child prodigies as music with Mozarts and Menuhins. Not so; there have been very few true prodigies, indeed only two can be certainly given the title – Capablanca and Reshevsky. But it is true that, at least today, it is a young man's game, so arduous and taxing are its demands. That, of course, was the inevitable consequence of rationalizing the way championships and tournaments are arranged; it is far better than the old, haphazard system in which champions could avoid challenges for years on end, but – along with the huge sums of money that champions can now command – it has made chess into a business, and a very big business.

But only, of course, away from the board. There, nothing tells except talent. Chess is, I believe, unique in that it has no element of chance or luck at all; he who plays the better move wins, every time. Incidentally, I say 'he', because although there are some formidably powerful women players today, particularly from Georgia, for some inexplicable reason, none has yet established herself among the supergrandmasters.

One of the inevitable developments in the chess world has been its transformation into an entirely professional concern. No player could now hope to conquer the world while playing only part-time, particularly because it isn't only a matter of playing; continual research is essential, now that entire books have been devoted to one variation of a standard opening. All wise players, throughout the years, have studied their potential opponents' games, but today they do so meticulously, with bodies of assistants to work with them. And it follows that it is very unlikely that any world champion, or indeed aspirant to the chair, will be in any real sense a nice man.

Max Euwe was the last world champion who could be thus described, and he was also the last amateur to hold the title. (His parallel in Britain was C.H.O'D. Alexander, also too much of a gentleman for the modern game.) Euwe would have been eaten alive by either Karpov or Kasparov, or for that matter Fischer; but he wouldn't have minded, which is why he would have lost to them.

Chess has spawned a huge literature outside the literature of the game itself; Stefan Zweig's *The Royal Game* is still a masterpiece of excitement and allusion, even to those who do not know the difference between Zugzwang and Sitzfleisch. There is even a musical, running in London at this moment, called *Chess*, though strict obedience to honesty obliges me to say that it is a stupendously boring one.

As a mere wood-pusher myself, I can only stand on the sidelines and wonder as Karpov and Kasparov slug it out, with hundreds of thousands of dollars – millions, ultimately – riding on the outcome of their match. Yet still, when all the fanfares have died away, and all the politicking has stopped, and all the bets have been made, there will be two men facing each other across a board of 64 squares, alternately black and white, each with eight pawns, two rooks, two bishops, two knights, one queen and one king, and each with nothing to help him but what he can find inside his head. May the better player win. He will.

The Times November 9th, 1987

The red and the black

S UPPOSE YOU WERE reading the morning newspapers and there learned of the death of an elderly retired professor of literature. Glancing through the obituaries, you find him commended in the most laudatory terms: 'When I heard of his death', for instance, 'I was reminded of friends and admirers all over the world who would grieve as deeply as myself', or 'His outlook and methods were essentially "open"', or he was a 'lovable and genuinely modest man', or 'his many colleagues . . . regarded him as a man of complete integrity and generous humanity'.

The picture by now would be clear; a teacher of inspiring liberal qualities, rooted in a generous and tolerant set of beliefs, a lover of good, a man of an essentially humane temperament, detesting all systems which worked to control free thought or to bar the road to those seeking the truth.

Now suppose you read that he

. . . had joined the British Nazi Party in 1936 while at Cambridge, and he remained a life-long member, serving for many years on its executive committee . . . He neither flaunted nor apologized for his unswerving political commitment . . .

Wait. A feeling of astonishment is now growing upon you, and you start to read the obituaries more closely. Doing so, you also come upon this, referring to his politics:

His commitment was based on a deep ethical revulsion against greed and exploitation, and on staunch loyalty. It kept him in the party in 1944, much as events following the July 20th bomb-plot must have hurt him.

By now, surely, you must be thinking that there is a catch in it. So there is, as I shall explain. The dead academic was Professor Arnold Kettle. He certainly did *not* join the Nazi Party, let alone serve on its executive committee, much less exhibit staunch loyalty to it; nor, of course, did he condone the horrors of the July 20 plot even though hurt by them. He abhorred Nazism and all its works, and would have despised anyone who did not. Indeed, he fought it on the battlefield.

So what is he doing in this farrago? What am *I* doing in it? What I am doing is translating, word for word and event for event, from Communism to Nazism, from black tyranny to red tyranny, from black extermination to red, from greed and exploitation in the colour of night to the same in the colour of blood, from the executive committee of the British Nazis to that of the British Communists, from Nazi purges to Soviet purges, from the heroic, noble bomb plot against Nazism in 1944 to the heroic, noble Hungarian revolution against Communism in 1956, from inexcusable 'unswerving political commitment' to inexcusable 'unswerving political commitment'. For Dr Kettle matched in his life, step for step, all the gradations of adherence to an infamous creed that I listed, the only difference being that the infamous creed of his choice was Communism, not Nazism.

Let us climb the right ladder, step by step. He joined the Communist Party in 1936, at the age of 20. You would have to be a very harsh judge to condemn him for that, despite the abundant evidence, even then, of the true nature of the thing that ruled in the Soviet Union. There followed the purges, the show trials, the full Stalinist terror; still, it did not take clairvoyance to see the war coming, and anti-Nazi zeal could understandably reply 'Any port in a storm'. (Though did he have no unease at the Nazi-Soviet pact?)

He joined the army in 1941. Remember that as soon as the Soviet Union was attacked, the British Communist Party ceased to proclaim that the war was only a capitalist conspiracy and that we had no business to be fighting Hitler, Stalin's friend; from then on, the Soviet Union was our gallant ally (not only in the Communists' eyes), and many Communists fought bravely, and died, to defeat the Nazis. Again, Kettle can hardly be criticized for not learning the grievous error of his political commitment through his own war service.

But then the excuses run out. In a memorable phrase, Anthony Hartley said that anyone who remained a Communist after the seizure of Czechoslovakia in 1948 'had failed as a human being'. But Kettle, in 1948, was just getting into his Communist stride.

After the subjugation of Czechoslovakia there were the show trials in the Soviet Union's newly-acquired empire; in each country in turn the leaders whom Stalin himself had appointed were culled, the most terrible and most patently fraudulent of these inquisitions being the Czech one in 1952. Each time, the Communist Party of Great Britain applauded. So it did in 1953, when the 'Doctors' Plot' was devised, and the greatest purge even in the bloody history of Soviet Communism was averted only by Stalin's timely death.

That death was mourned by our – Professor Kettle's – Communist Party in terms which would have been excessive if applied to St Francis of Assisi; the world's greatest mass murderer was lauded as the purest and most benevolent democrat since Pericles. Still Professor Kettle exhibited his 'staunch loyalty' to those who worshipped evil.

Then Hungary, and the extinction of that bright, brave flame (to say nothing of the extinction of a very large number of human beings). Kettle was – or at least was deemed by Mr Angus Calder in his obituary in the *Independent* to be – 'hurt'. Despite his pain, he managed to carry on as a member of the Communist Party, which of course praised the crushing of the revolution as a heroic action by the Red Army.

The Berlin Wall and the 1968 invasion of Czechoslovakia no doubt caused him to be hurt all over again; once more, he bore up courageously, and remained in the party. Through Brezhnev, Andropov, Chernenko and Gorbachov, through the rising tide of antisemitism, through the torture of dissidents and their concentration camp sentences, through the crushing of Solidarity in Poland and the invasion of Afghanistan, the brave fellow nursed his pain and remained not only a loyal member of the Party but for years a loyal member of its executive committee.

Two weeks ago he died, and those colleagues, admirers and friends who were quoted in the obituaries recorded his 'loyalty', his 'deep, ethical revulsion against greed and exploitation', his 'open outlook and methods', his 'unswerving political commitment' which he 'never flaunted nor apologised for'.

And now I think it is time to ask the late Professor Kettle's admirers a few questions. For this article is really about them, not him.

How exactly is a Nazi's or a Communist's outlook 'essentially "open"'? How does a 'deep ethical revulsion against greed and exploitation' lead to 'unswerving political commitment' to a system which practices not only greed and exploitation but mass murder? To join a Communist or Nazi party at the age of 20 can be easily understood, even excused. But remember that Professor Kettle remained a member of his chosen cause to the day of his death at the age of 70, and served for many years on its chief policy-making body; is it not matter for censure as well as wonder that he never 'apologised for his unswerving commitment' to abomination? How do those 'friends and admirers all over the world' answer that?

Moreover, his commitment was based also on 'staunch loyalty'. Staunch loyalty to whom and what? How *dare* any man be 'staunchly loyal' to a system notorious for treachery (whether demonstrated in Hitler's Night of the Long Knives or Stalin's massacre of his most loyal and devoted followers) and leaders loyal to nothing but butchery and persecution? And just what was the nature of the 'hurt' that he 'must' have suffered from the 'events' in Hungary in 1956, and wherein did it differ from that of any 'staunchly loyal' Nazi who was 'hurt' by the 'events' which followed July 20, 1944? In both cases, the principal hurt would have been to the victims who were tortured and killed; in the circumstances, what precisely did those colleagues of his mean when they called him 'a man of complete integrity'? *Complete?*

No doubt I shall now be told (I never met Professor Kettle) that he truly was, in his personal nature and conduct towards his colleagues and students, 'lovable and genuinely modest'. I have no reason to suppose otherwise. But that does not excuse his shameful *political* nature and conduct, and if his admirers think it does, let them answer this question: would they apply the same test (and give the same answer) to a man who had 'unswervingly' supported Nazism for half a century, whatever his private character? I shall answer the question: No, they would not. And those who 'regarded him as a man of complete integrity and generous humanity'; would they still thus regard him, as a man, even if his politics were of the Hitlerite rather than of the Stalinist variety? Again, I shall answer for them: No.

A case, strictly theoretical, can be made for taking Communism seriously, for treating it, despite all its evils, as a serious system of thought, worthy of respect even if to be rejected. Its ideas, however perverted, *are* ideas, and in that sense it can be distinguished from Nazism, which was nothing but hooliganism enthroned. But Communism must also be known by its fruits; if it is argued that Stalinism was the corruption of Communism, not its essence, then Stalinism must be condemned for all its bloody cruelty, its exterminations, its brutal imperialism, its destruction of thought, freedom and art. While all that was happening, Professor Kettle remained a leading member, 'staunchly loyal', of an organization that existed solely to serve it; let no one try to prove that the Communism he espoused was the harmlessly theoretical kind.

De mortuis, as Mencken remarked, *nil nisi bunkum*. But the comments and attitudes I have discussed here amount to something more than the natural and even admirable desire to speak well of the lately dead. It is more than affection blinding itself to the feet – feet, ankles, shins, calves, knees, thighs and hips – of clay. It is yet another entry in the bulging catalogue of the *trahison des clercs*. It is not that these clerks excuse Kettle's adherence to Communist evil because of his personal qualities; how could *any* personal qualities excuse it? The truth is that they cannot or will not see the evil itself.

Well, I can. I shall now be accused of a cowardly attack on a dead man, and of spitting in his grave. Allow me to reply, in advance of the accusations. It would have taken no courage for Arnold Kettle, in free Britain, to tell the truth about Communism. By his lifelong refusal to do so he spat in the grave of Communism's millions of victims.

The Times January 5th, 1987

The evil that men do

O UR CENTURY HAS seen enough massacres, pogroms and exterminations to turn the seven seas red with blood. But even among a list which includes Stalin's slaughtered millions and the Holocaust itself, a peculiar and unique horror still clings to the genocidal madness of the Khmer Rouge in Cambodia. It certainly has one distinction: they murdered a larger proportion of the population than any of their competitors. (An equivalent proportion in Britain would number eight million.)

The story has been told many times (most memorably, perhaps, in the film *The Killing Fields*), and it has recently been told again in a book called *Cambodian Witness* (published by Faber). It is the autobiography of a Cambodian who went through the nightmare, and woke to find it true; his name is Someth May, and his story is edited and introduced by James Fenton. Please read the following extract: not because it is the most dreadful thing in the book – there are episodes far worse – but because the point I want to make turns upon a particular aspect of it.

> Comrade Tek . . . had worked himself up into a rage. He approached the pile of struggling monkeys [he had broken their arms and tied their feet together], and killed them one by one . . . with a blow to the back of the skull . . . 'And now,' he said, 'I'll show you the way I used to kill the Lon Nol soldiers when we caught them, and the way to get the liver out.' He laid the last monkey flat on the ground . . . He made a cut to the stomach. Then he pressed hard on the incision with both hands. The monkey screeched. The liver

came out whole. Comrade Tek then slit the animal's throat. He said, 'If it had been a man, I would have put my foot in the cut to get the right pressure – otherwise the liver never comes out properly.'

Reviewing the book, in the *Guardian*, Salman Rushdie finished like this: '. . . how can men become like Comrade Tek? I don't know the answer . . . But the terrible lesson of our century is that *it isn't difficult*. I could be Comrade Tek. And so could you.'

It is Mr Rushdie's conclusion that I wish to examine, for I do not believe it is true. I do not believe that Salman Rushdie could become such a man as Tek, and I do not believe that I could, either. I do not believe that, in societies like ours, perhaps in any society, more than a very small number of people are like Tek, or could become like him.

I can do, and have done, many bad acts; hurtful, harmful, inexcusable. So have we all, other than the saints. We could all do things worse than we have done already, and under intolerable pressure we could do worse still; I know that if I were tortured to reveal information that would lead to someone else's death, I would not have the strength or fortitude to resist. There are other kinds of pressure, too, less direct but more insidious. Choose your own – money? power? flesh? – and while you are choosing tell me whether if the Devil offered you all the kingdoms of the earth you, too, would say 'Get thee hence, Satan'. It has just occurred to me that I have in my time broken a majority of the Ten Commandments, and of the ones I have not broken, I could not swear that I am incapable of adding them to the list, not even 'Thou shalt not kill'.

We are all sinners. In certain circumstances almost all of us could rob, perjure, do violence on another. Some could do these things more easily than others; there are gradations of badness. But there is a gap in the spectrum; and almost all of us, including Salman Rushdie and me, remain on the safe side of the gap, and always will, while Comrade Tek and a handful more are beyond it.

But this is not simply a fact, without antecedents or progeny; it enshrines two enormous and vital truths. The first is that some people are evil; *are* evil, not *are made* evil. The greatest and most dangerous lie of our time is that we are *solely* the result of our upbringing, our milieu, our physical surroundings, our schooling, our degree of affluence or poverty, our employment or employment prospects, our social or familial relationships and our sex lives, along with the weather, the threat of war, other people's smoking, Sellafield and the Freemasons.

I said that that is the most dangerous lie; wherein is the danger? In the determinism to which it leads; the effects of that determinism can be seen all round us, and the most pernicious of its effects are the condonation of guilt and the dismissal of responsibility. When there is next a riot in Toxteth, Bristol or Broadwater Farm, who will dare to say, amid the deafening chorus of exculpations – unemployment, sub-standard housing, racism, police brutality – that some people have a propensity to criminal behaviour by reason of what they wish to be, not of what has been done to them?

In any urban riot in this country, those doing the rioting are a small minority of those who live in the area of the riot; the peaceable majority, however, live in the same conditions as the violent few, and are therefore subject to the same riot-inducing pressures. Why do they not join in? But to ask the question that way round is already to surrender; let us ask, instead, why do the rioters riot? The correct answer is: because they want to. But that answer is never given. For that matter, why do you think that almost all talk of the drug problem is couched in terms of the peddlers and pushers, who are seen as uniquely evil figures because they thrust their poisonous wares into the hands of their victims. 'Victims'; what do you suppose would happen if we started to refer to them as accessories?

If our era needs an epitaph, and it may need one sooner than it thinks, how about 'It's not our fault'? For assuredly the now dominant ideology may thus be summed up. It is no longer fashionable, of course, to rely on Freud for an excuse; Marx is much more comprehensively satisfying. But amid the satisfaction responsibility dissolves.

And I believe that Mr Rushdie's argument – that we could all learn to do unspeakable evil – is only the other Janus-face of that state of affairs. No doubt we all have in us the impulses which, if given rein, will lead us into real wickedness. But most of us do not give those impulses rein, and we refuse to do so because we think that doing so is wrong. Some people, however, do not mind doing wrong, if it means they can get hold of somebody else's wallet. We call these people wrong-doers; or rather, we used to call them wrong-doers, but we are more likely today to call them under-privileged.

I ask again: are we or are we not responsible for our own lives? I think we are, and one very important part of that responsibility is ensuring that for us it is not, as Mr Rushdie says, easy to become like Comrade Tek, but impossible.

We do have a choice, every minute of every day. I said that the inability of most people to behave like Tek bears witness to two great truths. I have dealt with one of them – the fact that some people are evil and don't mind a bit – but the other is more important. It is this: the inability to do great evil comes as much from our own will as does the propensity to steal, assault and burn. If we do not become Comrade Tek it is because we decide not to, just as we stab a policeman because we feel like it.

Yet we cannot leave the argument there, for there is the most tremendous question of all to be asked, though not answered. It is: Why do most people, given the choice of being good or bad, choose to be good? Whatever the answer to that question, it is an eternal reproach to Comrade Tek, and a no less enduring assurance that nobody has to be like him.

The Times November 24th, 1986

A lick and a promise

PHILATELY IS NOT a disease to which I have ever succumbed; it seems to me the only human activity sillier than ballet. So if I announce that today I propose to discuss stamps, you will understand that I have no intention of trying to undermine the authenticity of the generally accepted overprinted fourpenny green issued in Nigeria in 1899, or reviewing the fluctuating prices fetched at auction by mint condition penny blacks between 1923 and 1939. Instead, I sing a larger theme.

A quarrel broke out some time ago (it may have been settled by now, though I have heard nothing since the original skirmishes) between the local government of one of Britain's few remaining colonies and those who, in Britain, advise the Crown on matters philatelic. The colony wanted to put forth a stamp bearing the image and superscription of an American pop singer; Her Majesty (or those who speak for her in these matters) demurred. (The demurrer did not concern the choice of subject for the stamp; it was a matter, apparently, of the royal insignia, which the design for the stamp did not carry.)

Britain is the only country in the world which adheres to the international postage convention but is not obliged by the rules to put its name on its stamps; the Queen's head suffices. The reason is that Britain invented – in the person of Rowland Hill – the modern postal system, and the concession is a mark of respect for our priority. Britain's colonies come under the same provision; but the absence of the name entails the presence of the monarch, and it is there that the dispute arose.

It was Mr Anthony Wedgwood Benn, of all people, who, when in government, initiated the modern fashion for pictorial stamps; it has proved to be one of the few services that our spavined Post Office can operate at a profit (so I have no doubt that plans have been drawn up for abolishing it). Who chooses the designs, which have ranged from excellent (the bird series) to atrocious (every Christmas issue, the nadir being reached with last year's 12p), I do not know; the evidence suggests a committee, with a wide variety of tastes represented on it. And the news from afar about the colonial stamp gave me a surprise, for I realized that Britain had not yet issued a set of her own stamps bearing the faces (or other parts) of our own pop stars. Well, well, it can't be long; Harold Wilson gave the Beatles an MBE apiece, and as far as my recollection goes the only dissenting voice was mine.

While the Mother Country hesitates, her children act. Way down South, it is proposed that a pop singer shall be commemorated in this way, and I have no doubt that as soon as the problem of the royal presence on the stamp has been sorted out, those in Britain with friends or relatives in the vicariously sceptred isle under discussion will begin to receive letters with the pop star's phiz in the top right-hand corner. And the question that inevitably arises is: whatever next?

For what is the only thing of which we can be quite certain when we contemplate the life and art of the stamp-honoured singer? It is that, probably long before his retirement or death, and quite certainly soon after, he will be utterly forgotten, and forever. That does not matter, of course, where the real function of stamps is concerned; a letter will go as speedily to the wrong address (or as slowly to the right one) whoever's is the picture on the stamp, and whether or not the sender who licks it recognizes the face. But the symbolic function of a decorative stamp is, surely, to portray on the one hand such things as the beauties of nature and the works of man's hand, and on the other persons worthy of respect and admiration for their talents and achievements – for, you might say, their place in history.

In history's house there are many mansions; but I doubt if there are enough to find room for pop singers, fashionable dress designers, drivers of exceptionally fast motor cars, disc jockeys, proprietors of hamburger emporiums, editors of glossy give-away property magazines, nightclub greeters, comedians whose jokes concern nothing but lavatories, fashionable hairdressers, persons famous only for dyeing their hair orange, persons famous only for sniffing cocaine, persons famous only for appearing in gossip columns, and persons famous only for writing them.

The point about that list is not that it is made up of people whom history will ignore. History, after all, will ignore practically all of us, and quite rightly. But what sets off those people from the generality is not that they will soon be forgotten, but that right now they are being noisily remembered. Their fame flickers briefly, and not very long ago it would never have flickered at all, but the fact that for the moment they fill the circumambient air with their howling and grimacing and swearing and boozing and whoring and drugging and spending says something real and clear about our time, and what it says is not at all pleasant or comforting.

Mistaken judgements have existed as long as the human race; many great reputations have collapsed when really tested by time. The only reason that Benjamin Robert Haydon is remembered today is that he gave the 'Immortal Dinner Party' for Keats, Lamb, Wordsworth, Ritchie and the uninvited Comptroller of Stamps for Westmorland, yet he had his time of being praised and courted before people noticed that his work was no good. (And it must be said that he put a vast amount of hard work into his paintings; today, you can get £6,000 from the Tate for folding blankets or piling bricks, and half a page of eulogy in the *Guardian* for tearing up pieces of paper.)

But only in our festered time, surely, has so much froth and so many bubbles been blown by so many fools so vigorously for so long to so little purpose. That must say something about

us, must it not? And if what it says is to your taste, you must
have a nonpareil strong stomach.

Take a single, fully representative, example. Will not that
same history which sweeps these people into the rubbish
bin marvel, even while plying the crumb brush, that for
years on end it was possible to make not just a living,
but a stupendously rich living, by putting records on to
gramophones and taking them off again?

I think it will. But I think it will marvel even more at the
adulation received by those who made the noises on the
records. I am not going to go all tearful at the thought of
Mozart dying in want; the important thing about Mozart is
not that he died, but that he lived first. But even if I have got
his priorities the right way round, it is very certain that we do
not honour him today, and his contemporaries did not honour
him yesterday, for his prowess at billiards. Oh yes, the froth
will be blown away soon enough; I think I shall live to see it
happen, and to see people all around me rubbing their eyes in
astonishment that it floated so long in the air:

> Weak if we were and foolish, not thus we failed, not thus;
> When that black Baal blocked the heavens he had no
>   hymns from us.
> Children we were – our forts of sand were even as weak as
>   we,
> High as they went we piled them up to break that bitter
>   sea . . .
> But we were young; we lived to see God break their bitter
>   charms,
> God and the good Republic come riding back in arms:
> We have seen the city of Mansoul, even as it rocked,
>   relieved –
> Blessed are they who did not see, but being blind,
>   believed.

When that happens, the Stanley Gibbons stamp catalogue
will no doubt still list the stamps that bore the portrait of a pop

singer. And if they are sufficiently rare, I am equally sure that dealers and collecters will buy and sell them. But I do not think that any of them will recognize the portrait.

The Times July 14th, 1986

See the conquering hero comes

For reasons too uninteresting to explain, I very rarely go to the cinema. When I do go, therefore, I choose the film with more than ordinary care. Four-hour Japanese epics about people disembowelling themselves in high-pitched voices are out; any French film made later than 1945 is out; American films tending to show that America is, or for that matter is not, the Great Satan are out; all films recommended to me by the people who recommended *A Room With A View* (the most over-praised phenomenon since the South Sea Bubble) are out, out, out.

These days, that doesn't leave very much. But among what it does leave is the film I saw last week: *Crocodile Dundee*. It was recommended to me by a friend who knows my exacting cinematic tastes, though my faith wavered when I learned that it was about an Australian with a funny hat who strangles crocodiles with his bare hands; my friend pressed the case for it, however, in such passionate terms that I gave in, and a few days later there I was in what when I was a boy would have been the one-and-nines. (Why are cinemas so dirty now? They never used to be. And why is the advertising before the film so bad?)

Crocodile Dundee (he does wear a funny hat, but at least it doesn't have corks hanging from the brim) kills a crocodile or two in the course of the film, one of them in a very scary scene, but that is not what the film is about. What is *is* about is what happens next. For the plot – slender but adequate – concerns an American girl reporter who is sent to do a story about his crococidal exploits, and thinks that it would make a more

interesting ending to the feature if she can persuade him to
come back to New York with her, the idea being to portray his
reactions when he finds himself in a great city. These, she
reckons, will be interesting, since he has never before been in
any city, large or small; his response to New York is indeed
memorably funny, and obviously he and the reporter fall in
love. The final scene is simultaneously touching and hilarious;
the audience burst into a roar of applause and cheers when it
became clear that she was going to end up with the right man.

But I did not come here today to review the film, quite apart
from the fact that it has already been reviewed by the appropriate man on the appropriate page. The point about *Crocodile
Dundee* is that it is more than splendid entertainment, and it is
in that 'more' that the extra interest lies.

The film is a fairy-story. To begin at the end, fairy-stories
invariably finish 'they lived happily ever after', and this one is
no exception. But even the smallest pause for reflection will
demonstrate that the sophisticated urban girl and the rugged
bushman would *not* live happily ever after. For a start, where
are they going to do their happy living? In her New York,
where he would curl up and die of polluted air in a month? Or
his Walkabout Creek, which consists of a pub and a few
shacks, where she would keel over from culture-shock in a
fortnight? Fairy-stories rightly take no account of such practical matters; nor does *Crocodile Dundee*. But it is important to
bear in mind that the film is a genuine fairy-story, not just a
romance; it is not Mills and Boon but the Brothers Grimm.
And the hero is not just Clint Eastwood off his horse (though I
don't go to the cinema, I like to be well informed, you see); he
is something much more significant. He is a true hero of
legend, and not just a hero but a particular kind of hero.

Crocodile Dundee is the perfectly pure, wholly innocent
(innocent in both senses of the word) figure who is found in
the epic literature of all the nations which have such sagas. He
is Beowulf and King Arthur, Roland and Oliver, Candide and
Bertie Wooster, Prince Charming and Bilbo Baggins and
Robin Hood. He is even – indeed, above all – Wagner's

Parsifal, '*durch Mitleid wissend, der reine Tor*' (the pure fool, made wise by pity), and if you think that that is coming it a bit strong, let me show you him in some of the New York scenes.

He encounters a pair of prostitutes; he has literally no idea of what they are offering him, because he has literally never heard of prostitution, and when their ponce appears and upbraids them for not getting on with their work, Crocodile knocks him unconscious, not out of revulsion for such a trade, but because the man used bad language in front of ladies. In the funniest single sequence of the entire film, he is at a *demi-monde* party; he comes upon transvestism for the first time, and his amazement (he had likewise never so much as heard of it before) is wonderful to behold, but not so wonderful as his encounter with a cocaine-sniffer in the kitchen. 'Blocked nose, eh?' says Crocodile sympathetically, then turns the snort into the old Friar's Balsam treatment; the addict watches in glazed incomprehension as Crocodile shakes his entire store of the costly white power into a bowl, pours hot water over it, drapes a tea-towel over the coke-sniffer's head and tells him to get his face right down and breathe deeply.

Now in real life there is nobody who has never heard of prostitution, few indeed who have never heard of gentlemen in ladies' clothing and vice versa, fewer still who think that cocaine is an old word for Utopia. When Crocodile is held up by a young punk with a knife and told to hand over his wallet, the puzzlement with which he says 'Why should I do that?' is absolutely genuine; the man who has never heard of prostitution has never heard of theft. More; the truth is, *he has never heard of sin.*

Those who are without sin are rare; perhaps only a few saints could be thus described. But he who does not know what sin *is* obviously does not and cannot exist. And yet there he is on the screen, in a product made by an exceptionally sinful industry, and there he is, too, throughout history and literature, the avatar who comes to announce glad tidings of great joy, and who can walk through the sinful world untouched, as the fire-walkers can stroll over red-hot coals.

If you think that I am making heavy weather of what is, after all, only a film designed to entertain, I reply that many, indeed most, of the sagas to which I have referred were designed only to entertain:

The wild village folk in earth's earliest prime/ Could often sit still for an hour at a time/ And hear a blind beggar, nor did the tale pall/ Because Hector must fight before Hector could fall . . .

Here, though, is the most important element in the story. All over the world, wherever the film is being shown, it is the most enormous success. But I do not believe that that is due solely to the film's entertainment value. To my ears, the applause I heard around me at the end of it seemed to have an additional cause, rare in today's popular entertainment. For *Crocodile Dundee* offers a story that is not only wholly positive throughout, but is positive on a plane far above the level on which mere entertainment (though I see nothing mere about entertainment) operates.

It tells us that innocence exists, and not only exists but triumphs. Never mind our knowledge that it usually doesn't; for the hundred minutes of the film we *believe*, and the triumph of innocence, clad in the infinite power of belief, becomes the normative reality. Why do you suppose that the legendary figures whom Crocodile resembles have lived on so long in stories of such richness and meaning? Because they tell us that the world will be saved, that good is not only better than evil but stronger, that there is not enough darkness in all the universe to put out the light of one small candle. They give us something to aspire to, but they also give us a renewal of the oldest promise in the world: Blessed are the pure in heart, for they shall see God. Or, to put it another way, they shall live happily ever after.

The Times February 9th, 1987

The Archbishop's voice*

D O YOU SHARE a widespread feeling that there has been a considerable decline in the last 20 years or so in personal morality – by which I don't mean only sexual matters?

Yes; I think that in all sorts of areas like debt, truth-telling, respect for property and sexual indulgence, there has been a general decline. It is always difficult to judge whether this means, in great balloon statements, 'we are a less moral society', but there are plenty of examples, such as crimes against the person, which are not simply attributable to better detection or a more widespread police force.

What do you feel has caused this?

I think that there are many reasons. I think the lack of neighbourliness in our society, and the more impersonal character of high technology and so on, means that the ways in which we communicate are less person-to-person. We are distanced very often from the results of our actions or our communications. I think also that we are a less reflective society, and can be desensitized by the amount of experience which we are asked to absorb by the mass media.

There is a lack of responsibility; a decline in a sense of God; a decline in a sense of respect for other people – we are too ready to find reasons why people should behave in certain ways, or adopt certain attitudes. I think that the amount of analysis of

* Interview with the Archbishop of Canterbury, Dr Robert Runcie, in *The Times*, March 30th, 1987, reprinted with his kind permission.

why people are led to behave in certain ways, the amount of sociological knowledge, the behavioural sciences generally, have induced in many people a sense that 'I am not the master of my fate'.

That is the determinist argument?

That is the determinist argument. It is very insidious in the way in which it has seeped into our society. There is almost a *trahison des clercs*. I think that the behavioural sciences may have produced a wealth of explanation, but it's tended to reduce our morality to explanation, and when we look at moral questions, there is a temptation to solve them by research or by resources, rather than by moral energy.

We have moved very considerably from a pattern of absolute standards to a pattern of relative ones. Is that a good thing?

There is a danger that the preaching of absolute standards is insensitive and can lead to an attitude of 'people must be made to behave' according to the simple absolutes adopted by the majority, or by those who have authority. But that doesn't work, because it is based on fear, and on an idea that is incongruous with a free society, the idea that there are some who know and they 'inject' moral values into those who don't know. On the other hand, there is also a danger that in the move to relative standards anything goes, or you get a tendency to elevate compassion to the one absolute. So society divides between the 'stiff' or the tough and the 'woolly' or the soft – those who are all for law and order and making people behave, and those who are all for understanding people and forgiving. Stiffness can become self-righteousness, but woolly forgiveness often comes to mean forgetfulness.

I think myself, with Iris Murdoch, that a person's morality is not only their choices but their vision, and therefore for me morality has to do with taking responsibility for what I am as well as what I do. Penitence is an exercise in realism. It is facing the facts under the guidance of something from outside, whether it is the Truth, or as I would say, God, and allowing it or Him to draw out of me that response which I am led in all honesty to give.

How do we infuse that moral energy, or reinfuse it?

By giving us a sense that life is worthwhile, by recovering some sense of wonder, recovering some sense that we have a purpose in being here. The Victorians had moral energy because they thought that you were put on this earth in order to leave it a better place than you found it, and that did create a sort of moral energy. It wouldn't be enough for me, because I want to bring in another dimension, and however difficult it may be for me to explain this, I think that when people leave out God they become less than human, and when people eliminate eternity they can't find contentment on earth, and when they leave out the heavenly city, they don't seem to be able to build a tolerable society on earth.

There are other visions. These can become demonic. They can produce short-cut moralities where, since Utopia is long delayed, they take short cuts to it. All men then are brothers except those who need to be eliminated in the name of brotherhood.

The demonic ideologies and the horrors they have perpetrated clearly do so in the absence of God. They have no spiritual dimension and therefore in the end murdering millions of people is of no consequence.

So, too, seeking fulfilment solely in self-indulgence and hedonism is also destructive. The two alternatives that modern godless man poses for himself, between atheistic Marxism on one hand and a hedonistic self-indulgence on the other, highlight the need for us to find fulfilment in something outside ourselves. What gives me the vision I need for my choices and the moral energy I need to face up to my responsibilities is God.

As Solzhenitsyn puts it, all the trouble stems from the fact that man has forgotten God, but in that case how does man remember God?

If we are to have a free society, which is essential if love not power is going to rule the world, then we can't have some people – people who believe in God – in a position to order other people what they should believe and how they should behave. Of course it is difficult for the growing child to know what to do or to know how to behave; because there are many, many more options open nowadays. It is a matter of guiding and teaching, not commanding and ordering. It depends on getting the better things taught, truth, long-suffering, gentleness, tolerance and the fruits of the spirit.

Some people say that the multiplicity of options is precisely the problem; that when choice was simply limited in the sense that you knew where you stood and what was required of you, it was much simpler and it worked better.

The Church can't behave as in the days when it was alleged to be there to keep people in order. It can only guide, not compel. In a free society, the key concept is not obedience but responsibility. On this I agree with you, though I am cautious in making public pronouncements because of the risk of being distorted by the media, overheard by the self-righteous and used as a stick to beat the weaker. I say yes to freedom, I say yes to responsibility, I agree with your criticism of those who say we are all programmed by our genes; but on the other side, I must say no to any suggestion that we are all *equally* capable of realizing truth and goodness and moral values, and also I must say no to the idea that we couldn't enlarge the scope and remove some of the hindrances and obstacles that might enable people to do that.

It is a fact that most people don't feel the need for God in their lives. Why not?

Material satisfactions are thought to be enough; many believe that if everybody was educated and if pressures on people were removed then people would be sensible and rational and good. Greater scientific knowledge has led us to think big and doubt the significance of the particular. How could one particular man, born in Bethlehem, died in Jerusalem, have such a command over the way we behave? Yet I think that more and more at the present time, we are discovering that there is intellectual space for belief, and there's moral space and there's emotional space for belief, particularly if you begin with the particular, rather than the big system or the whole universe.

While all this has been happening, the Church has been in the battle, but it seems to have failed. Is that unfair?

It depends where you look at the Church when you say it has failed. Saints have been nurtured in parishes; it isn't the public debates of the Church about synods and about the ordination of women or even about social and political implications of the Gospel that really advance the Kingdom of God. Far more people than you might imagine, in comparison to the number in the pews, are motivated by Christian values as they support the nursing services or the welfare state or create Amnesty International or work for Oxfam.

But there are now situations where we have neither legislation, nor a moral code which is generally accepted, about a great number of things. Most notable, because it is the most talked about, is sexual morals. I think the Church has, amidst all the confusion, tended to latch on to the simple imperative of love and necessarily say something about the sort of society which we are trying to build; 'but this you ought to have done, but not to have neglected the other'.

We haven't thought of St Paul's great therefores – because of these things, because of these truths, therefore, walk worthy of the Lord's vocation, which means no immorality, no telling lies, no stealing and so on. Now some of the quick-fire moral apophthegms which you get in some of the Epistles are an example of how rules are short cuts. They save you thinking it all out from the beginning.

Well, there is one gigantic 'therefore' in your case, which is the therefore of the connection between sin and divine displeasure or punishment.

The Church has certainly moved away from preaching a gospel that makes people's morality depend upon fear. They have done that because the way in which it has been preached has obscured any idea of God's love. But I'm sure that a morality of natural law and a morality of grace, which is a matter not of the punishment fitting the crime, but of Christians doing what they do out of gratitude, may seem softer, but in fact, it's truer and firmer.

But where is the sanction? Obviously it isn't 'Don't do that or you will go to Hell' any longer.

The sanction lies not in 'Don't do this otherwise you will go to Hell', but rather in 'When I survey the wondrous cross'. That's what motivates me. Now I think that one quality which seems to be drained out of our present is wonder. Despite the fact that more people listen to music, perhaps more people have an appreciation of the arts, surprisingly when it comes to moral action, there isn't more respect, there isn't more reverence, there isn't more sense of wonder.

That sense of wonder is a sense of the numinous, isn't it?

Yes, it must be, and I can't eliminate that from a wholesome society. I've lived briefly in societies, particularly in eastern Europe, that have tried to eliminate that dimension, and it's like trying to eliminate aesthetic appreciation. It is not the same as aesthetic appreciation, but it is a human value whatever else you may say about its transcendent reference, and a human society is impoverished without it.

Solzhenitsyn has also been saying incessantly that in the societies where religion is not merely frowned upon but stamped out, there is a resurgence of faith, and in the

societies where anyone can pray to any god they wish, there is failure. Do we need persecution?

I remember Desmond Tutu saying to me quite genuinely, 'You know,' he said, 'I would find it very difficult to be a Christian in England because everybody is so generally nice.' Well, that may not be quite true, but all the issues are blurred and I think it's that blurring that tends to anaesthetize us from the religious element. We are taught not to seek persecution; but it is, though more comfortable, in a sense much more difficult to be a Christian and a Christian believer in modern England.

Should it be difficult?

It should be a delight, but it should be a mixture of duty and delight.

Can we do without the form of authority which is rejected in talking about personal morals in a matter like this? Nobody now talks in terms of blame.

Blaming and condemning can so easily produce the fruits of self-righteousness that don't make for the most constructive sort of penitence and reparation and renewal. People know well enough that it is their own fault, and it isn't usually constructive to counsel and support people by a method of 'I told you so'.

No. But of course a lot of people are taught that indeed it isn't their own fault. That it is the fault of society or living conditions.

There is a crucial difference between general ethical teaching and pastoral care. If I am asked about promiscuity, my answer as a teacher of Christian ethics must be immediate and unqualified.

Well, you remember obviously James Anderton getting into hot water – I'm talking about the original statement, about swilling around in a cesspit of their own

making – was he basically right, however unhelpful he may have been?

Well, by being so unhelpful I can't think he was doing right. I don't want to criticize, but that seemed to me to be an example of the failure to steer a course between the stiff and the woolly. New moral problems have come up. But the way in which Aquinas or the Caroline divines of the seventeenth century worked out the detailed problems of how to respond to questions of civil disobedience and so on was of an order and depth and sensitivity that makes our Christian talk about nuclear weapons or the threat of Aids very thin stuff.

There is a distinction in homosexuality between the nature and the action, or do you not make a distinction?

I make the distinction between the condition of being a homosexual by inclination and homosexual acts themselves. The action itself is sinful when it's against a Christian moral teaching based on the Bible; on the other hand, there are degrees of behaviour and also there is a pastoral way in which you treat people who, for example, are not promiscuous in their homosexual action; you treat them in a different way from people who are. I have seen homosexual couples in a stable relationship and actually providing in terms of simple human generosity, hospitality, artistic achievement and flair, what I can't gainsay as human good; on the other hand, they seem to do that out of what to me is a moral handicap, but then we learn to cherish the good things that come out of the handicapped.

Do you mind if I ask you – what would you do if you had only one hand? Do you not have to say that their sexual conduct, none the less, was sinful, or don't you? Or does the example, as it were, transcend that?

The example of an exception to the general rule cannot overturn what is the norm of moral behaviour. We have to teach the norms of moral behaviour and deal with exceptions as they come, recognizing any good they contain, without commending them as an example to be followed by others. We do not hold erotic homosexual genital processes to be a responsible way of living for a Christian. Although people cannot help the way they are made, they can act so as to strengthen their ability to cope and lessen the likelihood of destructive consequences. Of course it is easy for us to say that, as we should remember how difficult it is for some of those concerned. But we should say it none the less, without seeking to throw stones at those who fail.

There is an argument that the Church has given way far too readily over abortion. Some would say no Christian church ought to be condoning it at all.

Let me state a general principle. I think that abortion for Christians is not on. But it *is* a difficult issue. There are two contrasting thoughts in my mind, and this is simply how I struggle with the problem. I do believe that as knowledge increases, so moral horizons are enlarged, and new opportunities make new moral claims upon us. This is why a Christian might have become less firm on a simple statement that abortion is killing and abortion in any form is sinful. I myself used to hold the more liberal view, but now I think we ought to be extending the area of the sacred rather than restricting it. It's a whole way of treating sacred material; it's a whole way in which I feel I want to adjust the way in which we treat the environment, and all the biological and zoological threads which join us to the animal creation and so on make me feel a sense of reverence for the non-human as well as the human, and make me think that all this way of dealing with genetic material as if it were disposable waste makes for a sick society. So that I am just opening to you a movement of my own moral attitude, and I've changed. I used to be rather glib about this idea that with greater knowledge, moral horizons are enlarged. But I have become uncomfortable with those arguments, because I think that a great deal of our shallow morals springs from this lack of a sense of wonder, a sense of mythic transformation of attitude that comes from believing in God's creation.

You have clearly moved, as you described it, but why? What was it that sowed the doubts?

I think that I am less of a rationalist than I was. I am less of a pragmatic rationalist, and that's because it's important that moral attitudes should fit not into the logic of thinking which will be the same for a humanist or a believer, but somehow that will fit adequately into my vision of God's love for us. Salvation comes from outside, and I believe that we can be responsible. We can be responsible and we can respond; and that enables me to escape from this dilemma, this moral dilemma, of being either 'stiff' or 'woolly'.

When Cardinal Hume was asked some time ago what distressed him most about the modern world, there was an enormously long pause, and he said, 'The loss of truth.' That makes me sad; and when we've been talking about sex and debt and violence and drugs and so on, I think that the loss of truth has had an insidious effect; the need to entertain or to excite or to encourage at all costs has had a serious effect on attitudes, that people seem to me to get away with concocted simplicities, to such a degree that it seeps into the atmosphere, that it is more important to entertain or to comfort people than to tell them the truth. I think that's a moral area that needs to be explored.

One final question. You made the distinction between the stiff and the woolly; they are both pejorative terms, and I see exactly why you argued a criticism of both of them. But if you had to fall into one or other of the camps, which would it be?

Stiff with myself, woolly with others. Jesus never encouraged us to be soft with ourselves, and when I look at myself it's a tough judgement I must make. But when I think of the other sheep that have gone astray, it's the parable of the Good Shepherd that guides my thoughts.

Who goes there?

T HE HOUSE OF LORDS will today be debating the Criminal
Justice Bill. One of its most important and controversial
proposals is the abolition of the right of a defendant in a
criminal trial to object, without showing cause, to a prospective member of the jury, an action which has the effect of
obliging the juror to stand down. At present, a defendant has
the right to three such challenges; there was talk, at the time
abolition was mooted, of a compromise, which would have
left a defendant the right to deploy *one* challenge, but the
Home Office, ever assiduous in the noble cause of suppressing
justice wherever it raises its head, insisted not only that
injustice must be done, but that it should manifestly be seen to
be done, and the last chance for a defendant to object to a juror
without saying why was removed.

Or rather: it will be removed if the Lords do not insist that
it should be retained. I hope they will, and shall now say
why.

First, it may not be generally known that this right is one of
the oldest principles of our law and constitution; it may be
as old, or almost as old, as the jury system itself, and *that*
began in 1215. What is more, the number of challenges
without cause that were permitted to a defendant on a serious
charge was enormous; in 1533 the number was reduced
from 35 to 20 (except for treason, where 35 remained the
figure).

But history reckoned without the Home Office. In 1948, the
number of challenges permitted was reduced to seven, and in
1977 to three; that is where it stands now, but it will continue

to do so only if the Lords can summon up a majority for justice.

They will find that they have a remarkable body of support for resistance if they decide to make a stand. In Committee, the House of Commons passed the measure by only one vote, so great was the disquiet among Tories as well as Labour and Alliance members; but the whips were out in force at Report stage, and it was carried easily. Now the Lords, as they should be and so often have been, are the last guardians of a vital principle of justice.

Before I discuss that principle, there is some astonishing evidence to be considered. The argument of those who want to see the peremptory challenge abolished consists entirely of the belief that by allowing defendants to retain this venerable right the courts would also be allowing defendants to collect a jury of thick-eared villains. Since no questioning of a prospective juryman is permitted, and since, as Shakespeare so handily put it, there's no art to finding the mind's construction in the face, there is not the remotest possibility of a defendant, except by a lucky hit or two, doing any such thing. (Moreover, with the number of permitted challenges now reduced to three, the chance is still further diminished.)

The idea of abolishing the right entirely came from the Roskill Committee, which was considering trials for fraud. It provided no evidence above the level of the anecdotal, and the members of the committee, or some of them, were plainly so disturbed by the lack of any good reason for destroying this ancient and vital right that they decided to find out more about the use and effect of the peremptory challenge. The Crown Prosecution Service undertook to discover the facts, always a useful thing to do before coming to a conclusion. Here are some of the facts that were discovered.

First, the incidence of challengers. The average, for the most recent period for which figures were known, was 22 per cent – that is, in 22 per cent of all criminal trials there was at least one challenge. In cases involving more than one defendant the figure was 32 per cent. In all

trials, the rate of challenge was highest in inner London at
35 per cent.

The *tricoteuses* of the Home Office must have leaned forward
eagerly at that point; if up to a third of trials include challenges
to jurors, it can mean only that defendants are using their right
to get away with murder – in some cases, literally. But it was
the *tricoteuses* on whose necks the blade descended, because the
Crown Prosecution Service study revealed that *there was a
higher rate of conviction in trials in which challenges were made than
in those with defendants who made no challenge*. (The figures were:
convictions with challenged juries, 60 per cent; convictions
with unchallenged juries, 53 per cent.)

Only those who are capable of being surprised by the Home
Office were surprised when, in the face of that evidence,
abolition remained in the bill. As I say, it has now passed the
Commons, and the Lords debate it today; will they behave as
illogically and unjustly as the Commons did?

The wretched reply to critics of abolition is that the right to
challenge for cause remains untouched. I can think, without
effort, of a dozen reasons for a defendant to be unwilling to
challenge for cause a juryman whom he has good reason to
want excluded. Perhaps he recognizes a prospective juror as a
man with whom he was involved in some earlier criminal
proceedings; to state the cause would reveal that he has been
prosecuted, and perhaps convicted, before – a revelation
which our law rightly takes very great pains to prevent. Or
perhaps he has quarrelled with a juror over some shameful
though not criminal business; objecting, he claims that the
juryman may be biased, and on being asked why he thinks
so, is compelled to reveal sordid circumstances that may
increase prejudice. Or perhaps he owes a prospective juror
money which he is unable or reluctant to repay – again, the
kind of thing that any defendant would wish to keep
secret – and has the right to keep secret – while he is being
tried.

Or perhaps he feels that the principle of a defendant being
tried by a jury of his peers is rather an important one, and feels

also that if he is shabby, black, drink-stained, homosexual, inarticulate, afraid or half-witted, his peers may not be represented with a degree of exactitude sufficient to fall within the principle if the jury consists of three red-faced squires, three retired senior officers of the Rhodesia Scouts, a man with a cat-o'-nine-tails sticking casually out of his breast pocket, two replicas of Scrooge and a trio of Gorgons. I do not say that such people will be likely to do anything less than justice; but then, that is easy for me to say, for I am not shabby, black, drink-stained, homosexual, inarticulate, afraid or even half-witted. Others may not feel so certain, and they are as deserving of a fair trial as I am. And the ancient right was designed, and preserved through so many centuries, to make as sure as may be (which is even now not very sure) that anyone in the dock in this country will be tried by people who are unlikely to regard him with as much incomprehension as they would a Martian.

It is not without significance that those who recommended the abolition of the peremptory challenge also recommended the abolition of the jury altogether in fraud cases. That prize, at any rate, was denied to those who would whittle away still more of our liberties, our constitution and our laws, in the interests of what amounts to nothing more substantial than tidiness.

I like tidiness. But I like justice better. The peremptory challenge in our courts has been, for hundreds of years, one of the strongest and most handsome of the pillars which uphold our system of justice. Though it has been reduced to a splinter of its ancient bulk it has remained, however attenuated, essentially what it was.

And what was it? What is it? It was and is a beacon which shows that right will be done to the lowliest in the land as well as the proudest, and that while right is being done, those who look upon the process shall plainly see justice being dealt out with an even hand, for all the imperfections that must inevitably accompany any human endeavour.

Parliament has now been asked to topple that pillar, and

extinguish that beacon. The Commons have indicated that they are willing to do so. The Lords can still refuse.*

The Times April 27th, 1987

---

* But they didn't.

Darkness visible

Hermann Broch by Paul Michael Lützeler*
The Spell by Hermann Broch†

O F THE THREE great Germanophone novelists of the
1930s, the work of Thomas Mann continues to enjoy its
rich and rightful due, and that of Hermann Hesse, though the
enormous vogue it had in the 1960s (when he became a totem
for the *jeunesse enragée* of two continents) has much diminished, is still a living force. Hermann Broch, however,
remains a dim and distant figure, passionately championed by
a handful, read by fewer than a thousandth of those who
would think *Ulysses* and *À la Recherche* an essential part of any
civilized European's cultural baggage, and for the rest only a
name, if that.

It is hard to believe that the absence of an adequate biography (in German, never mind English) has been the cause of this
neglect and harder still to accept as the reason the difficulty
(great though it is) of translating him, for his masterpiece, *The
Death of Virgil*, has been available for 40 years in an almost
magically successful English version by Jean Starr Unter-
meyer, and with the exception of *The Spell* his other fiction
too has long existed in translation.

And yet I remain convinced that Broch, in his strange but
compelling philosophical novels, is the peer of his two great
coevals, and the appearance of *The Spell* in English for the first
time confirms me in my belief.

* Quartet, 1987.
† Deutsch, 1987.

It comes with the long-awaited biography, to be published on June 15; Broch was yet another of those Wandering Jews (some of them, like Mann, were Wandering Gentiles) who managed to get out of Europe when the plague came, and he settled in the United States. A tyrannical father, an unresponsive mother and a disastrously incompatible early marriage left their scars on his character, but remarkably few on his work; very little of what Mr Lützeler tells us can be deduced from his novels (least of all that he was an expert textile-engineer, a trade learned in the family business). He was fascinated all his life by mathematics, and published a great deal of philosophical, psychological and scientific work; he played a part in the long wartime debate over the future of democracy in the post-war world, and formulated an outline for a charter of human rights.

He also embarked on, though never finished, a massive study of crowd hysteria, and it was from his thinking and work on the subject that the idea of *The Spell* grew.

No wonder; for the story is of just such a derangement, leading to a highly symbolic ritual death, and a much more mundane injustice. Broch sets his scene in a remote mountain village, closely and lovingly described but carefully unlocated; we do not even know what country it is in. The even pattern of life and work, unchanged in essence for centuries, is disturbed when a stranger arrives, to challenge immediately the village's way. Such is his messianic urge, he rapidly gains sway over a faction of the people, seduced by his demands that the village should revert to a primitive form of living, in which machines, from radios to threshers, are banned, and chastity enforced.

Soon, the fanatic is talking about the mysterious holiness of the earth, and then he begins to rave about blood. Those who talk much about blood, history has shown, will sooner or later shed it, and Marius Ratti, with his repulsive acolyte, Wenzel (the name is taken from a card of ill omen in a game, and is also a dialect cognomen for a penis), eventually does just that. But the sacrificial victim is a true scapegoat, for Ratti insists that the death must be of an innocent, and the pure maiden who is selected embraces her ritual slaughter willingly.

It is right for the reader, at that point, to jump to conclusions, provided he does not jump too far. No writer of Broch's stature makes one-to-one equations; Ratti, obviously, is the fanatic who stole Germany, but he is very much more. He is myth itself, which must be worked out in darkness, though in darkness there is always danger; he is the yeast in the inert dough of the village lapped in its ancient traditions; he is the fire of Max Frisch's *The Fire-raisers* and the old lady of Dürrenmatt's *The Visit*. He is, in short, evil itself, but he comes with a terrible truth in his pocket; that a human universe without evil would be meaningless.

There are some who resist; of course there are. Sack, the innkeeper; the village doctor, who is the narrator, but who himself succumbs to the spell; above all, Mother Gisson, earth-mother, wise woman, witch and saint. In Wagnerian terms, she is Erda, who knows what is to be, but understands that fate must be worked out in full, and her death is as much a symbol as is that of the victim, whose spirit is present as Mother Gisson dies.

There are other symbols; the mountain, where the long-sealed gold-workings are to be opened up, is thus metaphorically violated, and it takes a grim revenge, while Ratti raves:

> He who lacks love for the earth is not man, he rapes the earth with each step he treads on it, such a man must be banished, for he rapes whatever he touches . . . all evil comes from those men who have become alienated from the earth, it comes from the city . . .

But the purged earth survives. One of Broch's most crucial themes is the slow revolution of the seasons; though we do not know where we are, we know at any moment what time of year it is. And it is the seasons, which not even Ratti, with his band of brutal yobs led by Wenzel, can touch, which triumph in the end. The seasons care nothing for justice, murder, persecution or love, and Ratti is still on the town council when the book ends. But there have been no more sacrifices, no more witch-hunts, and the pregnant girl who will carry on life dominates the final pages in partnership with the dying Mother Gisson, who is also mother nature.

For all its symbolism, its wealth of unspoken religious reference, its mystic, ambiguous distribution of roles, *The Spell* makes swift, compelling reading. The outer pace goes at nature's speed, the inner at frantic man's; it is when they can no longer synchronize that the catastrophe occurs. Nature knows best; but there will always be men who strive to pervert her knowledge to their own use, with frightful consequences to themselves and, far more often, to others.

Sunday Times May 31st, 1987

The dead lie less easily

W E MAY AS well begin with the old joke (attrib. Frederick the Great, Metternich, Bismarck, Lord Dacre *und so weiter*): 'In Prussia, the situation is serious, but not hopeless; in Austria, the situation is hopeless, but not serious.' For seventy years, ever since the end of the First World War and the consequent dismemberment of the Austro-Hungarian Empire (not a moment too soon), it has been impossible, and most of the time unnecessary, to take Austria seriously; the world has constantly looked at her with a smile on its face. Sometimes it has been a happy smile, sometimes an indulgent one, sometimes a pitying, sometimes a contemptuous; but always the visitors' frowns vanished from the moment they crossed her frontiers.

Well, it took Kurt Waldheim to wipe the smile off our faces; for a country renowned for her Baroque architecture, Austria has been landed by him with an ample ration of Gothic horror. But the chill in the blood comes not only from what he did in the war and the wakening of the dead that this episode has achieved; it springs also from the fact that, in the very teeth of credulity and indeed imagination, *he is still in office*.

Not only does he refuse to go; not only, which is worse, has the Austrian government declined to tell him to do so; the last public opinion poll on the subject, taken before publication of the report by the commission of historians, recorded some 70 per cent of Austrians holding the view that he should remain as president, and I dare say that, now the report has appeared, the favourable percentage has probably gone up to 80. ★

★ To my surprise, it fell.

Given facts like that, I think we are obliged to take Austria seriously. To set the context, try this test; think of another country, genuinely free in every sense, from elections to the press, in which the head of state has engaged in behaviour which would render it impossible for any self-respecting person to sit down at his table, and yet insists on remaining in office.

I can think of only two comparable instances in modern times (and they only remotely comparable). One was the forcing out of office of President Nixon, who had done nothing to match Waldheim's behaviour in the war, but had violated the American law and Constitution; the other was the sacking, from all his public offices, of Prince Bernhard of the Netherlands (who wasn't even a head of state, but only the consort of one), when he was found to have been taking bribes. In the United States and the Netherlands the swell across both countries drowned the defenders, and the guilty men had to retire, however reluctantly.

But I cannot think of any such figure who has *refused* to bow to the decencies, and the suspicion now grows that Waldheim will not bow to the decencies because he doesn't know what decencies are. And it seems that his country, or the great majority of its citizens, are behind him in this. Does any of that make you want to smile?

Before the commission's findings appeared, I was prepared to make one plea for him, a plea which seemed to me to be justified, and which was being denied him in advance. I have always maintained that only a man who is a hero is entitled to demand that other men should be heroic. Those who condemn Germans, and others, who did nothing to stop terrible evil, must ask themselves whether *they* would have been brave enough to resist, knowing that the penalty for doing so might be a hideous death. Only if they are certain that the answer is yes can they reproach those who feared to raise a hand. I could not be a hero at that price, and I, too, would have feared to raise a hand. You will therefore search my writings in vain for any condemnation of those who did not do evil themselves but did not throw themselves between the evil and the innocent.

Very well; but *Waldheim*? Hear the commission:

> The commission established a number of instances in which officers took on the responsibility of circumventing or even defying illegal orders, without any serious consequences to themselves . . . The latest research demonstrates that no case is known in which a soldier who refused to participate in the murder of civilians was court-martialled and punished . . . The commission has discovered no instance in which Dr Waldheim raised an objection to or protested against an order which he undoubtedly knew to be illegal, nor one in which he took any countermeasures in order to prevent an illegal act or at least render it more difficult to carry out . . .

But let us leave aside what may be called moral complicity; let us just take the question of Waldheim's veracity. Even before the commission got down to work he had been caught out in two shameful lies: he had claimed that he never joined any Nazi organization, whereas he had joined not one but two, and he claimed that after being wounded he was invalided out of the army and returned to his legal studies, whereas he had returned to service.

Now come with me through some of the commission's findings. He claimed that he did not know that his despatch of the transcripts of commandos' interrogations would lead to their death under Hitler's *Kommandobefehl*; the commission demonstrates that he did know, and proves him a liar. He claimed that he knew nothing of the deportations of Jews from Greece; the commission shows that he did, and proves him to be a liar.

He claimed to have been away from his unit when these deportations were going on; he wasn't . . . liar. He claimed that army units were not employed in the deportations . . . liar. He claimed that he knew nothing about the reprisal massacres in Greece . . . liar. He claimed to know nothing about the atrocities in Bosnia when he was there . . . liar.

(Indeed, he first denied that he was there at all . . . liar.) He claimed to know nothing about the fate of Russian partisans on the Eastern front . . . liar. He claimed that he knew nothing of the transportation of Italian internees to Germany . . . liar. He claimed that he knew nothing of the Final Solution . . . liar, liar, liar.

And he won't go! Let us look ahead a few weeks, to the commemoration of the *Anschluss* of 1938. What are the politicians going to say in their speeches, after they have once again pretended that Austria was a victim, not an accomplice? Are they going to speak of those Austrian soldiers who only did their duty? If so, will the television cameras at that point cut to Waldheim nodding his agreement? Will Waldheim, in his own speech, after forthrightly condemning those Austrian criminals, from Kaltenbrunner to Globocnik, who did monstrous evil, again proclaim his ignorance of the evil? If so, would somebody kindly throw a corpse at him?

Austria has had too many excuses made for her. She is now, at last, getting a more objective examination, one which is beginning to show the extent of her willing and enthusiastic co-operation with Nazism. New generations have grown up since then, and no one can blame them for what their fathers and grandfathers did; at any rate, I can't. But the new generations have helped to elect a vile and mendacious man to the highest office of state, and they seem to be helping also to keep him in that office, however much he defiles it.

If Austria wants those smiles back, to say nothing of the tourists' money, there is only one road open to her. *Der Schurke muss weg.*

The Times February 15th, 1988

That dare not speak its name

THERE ARE TWO reasons why I have never taken any notice
of the regular and frequent complaints by the theatre that
it is dying out for lack of funds, that hundreds of playwrights
and thousands of actors are hanging themselves in their un-
heated garrets, that the National Theatre is to be pulled down
and the site ploughed for sugar beet, that wolves have been
shot in Shaftesbury Avenue, and that *The Mousetrap* is a
terrible flop and its producers are about to go bankrupt.

The first reason for my policy of treating all such claims
with what the late George Brown called total ignoral is that
they never come true. For the past 17 years, for instance, Mr
Nicholas de Jongh has been saying three times a day after
meals that the Royal Shakespeare Company is going to close
down permanently next Wednesday, and the RSC has recently
opened its *sixth* playhouse.

My second reason is based on experience. I have been going
to the theatre for more than 40 years, and I have seen the yo-yo
climb and descend more times that I can now count. I do not
know why the theatre has its fertile and its fallow periods, but I
have lived through too many of the fallow ones to feel anxiety
lest no new fertile one should appear; I know that it always
does.

At the moment the London theatre is in a very fruitful phase;
why, it has even opened – strictly speaking, reopened – a
long derelict playhouse called, appropriately enough, the
Playhouse. Moreover, a new Stoppard is in rehearsal, Michael
Hordern is shortly to appear in *You Never Can Tell*, good
judges tell me that Richard Briers' Malvolio at the Riverside

Studios is not to be missed, Simon Callow, who must be – nay, manifestly is – mad as a hatter (long live lunacy), is about to do the whole of Goethe's *Faust*, and in little more than a week, I have seen three plays each of which is a giant credit to London.

First was the RSC's production (by Terry Hands) of *The Winter's Tale*. This mysterious and magical play, too rarely performed, is here played without a false note, and the great parable of redemption strikes home with memorable force. At three of the productions of *The Winter's Tale* I have seen over the years, I have had the good fortune to take a companion who had never seen or read the play, and each time I have shared the astonishment, wonder and joy sweeping over my innocent partner at the great *coup de théâtre* that ends the play; this new RSC version was the third of such experiences for me, and it worked better than ever.

The second splendid evening was spent at the new Peter Shaffer play, *Lettice and Lovage*. It is a deceptively fragile work; the director, Michael Blakemore, must have had fearsome problems to solve, not least of them the fact that each of the three acts seems at first to be entirely self-contained, until Shaffer's masterly stagecraft binds them together and illuminates all three at once. It is a beautiful, amusing, vigorous, touching play, and it contains a performance, by that glorious creature Maggie Smith (she is practically never off the stage), which is not so much for the record books as for history, and lavishly illustrated history, at that.

But it is the third of my recent theatrical experiences that I want now to discuss in detail, partly because of the play itself, but partly also because of the circumstances implicit in its quality and made explicit by its reception.

Ronald Harwood is one of our most interesting playwrights. Lacking the inborn genius of Stoppard or the dazzling imagination of Shaffer, he has cut his way to success (I don't just mean commercial success) like a mountaineer cutting steps with an ice-axe; Harwood (Michael Frayn is another such) has done the strenuous work of learning and refining his art by simply doing it in public, risking failure but always understanding more, testing himself with harder problems, knowing that there is no point on the mountain where he can sit and rest, knowing (which is even more important) that art is a mountain unique in that it has no summit, and the artist-climber must go on for ever.

His new play, *J. J. Farr*, is his most complex, arousing and advanced yet. It is set in a curiously suspended world, a kind of rest-home where Catholic priests who have lost their faith, or are seeking it, may talk, reflect, explore, suffer, be healed – all without commitment or obligation. The warden calls it a 'subsidized limbo', but a far more thoroughly mixed theological metaphor is required; the play is about the Harrowing of Hell, and the forces that make the assault on the last enemy, death, are accompanied by the Hound of Heaven:

> Whom wilt thou find to love ignoble thee,
> Save Me, save only Me?
> All which I took from thee I did but take,
> Not for thy harms,
> But just that thou might'st seek it in my arms.
> All which thy child's mistake
> Fancies as lost, I have stored for thee at home:
> Rise, clasp My hand, and come!

I am well aware, alas, that some of my readers, having read this far, are shifting uneasily in their chairs, unwilling, if they are not alone, to meet the eyes of others. I am aware of it, moreover, for an odd reason; when I saw *J. J. Farr*, the Phoenix Theatre was far from full. And why should that be a clue to the unease I sense? Because the reception of the play has emphasized what anyone who ever treats of matters of the spirit will know: that for many, in our enervated day, God is a four-letter word.

Ronald Harwood's play is not a sermon, nor a tract; much of it is very funny, and all of it is theatrical in the best sense. It also displays a remarkable prescience; the eponymous hero is a former priest who has been kidnapped by Middle Eastern terrorists and kept hostage for months, being beaten and tortured in his captivity. Yet Harwood had finished writing the play *before* Mr Terry Waite was taken prisoner. Moreover, the sinewy prose and hand-carved dialogue makes it a pleasure for the ear as well as for the mind; and there is an interesting and unusual performance by Albert Finney, at his subtlest and most original best.

Surely that is enough to have London scuttling to Charing Cross Road? Not quite, it seems, whence my search today for the 50 righteous men who will save Sodom. (I think that metaphor is probably *too* mixed.)

The hinge of the play is the gradual extraction from J. J. Farr of the story of what happened to his lost faith while he was in captivity, and the effect of the revelation on the others in the refuge, particularly the one who, not content with losing his faith, has taken to denouncing it in the most violent terms. (It is not difficult to see the appropriate psychological point here, even before the militant atheist demonstrates, in the most shocking and gory manner, that all is not well with his rejection of belief.)

The play has been called a debate, and to some extent it is, though it is much more besides; above all else it is a searching study of searching human beings. I do not know what Ronald Harwood's own deepest beliefs are, and in a sense they don't matter, though few playgoers will leave at curtainfall without wondering; whatever they are, he has given us a play with characters whose deepest beliefs matter terribly to them, from the one who has found the nirvana of indifference (beautifully played as an old queen by Hugh Paddick) to the one whose memories of sin are driving him towards a terrible vision of damnation (a rich, ripe part, seized and devoured by Trevor Peacock).

And yet there were those empty seats, preceded by the well-bred titters and dismissals that much of the comment on the play comprised. And the chief note struck by the titters and dismissals was, as usual, nervousness.

Why? Why, that is, the nervousness? What is it about the most important thing in the world that terrifies so many people today, and particularly those who occupy what I have called the tin thrones of comment? Why were some people indignant, of all things, at Shaffer's *Amadeus*, just because he asked the greatest question – if Mozart was a conduit for his music to come to earth, who was putting it in at the other end? It doesn't matter how you answer that question: but you must try to answer the other one – why did so many, faced with it, squeal in pain and rage?

It would not be quite true to say that Harwood answers either question in his play; but he could not have been unaware of the second one even before his play opened, and it would be interesting to hear his views on it now. (But I doubt if he will be invited on to *Kaleidoscope* to give them.) It is a truism that, at horror films, people laugh, as a way of dispelling fear. And perhaps today, those who laugh or smile so disdainfully at the sight of a gifted playwright handling such questions are demonstrating that they are not quite as sure of their position as they would like to be thought. Perhaps, even, they are tormented by the feeling that they are actually wrong, and must titter the louder to quieten the voice that tells them so.

If London lets *J. J. Farr* go, London ought to be ashamed of itself. Much more to the point, it will have missed an uncommonly fine and arresting evening at the theatre, where human beings wrestle aloud with their souls, learning as they do so that the referee never tires of picking up the fallen.

If you have just tittered at that last metaphor, go to the play anyway. You might stop tittering altogether.

The Times December 17th, 1987

Intimations of immortality

L AST WEEK, AN orchestral conductor, Mr Alan Hazeldine, suggested in a speech to a scientific conference that the strains, mental and physical, on the members of his profession were hardly to be endured by mortal man, and frequently led to the most appalling disorders, ranging from curvature of the spine to agonies of self-doubt.

I do not think I have attended any concerts or operas given by Mr Hazeldine, so I have no opinion of his conducting; let me assume that he can wag a stick with the best. What caused my eyeballs to revolve rapidly in opposite directions for several minutes was his complaint about the inevitability of bodily and psychological harm among conductors. I don't want to seem unkind to a stranger, but I have to say that Mr Hazeldine's complaint is well placed to carry off the coveted Levin Lemon for the most amazingly ridiculous statement of 1987.

For the truth is that, to judge by the tables of mortality, conducting must be one of the healthiest professions in the world. The average longevity of the leading conductors is so astoundingly beyond any ordinary expectation that it cannot possibly be a coincidence. So far from reality is Mr Hazeldine's picture of conductors wilting to death under the strain that it would hardly be an exaggeration to say that they are practically immortal. Indeed, if you want to despatch a conductor in his prime you have to drown him, like poor Kertesz at 44, or crash his plane, like Cantelli at 36, or persuade him to drink himself to death, like Konwitschny. (Who, even on the sauce, made 61. For that matter, Barbirolli was said to moisten his lips from time to time; and he notched up 71.)

A few have dropped the baton in their fifties and sixties; Fritz Busch at 61, Rudolf Kempe and Erich Kleiber at 66 (though the latter left an heir, Carlos, so greatly gifted in the same trade that for once I am convinced that heredity does run in the family), van Beinum at 58, Furtwängler at 68, Hermann Levi at 61. (I dare say Levi's troubles were accentuated by the fact that he was Wagner's principal conductor, and was for ever being reproached by his appalling patron – and even more by Cosima – for being a Jew. He was in the habit of apologizing half a dozen times a day for this lapse in taste, pleading that it wasn't his fault but that of his parents, but it did him no good.)

For the rest, let the figures speak.

Toscanini clocked up 90, as did Tullio Serafin, who looked more like Peter Rabbit than could have been thought possible. Vittorio Gui, the unflappable maestro at Glyndebourne for so many years, notched 90 as well. Leopold Stokowski booked the Albert Hall for his 100th birthday, and fell short of the date by only five years; it is true that he was a fairly lousy conductor, but never mind the quality, feel the length.

Adrian Boult threw in the towel at 93; I recall that the consort of Sir Henry Wood ('Timber' to his musicians), who hit 75, once insisted to me, in a box at the Proms, that Boult was the devil come back to earth, though a more unlikely candidate for Satanity than that gentle gentleman could not be imagined, and what Boult had done to upset her so much she did not reveal.

George Szell, who conducted the Cleveland Orchestra for an immense length of time, making it as he did so into one of the world's finest, scored 73; poor Rudolf Bing, in his memoirs, offered a rather crisp epitaph on him: 'He was a nasty man, God rest his soul.' (Some say Bing wasn't exactly the sweetest figure since St Francis of Assisi.)

But America is clearly bracing, at any rate for conductors.

Walter Damrosch lived to 88, despite his curious habit, which one might have thought calculated to bring on the lightning, of improving masterpieces. 'Now,' he would say, 'we shall make some changements.' Another of the immigrant Americans was Eugene Ormandy, who kept up the wonderful sound of the Philadelphia. Their party trick was the *premier coup d'archet*, the entry with a chord so stunningly unanimous that if you shut your eyes you could not believe that there was more than one player on the platform; whenever the Philadelphia came to London, Ormandy would start the programme with a piece that showed off his players in this particular form of excellence. He reached 86.

As you must have guessed, I am reliving my youth; most of these giants (well, not Levi) were part of the great river of genius on which I was swept into my lifelong love of music. Of the ones I heard most often, perhaps the very greatest (and, by all accounts, most lovable) was Bruno Walter (86); 'Sing, my friends, sing!' he would cry to his ranks of violins. I was present at the concert at the Edinburgh Festival, in its earliest days, when he conducted the Vienna Philharmonic for the first time since he had been driven from its podium by the Nazis. He was a long time turning round to acknowledge the applause, and when he did so the reason was plain to see; the tears were coursing down his face.

Koussevitsky (77) conducted what remains for me the finest performance of the Ninth Symphony I have ever heard. But will somebody kindly confirm (where the devil is Henry Pleasants now that I really need him?) the story that he once, for a bet, played the Mendelssohn Violin Concerto on (it was his original instrument) a double-bass?★

Charles Munch, the only man who has ever managed to persuade the world that a French orchestra could be taken seriously, died at 77; Richter, who conducted the first Bayreuth *Ring*, at 73; Mengelberg, the enduring conductor of

★ The omniscient and hundred-eyed Henry wrote immediately, correcting my errors.

the Amsterdam Concertgebouw (he was barred from it after the war as a collaborator with the Nazis), managed 80; Victor de Sabata, who used to leap two feet off the podium in the frenzy of the last movement of the Beethoven Seventh, finished at 75; Ansermet, another of those one-orchestra men (his, of course, was the Suisse Romande), went on to 86; Beecham (ah, you who never heard Beecham, be silent for us who did, and count their manhoods cheap whiles any speak Who fought with us upon St Crispin's Day) gave in at 82; Knappertsbusch, one of the very few conductors who really hated applause (there are many who pretend to), lived to 77, and Klemperer (also one of the few) to 88.

Pierre Monteux (89) deserves a paragraph to himself. When he was 80, the LSO appointed him their chief conductor, with a contract for 25 years, renewable by mutual agreement for another 25. He was a link with the past if there ever was one; he conducted the first performance of *Le Sacre du Printemps*, and also (though that doesn't exactly gladden *my* heart) played the viola in the orchestra for the première of *Pelléas et Mélisande*.

When we turn to conductors still on deck, it is clear that their habit of living for ever shows no sign of – well, dying out. The doyen is our own beloved Reggie; Goodall, the third member of the improbable trinity of applause-haters, is 86. He conducted act three of *Parsifal* at the Proms a few weeks ago, and although he is not quite as steady on his pins as he once was, I can assure you that there is nothing wrong with the rest of him; it was a performance of aching beauty, depth and meaning.

Runner-up to Reggie is von Karajan at 79, followed by Leinsdorf and Solti at 75; Georg gets younger every time I see him, and will shortly be accused of being his own grandson. Celibidache is 75, too; years ago, coming out of the Albert Hall on a fine night after one of his concerts, I was challenged to make up a clerihew on his name before, on foot, we reached Knightsbridge Underground. I did it before we crossed Exhibition Road, thus:

> Sergiu Celibidache
> Said 'Play it *allegro vivace*';
> But Mariano Stabile
> Sang it *andante cantabile*.

Then there are Giulini and Kubelik, both 73, and the rest are youngsters like Colin Davis (60) and prodigies like Rattle (14).

There *is* an explanation; at least, it's the best I can do. There you are, on the rostrum, with a little white stick; when you wave it, anything up to 105 musicians, many of them perfectly sober, simultaneously do precisely what you wish them to. That must give you a charge that is worth any number of little liver pills. But it is the second half of the charge that carries the day.

The Vienna Philharmonic was in town, at the Albert Hall. The second half of the concert consisted of the C major Symphony of Schubert, and the orchestra was at its very best. Loud and prolonged cheers; so loud and prolonged that an encore was clearly called for. The Vienna Phil is in the habit of playing the Blue Danube as its extra-curricular contribution, but that would hardly do after the Schubert Ninth, and when the beat came down, it came down on the *Mastersingers* overture. It was colossally well played, and by the time the conductor came back on to the platform for the fifth time 5,000 people were on their feet, cheering their lungs out. The diminutive figure of Karl Böhm bowed and smiled – and basked; after another half-dozen recalls, he went home, well satisfied, and slept a dreamless sleep.

He lived to be 87. I cannot say I am entirely surprised.

The Times August 31st, 1987

Applaud with the Lord

E VERY FEW YEARS, though I think the gaps get longer, there is a stir about applause after a concert, if the concert is given in a church. The latest re-run concerned an organ recital in Bath Abbey by Mr David Liddle; he was warmly applauded, though the Rector, the Very Reverend Geoffrey Lester, doesn't approve of applause *in diesen heil'gen Hallen*, and had had a note put in the programme to the effect that members of the audience wishing to indicate their approval of the performance when it was over should stand in silence. 'Some people like applause and some don't,' said the Rev of their scandalous disobedience, adding: 'We don't. Neither did Sir Adrian Boult. That is enough said.'

This good cleric seems to have wandered out of the pages of Trollope. It is not at all clear why Sir Adrian Boult, who was a nice old soul, and not too bad a conductor (he knocked me down once, but not with malice aforethought – he was hurrying round a corner on the other side of which I was loitering), should be the final *arbiter elegantiarum* in these matters, and even if applause in church shocked him beyond measure, he would hardly have insisted, as the Rev Lester did, that the audience at this particular performance should do no more than stand in approving silence, because the organist who gave the recital, as it chances, is blind. (If the recital had been given by Beethoven, the Rev would presumably have advised the audience to ring him up and say thank you.)

There really is only one way to characterize the objection to applause of a concert in a church: it is nonsense, *sans phrases*.

Before I say why, I must point out that there are occasions

when applause really is not appropriate; I can recall two specific instances, though they were in theatres, not churches. The first was at Rolf Hochhuth's play *The Representative*, at the Aldwych Theatre; there was no note in the programme forbidding or discouraging applause, but since the final tableau of the play showed the doors of the Auschwitz gas chamber sliding shut, the entire audience, without any need for instruction, left in silence. The second such occasion was the performance of *The Biko Inquest* at the Riverside Studios; the text was taken *verbatim* from the transcript of the hearing, and again the audience instinctively and unanimously responded by leaving without clapping.

Wagner is popularly but erroneously credited with forbidding applause at the end of *Parsifal* on the ground that it was too holy, and for many years – well into my opera-going – this imaginary decree was obeyed not only at Bayreuth, where, if some hardy or ill-informed soul started to clap, red-faced burghers would leap to their feet, the veins in their temples standing out as thick as frankfurters, yelling (with a decibel count close to brain-damage levels) '*Ruhe! Ruhe!*' (which means 'Quiet! Quiet!'), but everywhere else as well, certainly including Covent Garden.

What Wagner had in fact said was that he would prefer the audience to wait until the end of the opera before applauding, but that cow Cosima, and that even worse cow Winifred, saw to it that his instructions were disobeyed for nigh on 60 years.

Now to the nub or crux. First, what is applause for? It is, I take it, the audience's method of indicating that they have had pleasure from the performance, and wish the performers to know it. That seems to me to be a perfect exchange; without the second half of the transaction it would be sadly incomplete.

I am sure that when the Rev Lester was a little boy, he was told, as most of us were, that if the nice lady gave him a piece of cake, he should say thank you. What is more, I am sure he did. Indeed, I have no doubt that if one of his flock were today to hold a door open for him, he would in no circumstances fail to acknowledge the courtesy. And, of course, if he were to go to a concert in the Pump Room, he would join in the applause with everyone else.

There is, therefore, clearly nothing wrong with applause, provided, presumably, that it is not mingled with unseemly cries, piercing whistles or excessive swooning. The objection is only to applauding in church.

Now some would say that a clergyman who permits a concert in his church but then prohibits applause for it cannot recently have studied the 24th verse of the 23rd chapter of the Gospel according to St Matthew. But there is more substance than that to the case against the ban. It is that to deny audiences their opportunity to express their gratitude for music suggests that those who do the defying must have a pretty rum idea of God.

I must, obviously, defer to the Rev where the relative degree of our acquaintance with the Almighty is concerned; I accept that his must be closer than mine. But I doubt if it is so close as to lead to a confidential tip on the subject of applause in church; to be frank, I feel that God has more important things on his mind.

But even if that were not so, I shall be so presumptuous as to declare my conviction that if God gives any thought to the matter at all, he is overwhelmingly likely to be on my side, not his own man's. I assume that the Rector of Bath Abbey would agree that, among the works of God's hand, music, *du holde Kunst*, ranks high. I assume also that the good cleric takes some such view as Peter Shaffer does in *Amadeus*; that Mozart was a conduit from heaven to earth, through which his music flowed, much of it describable, with no sense of incongruity let alone blasphemy, as divine.

Now if Mozart was made by God to *be* God's servant, however unwitting, and Mozart's music was God's gift to the world *through* his servant, then surely the man or woman who re-creates that music by performing it is adding another service to the creator of Mozart, music and performer alike.

I take Mozart because the argument is there at its most powerful, but I suspect that God has pretty eclectic tastes in

music as in so much else, and for all I know Max Reger is in
heaven at this moment, boring the angels into the screaming
heebie-jeebies with incessant performances of his Variations
for Organ on *God Save the King*. And although God is
presumably as bored as the angels, I suspect he claps at the end,
lest he should hurt Max's feelings, as enthusiastically as he can
bring himself to.

Reverend Sir, they also serve. You serve your God directly,
as a Minister of his word. Others have to go about to find a
way. Mr David Liddle, who has no doubt wondered from
time to time just *why* he is blind, has found his in the gift of his
music-making. Shall those who listen to his gift be denied
their wish to thank composer, performer and creator alike, by
signifying their pleasure and gratitude in the usual manner?

Massenet's charming opera, *Le Jongleur de Notre-Dame* (we
had it at Wexford a few years ago), has a lesson for all
concerned in the applause argument. Jean, the wandering
entertainer who has entered a monastic order, is ashamed
because he has no artistic talent with which to lay a tribute at
the feet of the statue of the Virgin in the monastery chapel,
while other monks can sculpt or paint or compose. He wan-
ders up to the altar, and goes through his old routine of love
songs, juggling and acrobatics; scandalized, the other monks
rush forward to drag him away for this sacrilege, but the statue
puts out her arm over him in protection and thanks.

That seems a much better approach. Anyway, the matter is
settled on the highest possible authority: Psalm 47 begins 'O
clap your hands, all ye people; shout unto God with the voice
of triumph'. A compromise; if the Rector will lift his ban
on clapping, I shall recommend restraint when it comes to
shouting.

The Times June 22nd, 1987

They also serve

I HAVE ALWAYS maintained that salutations are due, and properly given, to anyone who can do anything better than anyone else. There is a man in Switzerland who cuts pieces of paper into fantastic and beautiful shapes by folding them cunningly first, then plying the scissors in an apparently random manner. We all did this, or tried to, as children, but the good Switzer has turned it into a real art, and it is hardly likely that he will find a challenger to topple him from his recondite pinnacle.

In a different field altogether, the late Arne Tollefson took the humblest and least regarded of musical instruments, the accordion, and played it so finely and expressively that he persuaded serious composers to write for it. And I have told before the story of the man so skilled at parachute jumping that he once jumped out of an aeroplane without one, having thoughtfully arranged to collect one from a passing colleague holding a spare.

These feats betoken respectively a unique skill in manual dexterity combined with a remarkable eye for shape, a musical gift so refined that its possessor could conjure sweet sounds from an instrument thought incapable of making them, and an alliance of courage with presence of mind that makes most of us, when we merely contemplate it, clammy-palmed and dry of mouth.

There is an obvious distinction here between these outstanding achievements and those of the delightful fellow (I met him once) who got into the *Guinness Book of Records* by balancing 11 of the old 12-sided threepenny-bits on edge, each standing on its predecessor. This was something that, given a steady enough hand and sufficient patience, anybody might do, whereas my three heroes must have had some innate quality that others lack. But there is an equally real yet less obvious difference separating the trio from champion athletes. The highest jumper, or faster miler, in the world is only a bar's thickness or a tape's breadth ahead of the runner-up, and he knows that in a year or two someone will have broken his record, who in turn will see his own surpassed. In other words, a champion athlete is not unique, but the Swiss, the musician and the madman all are.

And here comes another. His name (not easily forgotten) is David Schummy, and he is the greatest boomerang thrower in the world. (You may wonder – I did – how boomerang throwers are ranked; it seems that the champion is the thrower who can keep his instrument in the air longest before it returns to his hand.)

Mr Schummy, whom I found in an old copy of the *Sunday Telegraph* Magazine at the dentist's, has an established boomerang air time of 36.33 seconds (if your watch has a seconds hand, time it – you will be astonished at how long it is), and is now, he says, keeping the thing aloft for a whole minute. I have no such obsession, let alone skill. But I think I understand it, and I am sure that I admire it. The spirit which animates these eccentric champions is at bottom the same as that which drove Flecker's pilgrims on the golden road to Samarkand:

> We travel not for trafficking alone;
> By hotter winds our fiery lusts are fanned;
> For love of knowing what should not be known,
> We take the Golden Road to Samarkand.

That is surely an admirable attitude, is it not? And the envy that we feel for it is not, I think, grounded in a wish to be officially classed 'the best'; it is based on a yearning for perfection, or at least a longing to strive for perfection. Perfection is an end in itself, as indeed has been clearly demonstrated by the eccentrics who seek it in such odd corners, for few people are going to nudge one another and point just because the world's greatest basket weaver or tea taster has gone by.

I was one of the twelve million people who stayed up to watch that astounding snooker championship final in which the man with the upside-down glasses won with the very last stroke – and I am not interested in snooker, indeed do not even know the rules. What kept me in front of the television set? I was staying with friends in the country, and everybody had gone to bed except my host and I. He rose – he cares for snooker no more than I do – and bade me goodnight; on the way out of the room he paused behind my chair to glance at the screen, and he stood there, unmoving, his body still turned at the angle that was to take him to the door, for the next 45 minutes.

We could not know of the amazing finish; but we had both been seized by the realization that we were watching two men approaching very close to perfection; the knowledge was so enthralling that we had to see it out.

Of course, there are other relativities. To play snooker like that, or to juggle flawlessly with two dozen coloured rings, or for that matter to decipher Linear B, is not so great an achievement as to write *Fidelio*, or design the Baptistry in Florence. But in the house of achievement there are many mansions.

There was a French postman, called Cheval; his beat was a country one, near Hauterives. He conceived – no one seems to know why or how – a magnificent obsession, to build, from nothing but pebbles picked up on his round, a miniature palace and temple. For 35 years as he delivered the letters he filled his pockets with stones (he was repeatedly reprimanded and fined by his superiors for ruining his uniform by overloading his pockets) and at the weekends he would go to the site of his building and pile them one upon another.

He continued after his retirement, and his monument stands to this day; visitors can enter it, though a tall man might bump his head, and wander about its miniature arcades and galleries, halls and domes, statues and niches. Every bit of it he found, and every bit he put in place with his own hands. It has no great claims to be art or architecture, but it is now a national monument, and so it should be. For it testifies in its humbler way, as surely as Notre Dame does in its might, to the dream of perfection that every fully human being knows, but that a few, a very few, dream waking. It is today called 'Le Palais Idéal', which must surely please the shade of Postman Cheval.

You may smile at Postman Cheval, or the boomerang man, but they know a secret which eludes the rest of us. For the builder and the thrower, by devoting their lives to one aim, have done something more than can be measured by their achievements; they have touched the hem of perfection's garment. Only the hem, mind; it takes Mozart to grasp the sleeve. But I think it takes more time, more energy and above all more determination than you and I have got even to feel the fabric brush our hand. Of one thing I am quite sure, though; once experienced, that touch can never be forgotten.

The Times October 13th, 1986

Bombs away

T HERE IS A STORY, possibly true, about Theodore Dreiser, that somewhat ponderous American novelist. As the story goes, he left New York on a journey to the West, and when he returned to the metropolis and joined his cronies, they hardly had time to greet him before he was raving about a sight he had seen on his travels. It was, he insisted, one of the most amazing experiences of his life, it was a phenomenon unlike anything else in the world, it was unforgettable, magnificent, overwhelming.

When he finally paused, one of the group inquired as to what exactly it was, this unique wonder. 'Well,' said Dreiser, 'out there they call it the Grand Canyon.'

Something much like this has just happened to Mr Martin Amis, son of Kingsley and himself a notably successful novelist. He has discovered the Grand Canyon, in the form of nuclear weapons, and deems it his duty to acquaint a world hitherto unaware of them with their existence and the dangers they pose.

To this end, he has just published *Einstein's Monsters* (Cape), a book consisting of five short stories and an Introduction. The short stories are not all about nuclear matters, though it could be said that in one way or another they are all variations on that theme. But I shall not discuss them; fiction has its own rules of logic and truth, and a creative writer is not in the witness-box testifying on behalf of his characters. (Kingsley has suffered all his life from fools accusing him of philistinism because he put the phrase 'some filthy Mozart' into the mouth of Lucky Jim, though he is, as it happens, a devoted and very knowledgeable Mozartian.)

The introductory essay, however, is another matter. There, Mr Amis is speaking directly in his own voice, and what he says is open to discussion and criticism as is any publicly-expressed opinion. And it seems to me that his attitude and beliefs are well worth discussing, not because of his standing as an interesting and talented writer but because in what he believes and how he expresses it he is representative of too many people today.

Martin Amis says that he 'first became interested in nuclear weapons during the summer of 1984'. His reasons for taking an interest were twofold, and significant; he was about to become a father for the first time, and he had read Jonathan Schell's book *The Fate of the Earth*.

I dare say (I am a bachelor myself, so I cannot speak with much authority) that the first of these two experiences was sufficiently unsettling to render him an instant disciple of Schell and his book; for it is plain that on reading it he at once threw away any ratiocinative faculty that he might have had. From that moment on, like a man converted in a vision, his only response to the actuality and implications of nuclear weapons is what Aneurin Bevan, in exactly the same context, called 'an emotional spasm'.

Jonathan Schell's book states, over and over again, the start-ling truth that a war with nuclear arms (particularly if it took the form, so grimly and appositely known by its acronym, of Mutual Assured Destruction) would be a most unpleasant business. True, it might knock down the Hayward Gallery in London and the Trump Tower in New York, but even so notable a contribution to civilization would be more than offset by the hundreds of millions of deaths and the almost unimaginable destruction, torment and misery that it would inevitably entail.

Of course, it is not certain that a war between powers armed with nuclear weapons would lead to their use, let alone their indiscriminate use, but the risk is too great and too hideous to be run. It is therefore absolutely essential that we should avoid a war between nuclear powers. It seems to have escaped Mr Schell's notice, and it has certainly escaped Mr Amis's, *that we have*. Moreover, although there have been countless wars in the last 40 years, no nuclear bomb has been used on a non-nuclear combatant by a nuclear one; not in Korea, nor Vietnam, nor the Falklands.

Now there must be a reason for this reassuring state of affairs. Unfortunately, Mr Amis and those who think – or rather, feel – like him are precluded from seeking it; their Bosch-like vision of the nuclear apocalypse fills their horizon entirely, with not a square inch for the frail butterfly of reason to settle on. Mr Amis tells us, again and again, that nuclear weapons make him feel sick: '. . . I experience nausea . . . they make me want to throw up . . . they make me feel sick to my stomach . . .' It never seems to occur to him to swallow a couple of Kwells and do some thinking. Indeed, the very idea of applying human reason (what does he imagine we have it for?) to nuclear weapons fills him with indignation. Instead, it's vomit, vomit, vomit, all summer long.

And not only the old heave-ho. Like many another uni-lateralist Fat Boy, he loves to dwell upon the very horrors that make him spew:

> Suppose I survive. Suppose my eyes aren't pouring down my face, suppose I am untouched by the hurricane of secondary missiles that all mortar, metal and glass has abruptly become: suppose all this. I shall be obliged (and it's the last thing I feel like doing) to retrace that long mile home, through the firestorm, the remains of the thousand-miles-an-hour winds, the warped atoms, the grovelling dead. Then – God willing, if I still have the strength, and, of course, if they are still alive – I must find my wife and children and I must kill them.

That seems a most unkind thought. I am sure Mrs Amis is quite capable of deciding for herself whether she wishes to go on living in a post-nuclear world, and as for the little Amises, surely some compromise is possible; how about killing half of them, or perhaps half-killing the lot?

Some people, incidentally, are even sillier than that. Reviewing Mr Amis's book in the *Sunday Telegraph*, Mr Alan Ryan quotes that same passage, and adds: 'It is a fantasy which every parent I know has been afflicted with.' But that brings me to a phenomenon that I have described before. There is something about the more gloomy folk in the anti-nuclear camp that does not ring quite true. Their words are full of unquenchable horror and fear at the impending Armageddon, they wring their hands, they proclaim their regret that they ever brought children into the world to be fried in a nuclear holocaust, they declare that nothing – art, love, reading, travel – means anything to them any more; and a powerful effect such anguished speeches have on me, as you may imagine.

And yet I have noticed, at dinner parties in Chelsea and Hampstead, that however loud and lurid the litany of doom, nobody in my experience has ever been so overcome as to push away untasted the taramasalata, the beef casserole, the kiwi-fruit sorbet or the Wine Society claret. I have met Mr Amis the younger only once, but he seemed a merry enough soul; what is the compulsion that drives him and his like to convince themselves that they can scarcely swallow, let alone sleep, for worrying about the possibility of nuclear war?

Well, precisely why do they think that it has not happened in the 40 years that it has been possible? Can it be that somewhere in their affronted subconscious there is the thought that, despite their fevered scenarios, deterrence – horrible, crude, dangerous, immoral – *has worked*? And that nothing else would have worked? And if so, is it their buried suspicion that they may have been wrong all along that drives them to such limits as calling Lord Chalfont (as Mr Amis does), solely because of his support for SDI, 'subhuman'? I have known Alun Chalfont for many years, and I have never noticed that his knuckles brushed the ground as he walked, nor that he was much given, while taking part in a conversation, to chewing absent-mindedly on the severed leg of a baby. Surely 'subhuman' is coming it a bit strong?

Every cliché of CND and its arguments is pressed into service. Civil defence? 'There are only two words to be said, and they are *forget it*.' It is no use my inviting Mr Amis to read John McPhee's *La Place de la Concorde Suisse*, which shows without question that the Swiss, if there is a nuclear war, will survive in enormous numbers (millions, probably) and survive in a meaningful sense, too; *they* aren't going to rush home and murder their wives and children. But the reason it is no use my urging Mr Amis to read the book is that nothing must be allowed to suggest hope; universal darkness must cover all, lest they should have to abandon their delicious Byronic poses and face the unheroic truth.

The whole tenor of Mr Amis's essay, and of CND and its adherents, is despair – despair mixed with relish, but still despair. They sometimes seem to long for the catastrophe to be total. For instance, it should be obvious that if the terrible thing happened, many hundreds of millions of people in addition to the Swiss – in China, for instance, and Australasia, Africa, South America – would survive, even though Europe, the Soviet Union and North America might be obliterated. Yet throughout Schell's book and Mr Amis's essay there is a continuous harping on the claim that the human race will inevitably become entirely extinct: '. . . neither we nor anyone else will ever get another chance . . . end the human story in all place for all time . . . no dead will rise . . . the risk is that of ending the course of human history . . .' Do they want it, these people who talk, as Mr Amis does, of 'the hyperinflation of death that has cheapened all life'? What does he imagine he means by that idiot catch-phrase? That living decently, honestly, deeply is no longer necessary, because a nuclear war may one day break out? But the human race has known, ever since it came into existence, that every member of it is destined to die; that is the only fact of which we can be quite certain from the day we are born, and that would be true

even if every weapon in the world, from 50-megaton hy-
drogen bombs to knitting-needles, vanished forever from the
earth tonight. How, then, is life – inevitably as transitory as it
is mysterious – 'cheapened' because we have invented a means
of ending a lot of it at once?

Again and again, Mr Amis quotes Schell's most absurd and
illogical arguments as though they proved his case. This, for
instance, which he calls 'Schell's noble syllogism'. 'He, thinking I was about to kill him in self-defence, was about to kill me
in self-defence. So I killed him in self-defence.'

And Mr Amis does not fail to add, on his own behalf,
'Yes, and then he killed me in retaliation, from the grave.'
But nobody, in nuclear terms, has killed anybody in such a
scenario; Schell and Amis alike have adopted CND's
sleight-of-hand – the argument that nuclear war is the same as
the *danger of* nuclear war. They have also adopted CND's
greater, and more dishonest, sleight-of-hand, the implicit
claim that the horrors of nuclear war demonstrate that the
unilateralist solution is the correct one, whereas all that the
horrors demonstrate is that peace must be pursued; they do not
in themselves indicate any particular path for the pursuit. (Mr
Amis does – just – manage to avoid the third and greatest of
CND's dishonesties – the use of the word peace, as in 'we of
the peace movement' to imply that those who oppose
unilateralism do not want peace.)

Now then. In 1945, Western Europe was destroyed, pros-
trate and exhausted. So was the Soviet Union, but the numbers that the Soviet Union could deploy were such that no
conventional weapons would have sufficed to stop Stalin
adding Western Europe to his Eastern empire. (The threat was
considered so urgent that there was a contingency plan to arm
the defeated Germans.) But Stalin knew that the bombs
formed a barrier that he could not cross. It is certainly disagreeable to think that we owe to these terrible weapons the
fact that we are still free, but to be unfree would, I think, be a
good deal more disagreeable.

I do not believe that the Soviet Union contemplates the

invasion of Western Europe; I do not believe that she has contemplated it for a good many years now. But I am quite sure that the initial suspension of such an ambition was caused by the existence of the atomic bomb, and the subsequent slow weakening of the ambition was the result of the West's determination to remain armed with the most frightful weapons that could be devised. And I would fear to stake my life against the re-awakening of the ambition if the West were to give up those weapons unilaterally. Hear Mr Amis again:

> What is the only provocation that could bring about the use of nuclear weapons? Nuclear weapons. What is the priority target for nuclear weapons? Nuclear weapons. What is the only established defence against nuclear weapons? Nuclear weapons. How do we prevent the use of nuclear weapons? By threatening to use nuclear weapons.

And that catechism, every word of which is true, is put forward not in explanation and gratitude for the way the peace has been kept, but as matter for scorn and jeering; an emotional spasm indeed.

Amis goes on: 'I still don't know what to do about nuclear weapons. And neither does anybody else. If there are people who know, then I have not read them.' That, I may say, is all too apparent; but I now invite him to read me. Because I *do* know what to do about nuclear weapons, and I claim no psychic powers, nor secret information, nor superior wisdom.

There is only one possible thing to 'do about' nuclear weapons. It is for us in the West to keep ours, plentiful and powerful, while the Soviet Union keeps hers likewise, and gradually, step by step over a long period – years, certainly – to negotiate reductions in their numbers (on both sides) and to make inspection agreements, equally bilateral, until the world is a reasonably safe place (it will never be entirely so) to live in. There is nothing glamorous or exciting about such a programme, which will be carried out by boring men in boring suits, sitting on ugly chairs in Geneva until they get permanently calloused behinds; but that is what can usefully be done, and the *only* thing that can usefully be done, about nuclear weapons.

Note that I insist on the 'usefully'. There are many useless things that can be done, and one of them is to adopt Mr Amis's policy, which is to crawl under the bed and shout 'Nasty bombs! Awful bombs! Shan't come out till Nanny takes horrid bombs away!' But Nanny doesn't exist. There are only ordinary fallible human beings, picking their way through a dark forest, in search of a distant, sordid, unmoral, shabby, yet ultimately glorious goal, which is to pluck this flower, safety, from this nettle, danger, and by doing so enable the world to survive and thrive, despite all the terrors of earth and sky, through our eternally unquiet day.

The Times May 11th, 1987

Condition critical

I SEE THAT Alexander Walker, film critic of the London *Evening Standard*, has been banned from attending press previews of the presentations of Cannon Films; Mr Walker has been denied the facility because Cannon don't like his critical views.

Mr Walker tells me that he has already seen most of Cannon's forthcoming output at foreign film festivals, and that Cannon-made films are shown also in non-Cannon cinemas; in addition, he can in any case buy a ticket at any Cannon cinema as soon as the film opens to the public. The ban, therefore, seems somewhat porous, and one wonders what Cannon had to gain by imposing it. But then, one wonders what gain is hoped for whenever this ancient chestnut is turned over in the fire.

Both the theatre and the cinema are guilty of turning it over, though the theatre is much the worse; every few years, some management takes umbrage and declares a particular critic *persona non grata*. What is so extraordinary about the practice is that the managements always lose, and never learn.

Almost any critic you can think of has been banned at times, starting with Bernard Shaw and A. B. Walkley and going on with Hannen Swaffer, Milton Shulman and me. The management doing the banning always claim that the banned critic has been conducting a vendetta, though all they ever mean is that they think more highly of their output than the critic does, which is not very surprising when you come to think of it.

Milton Shulman provoked a different kind of ban, many years ago. The cinema people collectively decided that they didn't like the tone of his reviews (he, too, was film critic of the London *Evening Standard* – perhaps there is a rule that every thirty years the *Standard*'s reviewer is objected to), but they didn't forbid him entry, or even bar him from press showings; instead, they took all their advertising out of the paper, and indeed out of the *Standard*'s morning and Sunday sisters, the *Daily Express* and *Sunday Express*. That was a foolish thing to do; but what made the folly even greater is the fact that the cinema's representatives told Lord Beaverbrook, who then owned all three papers, that they wouldn't bring their advertising back until Milton was sacked.

Now whatever the villainy of Beaverbrook (which was considerable), he was the very last man to give in to a demand as gross, idiotic and impudent as that, and he sent them packing. The siege went on for something like a year, until Ken Tynan resigned as the *Standard*'s theatre critic in a fit of pique and Milton was asked to review plays, which he has been doing ever since.

There have been some merry battles over bannings. Hilary Spurling was banned from the Royal Court, and the present Chancellor of the Exchequer, who was then Editor of the *Spectator* (for which Miss Spurling wrote) devoted a weekly article to flaying the banners. The usually sensible Lindsay Anderson caught it hottest. The Court soon gave in.

Hannen Swaffer was not only banned, but slapped; an actress he had criticized gave him *la gifle* in the Savoy Grill. I don't know what he had said to provoke her so; possibly – you never know – he may have suggested that her bum was too big. Anyway, actual blows are almost invariably the product of a need for publicity for a failing show. (The failing show invariably fails, but the theatre never learns that, either.)

When I was a theatre critic I was banned several times, though today I couldn't tell you what the bannings were about if my life depended on it. (But that's how it goes; once, at a party, I ran into an Attorney-General with whom I had been having, only a year or so before, an immensely violent and prolonged ding-dong. Neither of us could remember what it had been about.)

If Milton Shulman holds the record for the longest siege, I think I must hold the Blue Riband for the shortest; it lasted a single day. I *think* it was the absurd Charles Marowitz who decided that my presence was not welcome at his work; anyway, whoever he was, my fellow-critics, led on that occasion by Michael Billington, declared solidarity with the persecuted Levin, and I began to see myself as a combination of Martin Luther, Ibsen's Enemy of the People and St Joan. Unfortunately, the enemy surrendered the following morning.

Milton Shulman insists that the Royal Court once banned me, and that on that occasion he led the rescue party; I have no recollection of being banned by the Court, though there were entire seasons when I fervently wished that I might be, and on one occasion, at a thing called *The Beard*, I came very close to shouting 'Fire!'

The theatre has got better in recent years, presumably because more intelligent managements have taken over. The Littlers and Shereks and their like have long since gone, and no one could imagine sophisticated fellows like Codron or White or Mackintosh making such fools of themselves, let alone those who run the RSC and the National Theatre. I often see that amiable fellow, William Douglas-Home, these days, and you wouldn't think, to see us in such friendly discourse, that once upon a time he would cheerfully have murdered me, let alone banned me, for my reviews of his plays. (But he never was one for bearing grudges.)

I often wondered why such theatres as the Whitehall in the Rix days bothered to invite the critics at all. The audience for those immensely successful trouser-droppers never read us, indeed probably didn't know there were such people as theatre critics, and would have thought it a very odd trade; so it is, as a matter of fact. The same was true of the Victoria Palace when the Crazy Gang was in residence; idling away a few minutes in the darkness (I never did find them funny), I once worked out that the combined ages of the six of them added up to 391 years, which, I said in my review, was nothing compared to the age of some of their jokes. They were forgiving fellows, too.

Eric Maschwitz wasn't; he was the only man to have walked out of a room *three times* solely because I had walked in, and when I tell you that one of the rooms was a restaurant where he was having lunch you may judge the strength of his feeling. I remember what I had done to enrage him, too. In a review of a terrible comedy, I described in detail the ghastly gurgling laughter coming from the man in seat E6 (I think I complained he was preventing me from getting to sleep).

A letter to the paper revealed, in indignant tones, that the man in E6 was Eric Maschwitz, head of Light Entertainment at the BBC, so there. The paper printed the letter, and I – never one for letting ill alone – added a footnote which read: 'I didn't know this gentleman's identity at the time, but now that I do I feel that it explains a good deal, hitherto mysterious, about the BBC's Light Entertainment.'

A somewhat parallel experience befell me at the first night of *Beyond the Fringe*, though I did not know of it until some time afterwards. In the interval, the cast of four, together with the director, held an emergency council of war, to decide whether to send round a note asking me to make less noise; I was screaming so loudly in my mirth that they were genuinely afraid that the rest of the audience could not hear the cast. They let me scream on, and got a rave review. (Mind you, I wasn't the only one; Alan Bennett's sermon as the Rector of St Jack-in-the-Lifeboat must have brought several members of the audience close to death.)

Go your ways, Cannon Films; the egg will be on *your* faces, and the longer you leave it there the harder it will be to wipe off. As for the victim (or villain) my last word is: hang in there, Alex, you'll be back. Though whether that will gladden your heart is another matter.

The Times January 25th, 1988

Devil's advocate

The Stories of Muriel Spark*

THERE IS SOMETHING peculiarly appropriate about the fact that although this book is said to contain all 27 of Mrs Spark's published short stories, and indeed does, the contents page lists only 26. The longest story in the collection exists in a kind of anonymous limbo; there it is, from p. 221 to p. 262, but the reader will be unaware of its existence before stumbling upon it.

This has all the most characteristic of Mrs Spark's qualities. It is mysterious; it provokes unease; it makes us search for a hidden meaning which may not be there; it leaps out abruptly at the unsuspecting passer-by. Ever since, in 1959, *Memento Mori* announced that English fiction had acquired a new and original voice (it was followed in 1960 by *The Ballad of Peckham Rye*, in case anyone was wondering whether she could repeat her success), *la belle dame sans merci* has had us in thrall. The pictures she paints are lit by fire, and no one can be quite sure whether the fire is an innocent burning of leaves, the result of arson, or the flames of Hell. Whatever the answer, if she had been born a few centuries ago, she would certainly have been burnt as a witch.

A cold moral order rules these stories. There is violent death in them, animal as well as human; there is madness – quiet, inward and deadly as well as loud and lurid; there is horror, of which we would not find it easy to say exactly why it makes us

* Bodley Head, 1987.

shudder; there is comedy, too, of course, but I rather feel that when Mrs Spark introduced the Devil into her fiction under the name of Dougal McDougal he decided he liked it there and has ever since refused to budge.

She tries to tempt him out with wit, irony and startling aphorisms like '. . . truth has airy properties with buoyant and lyrical effects, and when anything drastic starts up from some light cause it only proves to me that something false has got into the world'. When these approaches fail, she tries, in desperation, whimsy: 'The Playhouse Called Remarkable' and 'The Seraph and the Zambesi' can set your teeth on edge, though even in those there is more than a hint of the macabre to stop them cloying. But Satan folds his arms and stays put.

He has work to do; among the best of these stories are those set in Africa, long before independence, in which adultery and revenge stalk the pages. But the tales are far too complex, subtle and deep to permit comparisons with Maugham; 'Bang-bang You're Dead' ends in blood, but the conclusion, rooted in land innocently tilled earlier in the story, is that human lives can be wasted in a great variety of ways, of which being murdered by mistake is only one.

The longest and best of the book's stories, 'The Go-Away Bird', unfolds its tangled Norn-ropes slowly and with deliberate untidiness; it is the story of a girl growing up in an unnamed British colony, gradually learning the rules of safety, exploring the lusts, loves and darkness in people who have too little to do. The atmosphere, the tension, the savage sun, the cleared jungle that waits to spread into the human heart, much as it creeps back on to neglected ground – these are caught with an almost miraculous precision, though the 'almost' is really unnecessary, for there *is* a miracle or two in the book, and a few ghosts as well (one of which is the narrator of the story in which she occurs). But the end of 'The Go-Away Bird' is as abrupt as it is appalling, for the way the story slows down suggests, and is plainly meant to suggest, that it is going to trickle away into the earth, leaving the reader to think of Daphne's barren life, now set to be wasted. When she cries out

'God help me. Life is unbearable', we are sure that that is what is to happen; 30 lines later Daphne's life is indeed wasted, but not at all in the manner which we have been led to expect. Yet so skilful is the construction, and so powerful and impassive the imagination, that we do not feel cheated or tricked.

The Devil certainly won't go away. It is not clear, in 'The Twins', whether he has taken over the children or the parents or both (there is more than a touch of *The Turn of the Screw* in the story, for all that it is less than 10 pages long), but although nobody in it is killed, either quickly or slowly, and nobody goes mad, either seriously or comically, there is such a presence of evil in it that devout readers would be well advised to have a basin of holy water beside them, and the rest a stiff whisky.

You will have noticed that I have said nothing about the prose. That is because it is practically impossible to describe; I have never reviewed a book and found so few direct quotations among my notes. 'Elusive', the usual word, won't do; the writing is all but invisible. Yet there is not a page, hardly a paragraph, in which the writing is blurred or flat; however dramatic the events, the words remain ordered, calm, precise, and exactly equal to the task set them. Does she make thousands of drafts, or do these chiselled lines spring fully-armed from her pen?

Though themes, settings and human types recur, every one of these stories, even the slightest, has its own self-contained richness and force; few books of short stories can be read straight through, but this one can. The Devil has certainly found himself a comfortable billet.

Sunday Times April 12th, 1987

Kindly take the blame

PHARAOH DIDN'T KNOW when he was well off. Only *ten* plagues? In this country, vast and well equipped armies, private as well as public, have turned the search for new horrors to warn the nation against into the most promising growth industry of our time, and every day, as they roam the land with their trained ferrets, their search is rewarded by the discovery or invention of at least a score of problems, dangers, deficiencies, threats, shortages, surpluses and potential disasters, each of which, let alone all of them together, will inevitably entail the collapse of civilization by the following Wednesday at the latest.

Everything we eat is poisonous; everything we drink is immoral; everything we touch is contaminated; everything we smoke is fatal; everyone we go to bed with is diseased; every child is sexually abused; every adult is a racist; everyone who is not a drug addict is a drug pedlar; and every household that does not possess a colour television set, a compact disc player, a video recorder and a motor car is under-privileged AND SOMETHING MUST BE DONE ABOUT IT.

The latest of these attempts to save us all from Satan's power when we have gone astray surfaced a few months ago; I whacked it on the head, but to no avail, for it immediately grew nine more heads, and it is now ravening about the country seeking prey to devour. Before it devours us all, let me have another, and this time a more comprehensive, whack.

The subject is debt: or, to look at it from the other end, credit. People, it seems, are getting too much of the latter and therefore getting into too much of the former. Sir Gordon

Borrie, head of the Office of Fair Trading, recently hoisted the storm warning (it was his jeremiad I was whacking), and he has returned to the subject, though this time, I am glad to see, in a very considerably calmer tone of voice.

Others have been less circumspect. Before I get down to detail, I must draw attention to the curious assumption which underlies – underlies because it is apparently taken so completely for granted that no need to argue it seems to trouble those putting it forward – the whole case. It is unanimously and without qualification assumed that when anyone gets into debt, the fault is entirely and always that of the lender, not of the borrower.

Now the strangest thing about that assumption is that as far as I can see nobody thinks it is strange. There has been not a word from even the driest of Tories; the Adam Smith Institute is silent on the subject; the providers of credit have clearly decided that a seemly discretion is their most fitting defence; and everywhere one looks the holders of the assumption are masters of the field.

Yet even they must surely realize that their assumption, right or wrong, is of remarkably recent birth, and that only a couple of decades ago it would have been regarded as very odd indeed by creditor and debtor alike. Whether the old attitude or the new one is the more valid, so abrupt a turnaround is worth discussing, is it not? Yet I have seen not a word of such discussion; here, then, are quite a lot of words to remedy the deficiency.

To start with, I offer a quotation from the author of a book on the subject, Ann Andrews, which I take from a feature on debt and credit in this very newspaper; the article was based on the ease with which the writer, Lee Rodwell, managed to obtain a set of store credit cards giving her no less than £8,000 of credit with practically no questions asked and certainly no security given. Interviewed by Miss Rodwell, Miss Andrews said this:

> The trouble with credit is that it erodes your normal common sense about money. It is made to look easy, attractive.

If a store says you can have credit, you think that if they say it's all right it must be all right.

Who is the 'you' in that paragraph? It certainly isn't me; I have a horror of debt so extreme as to be almost pathological, and none of my massive collection of credit cards is really a *credit* card at all, since I invariably pay the bill, as I pay all bills, the moment it is presented.

But no one has to be as weird as I am to see that getting into debt, and in particular getting dangerously deep into debt, is a very bad idea, however 'easy, attractive' it may look. Why is it assumed that the only thing anyone faced with temptation can do is succumb to it?

But that brings me to the heart of the mystery I have outlined. And there is unlikely to be a better illustration of the strangeness I speak of than a recent article in the *Listener*, written by Mr Martin Young, who presented a BBC television programme on the subject of credit and its cards. I did not see it, but obviously the ideas on the screen must have been the same as those on the page, since they were the ideas of the same man, and the article was in effect a summary of the programme.

Mr Young quotes from two women he interviewed for the BBC. The first, Rose,

. . . owed £21,000 on a social security income of about £80 a week . . . Yet there are still places in the high street where Rose can extract credit with almost no questions asked. It is an indication of how desperate the retailers are for new customers . . . And in case the image of Rose suggests a feckless waster living off the state and squandering her money, it should be stated that nothing could be further from the truth. She is, in many ways, a fine example of Mrs Thatcher's enterprise culture.

I somehow thought that it would turn out to be all the fault of Mrs Thatcher, but before I suggest that it isn't, let me quote a little more from Rose. Her excessive indebtedness began when her domestic problems led to her losing her job, so, she says, 'it's just circumstances, really'.

Now Rose has clearly had a very bad time; money worries following a divorce (and a messy one, by the sound of it) would lay most people low. She is plainly deserving of sympathy, and she has mine. But that is not the end of the matter.

It must have been clear to her that whatever work she was likely to get, £21,000 of debt would take years, if not decades, to pay off. The creditmongers who extended such irrecoverable sums are fools, and I hope they lose the lot, together with the bad debts of all the others to whom they supplied credit on note of hand alone. But Rose walked into that £21,000 hole by her own choice; a desperate choice, no doubt, but hers. The assumption behind Mr Young's comments is that because the lenders lent her money she could not pay back, *they* are altogether morally to blame for the choice she made, and for her 'it's just circumstances, really'.

I ask again; what is to become of us, as individuals and as a nation, if we continue to assert that we are inanimate objects rather than human beings, and that anything we do, from kicking the dog to getting into debt, and from getting into debt to cannibalism, is really nothing to do with us, but the fault either of other people, or – today even more frequently argued – 'just circumstances, really'?

I turn now to the second debtor on Mr Young's programme:

> Sandra was just 17 when she applied for her first credit card. To make it legal, she pretended she was 18. That little burst of bravado certainly brightened up the tail-end of her teens, but it is already ruining her twenties. Today Sandra owes over £3,000 on credit cards and loans . . .

Let us look more closely at that passage, for the unconscious attitudes Mr Young displays are wonderfully revealing. 'To make it legal, she pretended she was 18'; what he means, actually, is 'To make it *il*legal', but he is so imbued with the belief that it is not her fault that he turns the situation upside down. Nor should we miss the significance of the word he uses to describe what she did: 'bravado'. Come, let us all go *swaggering* into debt; we can have Cyrano's courage without his nose, and there is no need to think of those who are lending us the money because it's *their* fault that *we* are unhappy.

Now Sandra truly is unhappy. But within the catalogue of her sorrows unrolled by Mr Young, there is yet another nugget of unconscious irony on his part; at least, it seems to have altogether escaped his waking notice:

> I have to pay £12 towards my debt a week. Twenty pounds for my rent. Seven pounds for food. Five pounds for bills. I pick up £68, and I've got bus fares and I smoke as well, so it's very tight.

I'm sure it is, and again I sympathize. But has not the list turned into one of those quiz questions which have the form of 'Spot the odd one out'? She must, of course, pay her instalment on the debt. She must, naturally, have somewhere to live. She must, certainly, eat. To get to work she must, assuredly, pay her fare. And a fiver for everything else is little indeed. But – and here I brace myself for the reproaches – does she *have* to smoke? Are the cigarette sellers forcing her, with blackmail, threats of violence, to buy their wares? Physicians of the utmost fame assure us that smoking is bad for us, and I believe them; giving up cigarettes would be wise as well as honest. But even if smoking was the very best route to healthy longevity, doesn't something come before her simple pleasure – that is, paying off her debt at perhaps £13 a week instead of 12?

I said I braced myself for the reproaches, and I know they are on the way. Many people, following the path I have been discussing, have by now rendered themselves incapable of seeing that there is something blameworthy in running up a bill and not putting its repayment above everything except genuine necessities, however modest the luxuries. The reason they cannot see the blameworthiness is that they have forgotten the very concept of blame, because they have forgotten, or been taught to ignore, the concept of responsibility.

Let us go back to Rose for a moment. With all her debts, Mr Young says indignantly, 'there are still places in the high street where Rose can extract credit with almost no questions asked'. The more fools they, as I have said already. But why does it follow that if people *can* extract credit they *will*, or even *must*, extract it? Why (I quote from another passage in Mr Young's article) is it matter for outrage that 'credit is not only freely available but forced into your eager little hand'? Why can you not clench that little hand into a fist, so that no credit can be forced into it?

And this whole story is not the worst. How many times, in the last few years, have you read articles or letters in newspapers, or heard comments on radio or television, in which it is asserted that shops, and in particular supermarkets, are to blame for shoplifting because they make the display of their wares so inviting? Could there be a more terrible indictment of what we have become that the thief is excused not on the ground that his children are starving but because it is easy for him to steal? I ask again: Why is it assumed that the only thing anyone faced with temptation can do is succumb to it?

I do not expect an answer. I shall therefore supply my own. We assume it because we have been taught for so long that we are not the master of our fate and the captain of our soul that we have come to believe it. But it was a lie when the tuition began, and it is still a lie. It would be no bad thing if, among the good resolutions we made for the new year now dawning, we included a resolve to assert the truth in the face of the lie. If anyone needs a stiffener for that resolve, it can be found in my last quotation from Mr Young's article. It is in the form of a question:

> The worry is also ethical – should there not be a clear responsibility on every lender to check the debtor's ability to repay the loan?

For those who have still not taken the point, here it is. Should there not be a very considerably greater clear responsibility on every *borrower* to check the debtor's ability to repay the loan?

The Times December 29th, 1986

Man and music

THE OTHER DAY – days, actually, for the experience was repeated thrice more – I found myself sitting not a dozen feet away from two of the greatest living sages, those twin towers of wisdom, learning and civilization, Sir Isaiah Berlin and Sir Ernst Gombrich, together with their respective ladies.

Mind you, though I scored on propinquity, I was by no means alone in their company; we had been joined by some 3,000 other people, including the Lords Weidenfeld and Gowrie, the President of Trinity College, Oxford, Sir Claus and Lady Moser (the latter dressed from head to foot in a red outfit so stunning that I feared that people would try to post their Christmas cards in her collar), the artist Milein Cosman (widow of that maddening but indispensable fellow, Hans Keller), Sir Stephen Spender and his beautiful daughter Lizzie, Mr Ronald Grierson, who had three reasons for being there, though the rest of us had only two, Mr Humphrey Burton, Anthony and Catherine Storr, Kevin and Rachel Billington, the great Robert Muller (who is a real person, despite the widespread belief, which he has himself begun to share, that I invented him) and Mrs Alfred Brendel.

Never let it be said, then, that Levin does not mix with the *beau monde* and the *haut ton*. But what brought together so glittering and diverse a throng? The answer is: *Mr* Alfred Brendel. For we, under the benign presidency of Sir Isaiah, constitute the Brendel Groupies, mutually pledged not to miss any of his concerts or recitals unless we are abroad, jailed, in hiding from our creditors, undergoing open-heart surgery or fighting drunk. And our hero was playing, in the Festival Hall, a series of four recitals, all of them devoted exclusively to the music of Schubert, whence our two reasons to be there, viz., the music and the musician. (Mr Grierson, in addition, is the Chairman of the South Bank Board.)

Groupies excused for one or more of the disabilities above will be pleased to learn that Brendel has acquired a new *tic*, which takes the form of pushing his spectacles back as though they are about to fall off his face, though it is clear that they aren't; he takes appalling risks with it, sometimes doing it within a semi-quaver rest. Rather more to the point, those who missed the series missed some eight hours of piano playing that amounted to one of the most enthralling and affecting musical experiences of a lifetime, comparable to the seven-recital series in which, a few years ago, he played all the Beethoven sonatas.

There are still some very good pianists in the world. Though Richter plays no more (at any rate as far as the West is concerned), the veterans are well represented; Horowitz shows no sign of giving up, Michelangeli (should he actually appear) still displays a technique that none can rival, and Arrau, for all that he has to have a friendly arm to help him on and off the platform, sounds the depths as he always did. Meanwhile their juniors like Perahia, Ashkenazy and Barenboim (though the last two, particularly Barenboim, are doing more and more conducting) tend the flame. What is it, then, that seems to set Brendel off from even the greatest of living players, with only one or two exceptions such as Serkin and the *wunderkind* Schiff, and numbers him with such giants of the past as Schnabel, Backhaus, Curzon, Fischer and Solomon?

One word makes all clear: authority. But it can be put even better at slightly greater length: you emerge from a Brendel performance of, say, the Waldstein, thinking not 'What a great pianist Brendel is', but 'What a great composer Beethoven is'. And all the names in that galaxy inspired that feeling.

It is not a matter of self-effacement; not one of those pianists could have been mistaken for any other. But while listening, the listener was convinced that *this* was the only way it could be played, and that the composer was nodding his head in approval from the Celestial Box. Of course, there is no 'right' way to play any piece of music; provided it is approached with integrity (it isn't always, I'm sorry to say), a case can be made for almost any interpretation. But with most pianists, even including some of the very greatest, we murmur, even as we whole-heartedly applaud, a not entirely convinced 'Hm'. With Brendel, and the rest of the chosen few, it is an indisputable, fulfilled, 'Ah'.

With other pianists, there is talk, at dinner after the performance, of the daring tempos, of the delicacy of the playing in the last movement and the fiery quality of the first, of the dream-like quality the pianist achieved in the adagio. This may be followed by comparisons; do you remember how X attacked the scherzo, how Y's touch was so vigorous, how Z went too fast for comfort in the repeat? Played by our Olympians, however, the music dominates the conversation, and the effect of it upon our souls is what we remember when we hear it like that.

So it was with Brendel's tour of Schubert; eight Impromptus, six *Moments Musicaux*, three *Klavierstücke*, the Wanderer Fantasy and eight sonatas; the final recital consisted of the last three sonatas Schubert wrote, all of them in a single month, as though he knew (he obviously did) that death was approaching, and that he had to forge those three mighty swords before the fire went out. Do such geniuses always have an intimation when their lives are coming to an end? Are they warned? I ask because there seems, too often to be coincidence, an extra intensity, a greater depth, in the music composed in their final span. The Mozart Requiem, for instance; these Schubert sonatas; the last Beethoven quartets; perhaps even *Parsifal*. If they can indeed see into the future, and through that glimpse learn that their future is destined to be cut short, it is not surprising that they struggle to tell their ultimate truths, to grasp the ultimate secret, before it is too late.

There is a tiny clue to Brendel's artistic integrity in his attitude to encores. When he did the Beethoven sonata series, he played one encore after each of the first six recitals, but made clear, with the most tactful mien, that he would not add anything to the seventh and last programme. Superstition? Exhaustion? Eager for his supper? No; it was only that the work which ended the series was the Op. 111 Sonata, and, as he put it in his dressing-room, 'After the 111, *there is nothing more to say.*' And so it was with the four Schubert recitals. He played an encore after the first three, but he finished the final programme with the B flat major Sonata, and because after that, too, there is nothing more to say, he said nothing more.

It is hard to believe that, until very recently, the Schubert piano works were held in low esteem. (Well, his C major symphony was held in even lower, largely because those idiots in Vienna couldn't play it, and it was left to Mendelssohn to rescue it for posterity.) Yet it must surely be obvious to anyone with an ear on each side of his head that they are among the greatest musical creations in all history.

Take the Sonata D784, which Brendel included in the first of the programmes. Mysterious, dark, almost tormented, full of strange harmonies and stranger modulations, it challenges the very idea of what music is, just as Beethoven's last quartets challenged not only the form but the substance. Brendel's playing of it found all the pain, yet instinctively and unerringly found also the resolution, as a great theatre director – and *only* a great one – finds the resolution in *King Lear*; any production of *Lear* which leaves the audience in despair has failed, and anyone who misses the exaltation in the D784 is – well, is listening to someone other than Brendel play it.

And then there was the D959, Schubert's penultimate sonata. Every time that astounding theme in the last movement – part hymn, part military march, part glorious Schubertian song – came round, Brendel gave it more meaning and more delight – yet the earlier versions lacked nothing of either; this wonderful musician had simply (simply!) felt Schubert's mounting excitement as the flames of the music burned ever higher, and conveyed that excitement in full.

Again, take the Impromptus, particularly the second and third from the D935 set. The principal idea in each of them is of the most simple, almost childish, construction, and it is perfectly possible, and indeed perfectly legitimate, to play them that way. It needs a Brendel, with his magisterial, humble certainty, to show that they have great depths beneath the innocence. No, he doesn't show that; he doesn't 'show' anything. He plays the music, without histrionics, eccentricity or vainglory; and it sweeps us away with *its* beauty and *his* impeccable judgement.

These four programmes were not just wonderful and memorable musical experiences. They were life-enhancing in the most profound and enduring sense; my life, and the lives of all in those audiences who took the measure of what they were hearing, are permanently enriched by those eight hours. The greatness of Schubert is infinite, yet it continues to grow for anyone who explores it, because the solace, joy, truth, and – above all – understanding that he offers are literally endless. To explore it in the company of Alfred Brendel's playing is to reach as far into the mystery as mortals can hope to get.

The date of the Brendel Groupies' AGM will shortly be announced by Sir Isaiah Berlin. The first item on the agenda will be a discussion on the question: Since he doesn't look at the keyboard anyway, why does he bother to wear his spectacles if he is afraid of them falling off?

The Times December 21st, 1987

As she is wrote

THE CAMPAIGN FOR Plain English provides much merriment. Its founders and organizers realized early on that to commend and encourage the writing of good English was not enough, particularly where publicity (on which any such body must rely) was concerned. This wicked world being what it is (viz., wicked), few column inches would be devoted, in most newspapers, to the news that the Market Harborough Watch Committee or the Prudential had put out a statement in intelligible, and even grammatical, English; what the campaigners had to do to gain attention was to publicize examples of officially promulgated *bad* prose. Every year, therefore, they hold a ceremony at which wooden spoons are liberally distributed among those who have sinned against our tongue; some of the verbiage thus denounced is so grotesque that if I did not have complete faith in the directors of the campaign I would suspect them of making it up.

But they have included in their most recent roll of dishonour an item which has implications far beyond the salutary castigation of bad English that the campaign metes out; it sums up something much more significant about our society. It comes from the department of community affairs in the local government of a London borough,* and here it is:

> Community Affairs delivers decentralized services with specific targeting and outreach techniques to achieve manifesto objectives. The front line interface with the public and

* It was Haringey.

community groups provides a catalyst input to services across the council, supporting initiatives in priority areas.

Illiteracy, these days, is nothing to be surprised about. The interest, and the significance, of the item lies in the particular kind of illiteracy displayed. Ever since the English language was created there have been dreadful and murderous assaults upon it by people who didn't know how to use it; but until very recently – I think only some 30 years ago – this form did not, and could not, exist. All language, after all, reflects the minds of those who use it, and it is only yesterday that people's minds began to work like that.

Let us look at the passage more closely. It contains 39 words. Of these, 11 are inert or neutral, being only auxiliary terms – conjunctions, articles, etc. The remaining 28 either mean nothing whatever (outreach, interface), or mean nothing as here used (targeting, community, input, across, front line, areas), or can mean anything that any reader might take them to mean (techniques, objectives, initiatives, services, groups, priority, supporting), or are largely tautological (affairs, manifesto, provides, delivers, decentralized), or are *entirely* tautological (specific, public), or have a real meaning which the author cannot be bothered to look up in the dictionary, preferring his or her own imaginary meaning (catalyst).

That leaves 'achieve' and 'council'; it's not much to show for a 39-word paragraph which is, after all, supposed to be explaining the department's work to those who pay for it.

What has happened here? How did we get to the point at which such jabber cannot be seen to be jabber either by those who do the jabbering or by those whose job is to scrutinize it?

What has happened is the rise to power of the half-educated. The mark by which you may know the half-educated is their attitude to their own lack of a real education. Half of it is an aggressive certainty that they know all it is necessary and useful for them (or anyone else) to know; the other half is a desperate unease and resentment at the evidence – which is all around them – that they don't really know anything. The combination has a devastating effect on them, and in particular on their vocabulary. The *uneducated* are content to use their smaller, yet perfectly effective, vocabulary, together with their rudimentary, yet equally satisfactory, instinctive grasp of a working grammar; the *educated* can deploy a wider knowledge of words and a deeper understanding of the use of them; but the *half-educated* despise those who have never had their own educational advantages, and are therefore unwilling to limit themselves to a vocabulary and syntax they can understand. The result is inevitable; they try to rise above their own educational station – and in doing so they write that paragraph, and countless more such paragraphs, up and down the land, every day.

What is the most obvious thing about that paragraph? It is that it has never occurred to the author of it to discover what the words mean – not even the ones that do mean something. The author has seen such words in print, and concluded that they are important ones, and therefore thinks that to write a statement largely composed of them is a sign of learning, which will be recognized and applauded and earn credit and respect.

But the author has missed the point twice over; first, it is impossible to write a coherent paragraph by jumbling together, in more or less random order, a series of words conveying no intelligible meaning to the writer, and second, these words, whatever they mean (if anything) are among the most threadbare clichés the language contains.

Repulsive, meaningless English is not the province of only one variety of politics; both the strangulated pomposity of the right and the windy falsehoods of the centre are debased and corrupting. But the kind of lifeless jargon that I have quoted is, almost without exception, of the left. And it signals danger, for it implies an attitude which is already to be found in actions, which in any case can never diverge far from the words they are described in.

An impulse to write such rubbish comes from the same mind-set that leads to the removal of books from public libraries on the ground that they are 'racist', 'sexist', and every other variety of 'ist' that intolerance can put its hand to; another demonstration of contempt for the uneducated, who cannot be allowed to make up their own minds as to which books they think fit to read. It is, indeed, the kind of thinking that has led to the most dangerous and fanatically pursued of all the new, half-educated left's yearning, which takes in a vast variety of essentially totalitarian aims, of which book-burning is only one; the drive for uniformity, called equality.

Years ago Kingsley Amis said 'More will mean worse'. Even in those days he was greeted with howls of execration for suggesting that not everybody should have the 'right' to a university education because not everybody is capable of benefiting from it. Mr Amis's prediction has come true tens of thousands of times over, but even he did not foresee the political dimension in what he was prophesying, the desire of the half-educated to take their revenge on society by restricting society's vision to their own limited horizon.

The dead jargon of that terrible paragraph is not something isolated, to be jeered at and forgotten. It has been encouraged in the universities, in Parliament, in the schools, in broadcasting and newspapers. It is, literally, dehumanized and dehumanizing; it poisons not only our beautiful, infinite and unique language but our national life; when words have been emptied of meaning, meaning itself fades.

There are those who want meaning to fade and die, who tell us that there are no differences between human beings; they would, if they had their way, make all of us live, think and act according to one sterile rule. Such attitudes lie behind the jabber and jargon that fills the air, a perfect demonstration of the fear and hatred of divergence, which is the most precious and the most significant of all our human qualities.

The Campaign for Plain English is concerned to keep our language fresh and untarnished; an admirable ideal. But those in charge of it little know how much more important a task they are engaged upon. Because a language defines a people, the campaign is now charged with the preservation of our national character and our individual identity. In that great cause we shall need all the specific targeting and outreach techniques we can get, if we are to provide a catalyst input supporting initiatives in priority areas. The frontline interface is nearer than we think.

The Times January 4th, 1988

The busy bureaucrat

THERE IS AN old story, which may be less apocryphal than is comfortable to think about, of a farmer being chivvied by the Ministry of Agriculture because he had not sent in details of crops and yields by the date specified. He wrote to say he had been very busy, as it was lambing time, whereupon the Ministry told him, severely, that he was in breach of the regulations with his delay, and should have postponed the lambing.

The gentleman in Whitehall does not know best; who, including the lambs, would think he does? But his latest wheeze, which is very far from apocryphal, is beyond patience. The Department of the Environment, whose selfless and never-ceasing efforts to destroy the environment altogether are all too little appreciated, has produced a Green Paper, for consultative purposes, about 'pests', which, it seems, does not refer to officials of the Department of the Environment but to such undoubted nuisances as wasps and cockroaches. The idea behind the Green Paper is that local authorities should be given powers to destroy all the wasps, cockroaches, etc. that they can find. (A wasp can fly faster than any member of Ealing Borough Council can run, but let that pass.)

So far, so good; unless you are a wasp, a cockroach or a Buddhist, you will probably be unconcerned at the forthcoming *battue*. You may, however, pause for reflection when you learn that the DoE wishes to include bees in the list of *hostes humani generis*.

Possibly the gentleman in Whitehall was once stung by a

bee; certainly he has been stung by the reaction of the Bee-keepers' Association (who were not, of course, consulted in advance, or even informed, about the Green Paper), for he has tried to make the proposal look less grotesque by claiming that there is no intention of encouraging local authorities to exterminate all the bees for miles around. But he is trying to close the hive door after the bees have flown.

Apiculture is one of the earliest activities of man; there is a cave-drawing in Spain, probably at least 100,000 years old, showing two honey gatherers climbing up to a bees' nest, and bees were domesticated almost as long ago. Moreover, the bee begins to buzz in history and literature from the earliest beginnings of both; the Egyptians have had hives for 5,000 years, and St Ambrose and Plato were among the many historical figures of whom it is related that a swarm of bees alighted on their mouths while they were in the cradle, thus indicating that their adult words, spoken or written, would be as sweet as honey. And do not imagine that 'honey' as an endearment is a 20th century American coinage; it occurs in Chaucer.

Shakespeare seems to contradict himself in his use of the bee as metaphor. In *Pericles* he gets it right: 'We would purge the land of these drones, that rob the bee of her honey', but in *Henry IV, Part 2* he seems to think that the drones go foraging:

> When, like the bee, calling from every flower
> The virtuous sweets.
> Our thighs packed with wax, our mouths with honey,
> We bring it to the hive, and like the bees,
> Are murdered for our pains.

And it is not only honey-gathering that is of such antiquity; the Bronze Age was familiar with the *cire perdue* method of casting, and the wax used seems to be the product of the bee. There is a curious reference to bees in Herodotus, who says that the country beyond the Ister (which we call the Danube) is impassable, owing to the swarms of bees; modern scholars say that he must have meant mosquitoes.

The Bible is in no doubt. 'My son, eat thou honey', says *Proverbs*, 'because it is good', but honey has been admired for purposes far removed from eating; Alexander was embalmed in it, for instance. After all, sugar has been long known (though not nearly so long as honey), but its widespread use is of fairly recent date; most of the centuries have preferred honey, a most sensible attitude. I have heard tell that Drambuie incorporates honey, but I have never tried it.

Bees, of course, are held up for our emulation as the most industrious of all creatures, and have been revered for their wisdom. In some bee cultures, a black ribbon is tied to the hives when their owner dies, and in others the bees are solemnly told of his death.

Among the most wonderful of all books of natural history is Karl von Frisch's *The Dancing Bees*; when I first picked it up, more than twenty years ago, I had little interest in bees and none in bee-keeping, but by the time I finished it, two rapt and unbroken hours later, I was looking out of the window on to another world. Frisch must have been a marvellous man; in more than half a century of bee-study, he made a vast range of contributions to the knowledge of his bombinating little friends, starting in 1915 with his discovery that, contrary to the then settled belief that bees are unable to distinguish colours, they are very substantially dependant on colour for their choice of flowers to forage among, and for orientation. The words with which he chides the old conviction are a model of what a scientific attitude should be (but too often isn't), and says more about the sweetness of his own character than the sweetness of an entire hive:

If we use excessively elaborate apparatus to examine simple natural phenomena Nature herself may escape us. This is what happened some forty-five years ago [he was writing in 1927] when a distinguished scientist, studying the colour sense of animals in his laboratory, arrived at the definite and apparently well-established conclusion that bees were colour-blind.

It was this occasion which first caused me to embark on a close study of their way of life; for once one got to know, through work in the field, something about the reaction of bees to the brilliant colour of flowers, it was easier to believe that a scientist had come to a false conclusion than that Nature had made an absurd mistake.

Frisch went on to discover the 'language' of the bees, unsuspected before he came on the scene; he describes the 'dance' that a foraging bee performs on returning to the hive, a meticulously choreographed ballet that gives her sisters an exact geographical fix on the source of provender that she has found. There is, indeed, little modern knowledge of the bee that Frisch did not either reveal or add to, and the reverence with which he approached the subject must have had a great bearing on his ability to discover so much more about it.

I do not remember ever being stung by a bee, though I did once meet a wandering queen, and made myself scarce before the swarm arrived; apiarists insist that a bee will not sting wantonly, but I was taking no chances.

There are many millions of bees in this country, which is not surprising in view of the fact (which is) that in a normal hive there will be quite 50,000 adult bees. Only the other day, bee rustlers stole well over a million from a bee-keeper in Norfolk, who observed, rather pertinently, that they must have been stolen by an expert, 'because no one else would have been brave enough'.

The only negative attitude to bees I know of is the Roman belief that a swarm of bees was a presage of disaster; just before the battle of Pharsalus, Pompey was making the appropriate sacrifice when a swarm settled on the altar; he went on to fatal defeat by Julius Caesar.

Today, it seems, the wax is on the other thigh; it is bad news for the bees when officials of the Department of the Environment are swarming. I hope the bees sting them all, on the nose, ears, knees and bum for a start. If the officials have enough sense, which is unlikely, they will withdraw the Green Paper, and replace it with a Honey-Coloured Paper on which they will write out one thousand times: The bee is not a pest.

The Times May 4th, 1987

'Tis pride that pulls the country down

M R TERRY WOGAN, already justly famous for inviting me
to display my knees to the nation in close-up, is the
subject of a thoughtful article in *The Listener*; it is now two
years since his television talk show started on BBC1, and the
writer, Mr David Berry, has come to some conclusions
about it. These conclusions seemed to me so remarkable
that I promptly came to several of my own, and I think it is
worth revealing them to my readers today, as once I did my
knees.

Mr Berry, after remarking on Wogan's popularity (he does
not scorn it), argues that the success of the programme 'has
come at a price', and it is this price, which he plainly believes is
too high, that forms the substance of his criticism of Wogan,
and mine of him.

It is a long time before we discover just what Wogan's crime
is. It is not that he behaves badly to his guests; on the contrary,
Mr Berry rightly commends mine host's invariable courtesy
and his skill at putting potentially nervous visitors at their ease.
Nor does Wogan have any political bias; nor does he favour
among his guests BBC stars over ITV ones. All in all, he is 'a
likeable bloke'.

Nevertheless, there is the Price of Wogan to be considered.
We learn that the guests on the show come over as the kind of
people 'whom viewers would welcome as neighbours or
friends . . . Voyeurism is replaced by curiosity, hatred by
admiration, envy and resentment at success by a good-natured
respect for the successful . . . despite conflicts of race or sex
or class . . . Britain emerges as still essentially one nation.

Despite the country's decline, there is still much in the British character we can celebrate.'

Wogan 'can see from the outside the desire of the British public to escape from present uncertainties back to what made Britain great: the fortitude and modesty of her people. Only an Irishman could see this and . . . gently mock it in a way which comes across to the British viewer not as an attack but as a celebration.'

And at last, in the penultimate sentence, the worst is revealed: Wogan 'has built a rapport with viewers by confirming our need, amid the challenge of other cultures, to be proud to be British.'

String the bastard up, that's what I say; Wogan's popularity and success have clearly been earned by painting a wholly spurious picture of Britain. It must be said that Mr Berry's case is put forward in quiet and civilized tones; he does not sneer at Wogan or at those whom Wogan is thus leading astray. All the same, his view seems to me to be nonsense, and nonsense of a peculiarly characteristic kind – characteristic, that is, of a section of our society which is unable to come to terms with the dramatic changes in Britain's view of herself that have taken place in the past few years.

Nobody but a lunatic would deny that there are many things wrong with this country; sloth, obstinacy and cowardice on both sides of industry, a rising tide of political as well as physical violence and intolerance, a level of public lying for which we would have to go back many decades to find a precedent, the decay of ancient and essential institutions, the manifest inadequacy of so many of our leaders and potential leaders, together with the more obvious and visible problems such as unemployment, poverty, crime, greed, bigotry and Law Officers – these are but a few of the most persistent and serious of the problems from which Britain is suffering.

They will not be quickly or easily cured. But the view that Mr Berry puts modestly forward, and which others put forward more stridently and more politically, suggests that Wogan's crime is to disguise the fact that the country is done for, that mutual hatred is (in some mouths *should be*) the norm, that we are in the throes of an undeclared civil war (indeed several at once), that the desire to celebrate what was once great about Britain is a regressive infantilism, and that the pride in being British is an embarrassing folly at best, and at worst wicked.

There is some support for this view; the municipal authorities at Rochdale have just denounced the painting of the Union Jack on the sides of local taxicabs as 'racist'. Even among many of those who are convinced that the wretched country's up the flue, Rochdale's action might be thought a trifle extreme; but a less clearly daft equivalent can be found even in the most respectable circles.

Yet it seems to me that the nostalgia is on the other foot; the working classes (and does not the very phrase reek of mothballs?) *no longer know their place*. That, of course, is what the squire and his relations used to think, but the meaning of the words has changed dramatically.

The 'place' of the workers, in the eyes of those who claim to know better than the workers themselves what is good for them, is to form a resentful mass of downtrodden and effectively disfranchised proles, who believe, or who can be persuaded to believe, that there is no point in their hoping for anything better than their present lot, because the rich will never let them rise in the world. But in order to keep that reservoir of disaffection topped up, those who know best must constantly strive to limit the horizons of those who fill it.

As I have so often said, the only power the trade union bosses have is the power to keep their followers poor. That power is now being eroded at an astonishing speed, but before it began to crumble it was a symbol of what was wrong with the people known as 'organized labour'. What was wrong was that they were denied anything to aspire to – not, now, by the rich man in his castle, but by the shop steward at the gate. As their forebears had believed that the hierarchies of class, power and money were the natural order of things, so *they* accepted for decades the newer denial of their aspirations by those who claimed to speak for them; this in turn became the modern version of the natural order of things. Suddenly they began to awake to the realization that it was *not* the natural order of anything, but an irrelevance and a bluff, which could be brushed aside without the smallest difficulty. They began to brush; and found the experience to their liking.

Why do you suppose that when the present government gave the tenants of council houses the right to buy the roof over their heads (and on advantageous terms) the Labour Party, and its local government arm, screamed bloody murder? Why, having vowed to stop, indeed to reverse, this dreadful traffic, did they subsequently, and with ill grace, find themselves obliged to accept it? The answer to the first question is that Labour politicians saw their own power, parallel to that of the union *capi*, endangered; the answer to the second is that, to their horror, rage *and astonishment*, they found that it was popular among the very people whose unquestioning allegiance they had so long enjoyed.

I do not know who coined the term 'popular capitalism', but it is a good one, and describes something of immense importance. Never mind the floats of BT, British Gas, TSB; the revelation was what happened to British Airways. For months before The Day, there were warnings that this one was not like the others, that amateurs should steer clear, that it was a high-risk business, that the institutions would scoop the lot and that that would be better all round for everybody. Sid didn't listen; in the last few days of the campaign he stormed the *guichets* to get his couple of hundredworth. For Sid had seen his neighbours, friends and workmates getting a slice of the earlier sales, and had determined that he was not going to be left behind.

Good luck to him. But not just generalized good luck; he is demonstrating that Wogan is right, and Wogan's critics wrong. For him, Britain *is* still one nation, and a nation to be proud of; for him, 'envy and resentment at success' has indeed been replaced 'by a good-natured respect for the successful' (not least because he now wants to be one of the successful himself); for him, it is indeed matter for 'celebration' that Britain is looking again to 'what made Britain great – the fortitude and modesty of her people'.

What has surprised many, horrified some, and presumably driven Mr Jeremy Seabrook almost to distraction, is that this movement is outwardly expressed in economic terms. Those who were once assured – by those who insisted on representing them – that it would always be their fate to be poor have now realized that they do not have to accept that fate. Mr Eric Hammond's merry men are in the van of that realization, of course, and have been putting it into effect for years; but a huge wave is building up, to crash on the shore very soon, as more and more people aspire to that which they had so long been told was beyond them.

And this is the precise moment at which Mr Roy Hattersley comes out with a plan for *equality*, the eternal enemy of prosperity for the very people in whose name the egalitarians claim to speak! That, you may say, is a far cry from Wogan. I disagree; Wogan does indeed represent those values, those attitudes, those aspirations which were so politely put down by Mr Berry and which elsewhere, amid foaming hatred, are proclaimed evil. But in doing so, he is a prophet, and more truly embodies the future of a Britain proud of herself than those who declare, with relish, that there is nothing to be proud of in Britain, and that those who feel such pride are enemies of the people.

The Times February 17th, 1987

Vice versus

S OME TIME IN the early 1980s, Mr Tony Harrison, one of the finest and deepest poets now writing in English (he is in addition our leading translator of dramatic verse, with versions of *Le Misanthrope* and the *Oresteia* that have never been bettered and probably never will be), was in the habit of making time to visit his parents' grave whenever (he no longer lived near the cemetery) he had to change trains in the area. On one such visit, he found that the cemetery had been desecrated by skinheads, who had sprayed aerosolled obscenities – though not, as we shall see, only obscenities – on the head-stones and monuments, including the grave where his parents lay.

This gave him a shock; it also, however, became the seed of what later flowered into one of the most powerful, profound and haunting long poems of modern times; some 3,500 words in 112 four-line stanzas, rhyming ABAB. The poem is a meticulously controlled yell of rage and hope combined, a poisoned dart aimed with deadly precision at the waste of human potential, shaped by a master poet with a rich and instinctive feel for the language, a penetrating eye that misses nothing it looks on, and an exceptionally ingenious capacity for using innocent word-play to make a telling case. The poem was published in the *London Review of Books*, and later in an anthology of his poetry; his verse in general, and this poem in particular, has received the highest commendation from a very wide range of critics and fellow poets.

The poem is called *v*. Just that; *v*. The v stands for versus; it is the symbol that links football clubs to their opponents of the

week, and since the graveyard graffiti were spray-painted by
supporters of Leeds United, the theme recurred throughout
the area of desecration. Mr Harrison's use of it, however, is far
wider; he uses the v as a symbol of division, as he uses the
United of the football club as a symbol of harmony. Let him
speak in his own words:

> These vs are all the versuses of life
> from LEEDS v. DERBY, Black/White
> and (as I've known to my cost) man v. wife,
> Communist v. Fascist, Left v. Right,
> class v. class as bitter as before,
> the unending violence of US and THEM,
> personified in 1984
> by Coal Board MacGregor and the NUM,
> Hindu/Sikh, soul/body, heart v. mind,
> East/West, male/female, and the ground
> these fixtures are fought on's man, resigned
> to hope from his future what his past
> > has never found.

The poem is a threnody; for his dead parents, for the 'skins'
who have deadened themselves, for all the wasted hopes of the
world. It is written in fire, and the fuel is a monolithic
integrity; Mr Harrison is not only a poet of consummate gifts,
but evidently (I have not had the pleasure of his direct
acquaintance) a man of exceptional quality.

So much by way of introduction; now for what this is all
about. The befouled cemetery, strewn with empty beer cans,
bore also in graffiti form words other than those connected
with the skinheads' favourite team. Obscenities (have you
ever noticed how few they are?) were repeated incessantly
throughout the burial ground – as, indeed, they are repeated
on any available bit of wall, derelict building, underpass or
other structure wherever two or three skins are gathered
together.

Now the words in question, though on the whole they are
not used in polite society, or for that matter in society

sufficiently literate to express itself more eloquently, are known, with their meanings, to everyone in the country except *very* young children. They are, however, subject to a strict taboo; not the taboo which simply excludes them from most civilized discourse, but a much stranger form, which is based on the conviction that, first, the words are *not* known to anyone other than habitual users of them, and that, second, if they are spoken in ordinary conversation they may provoke no more than distaste, but if they are published, either physically in a newspaper or verbally on television or radio, they will have generally unspecified but very terrible consequences, which will have the effect of undermining all moral standards and restraints, leading in turn to a state of affairs in which the very sheep in their pens and the spaniels in their kennels will not be safe from even the most extreme forms of depravity, while as for the au pair – but a veil must be drawn somewhere.

The taboo has one subsidiary form which is actually odder than the basic theme. If the words are printed with only their initial letters, followed by asterisks or dashes ('F★★★', say, or 'Sh—'), they are at once and entirely robbed of their dreadful power, and may be read by the most sensitive souls without harm or danger. (No one has ever been able to explain this phenomenon; come to think of it, no one has ever been able to explain the main taboo, either.)

We return to Mr Harrison. In his poem, he uses these words very freely in two distinct modes. The first is, so to speak, quotation; he records the spattering of the words amid the graves. The second is in the form of an imaginary dialogue, conceived as the skins' answer to his implied rebuke, in which they express themselves as best they can – the best being, because of their limited vocabulary, with a profusion of the words in question. As, for instance:

> Aspirations, cunt! folk on t'fucking dole
> 'ave got about as much scope to aspire
> above the shit they're dumped in, cunt, as coal
> aspires to be chucked on t'fucking fire.

Yer've given yerself toffee, cunt. Who needs
yer fucking poufy words. Ah write mi own.
Ah've got mi work on show all over Leeds
like this UNITED 'ere on some sod's stone.

The scene now shifts to Channel Four, which has
announced its intention of broadcasting the whole poem, read
by Mr Harrison himself, on November 4 at 11 pm. To hear a
poet of such talent read a poem of such quality will be a rare
and memorable experience; I shall ensure that I see the
programme.

So, I hope, will anyone who despairs of modern poetry; so,
inevitably, will be many who think (rightly, for all I can say)
that they might get a thrill from hearing impolite words on
television. But so, alas, will the inglorious company of the
smut-hounds, the book-burners, the sniffers-out of words and
expressions that awake (as well as their prurience) both their
alarm at, and their fascination with, such terms.

Most of them have not waited for the broadcast, nor have
they thought it necessary to read the poem before denouncing
it. In addition to the usual dial-a-quote MPs and Mrs Whitehouse (oozing self-righteousness as usual), a wholly factitious
campaign has sprung up, demanding the cancellation of the
programme (which is no more likely to have been seen by the
demanders than the denouncers). In particular, the *Daily Mail*
covered most of its front page the other day with a headline
reading 'TV FOUR-LETTER POEM FURY' (in newspaper
parlance such words as 'fury' and 'storm', used in that context,
signal to the knowledgeable that the entire campaign is spurious), and as the terrible hour approaches, we may expect
them to intensify their imaginary indignation.

Here I pause, to peach. I have heard the editor of the *Daily
Mail*, Sir David English (a very parfit gentil knight, too!) say
'Fuck'. He did not say it loudly, nor with great emphasis, and I
think he looked round first to see whether there were any ladies
within earshot, but say it he did. (In all fairness, I must add that
I have used the word myself, but many years ago Sir David

and I both worked at the *Daily Express*, so perhaps I picked it up from him then.)

Oh, asterisk, dash and blank; have we really got to go through all this yet again? Must the ghost of Mervyn Griffith-Jones rise gibbering in its winding-sheet to demand that our wives and servants should be protected from such things? Is Ken Tynan (what a fine, honest and beautifully written biography his widow has just published, incidentally) to be hauled out of Purgatory to testify to the fact that he was the first man to say 'Fuck' on television, and that the world did not come to an end because of it, either at once or gradually? Do we not show ourselves as a nation of laughing-stocks when one of our most outstanding literary artists proposes to read one of his most telling creations in public and is greeted by screams of hysterical outrage from people who have almost certainly never heard of him, and have probably not read any poem written later than Wordsworth on the daffodils?

Well, if we must, we must. For my part, I think I have made my position fairly clear, and all I need to add is that I hope Channel Four will stand firm against the Yahoos. And, perhaps, that Mr Harrison's *Selected Poems* is published by Penguin, is in print, costs £4.95, includes *v*., and demonstrates, far more conclusively than any article of mine, what squalid nonsense the campaign against him is.

The Times October 19th, 1987

Dust to dust

WHY IS THE MACABRE farce on Saddleworth Moor permitted to continue? Whose decision was it to suspend
the operation for the winter and resume in the spring? Who, if
anybody, is in charge, and what does he think he is doing? An
MP has described the exercise as 'an expensive publicity stunt',
but it is not even clear what it is supposed to be publicizing,
apart from the fact, fairly well known already, that there are
enough ghouls around to put a degree in necrophilia on the
curriculum of half our universities.

So many lies have been told that it is now impossible to
discover when and how the idea of an expedition to the moors
arose. What Myra Hindley's motives were when she suggested or agreed to the visit, and what the police supposed
could be achieved by it, I do not know; it is inconceivable (or at
any rate it should be) that the Home Office was not consulted,
and although there is practically nothing too disgraceful for
that horrible place to connive at, I find it difficult to believe
that even a Home Office minister could have authorized those
pointless and distasteful happenings.

In the first place, there is not, and never was, the slightest
chance that Miss Hindley, except by an accident which could
have happened to anybody, would have been able to find the
bodies of other murdered children even if she had wanted to.
You do not have to be an Ettrick shepherd to know that on
such bleak and forbidding ground, where a walker could get
lost in ten minutes, the landscape is such that any hundred
square yards looks like any other. Dips and gulleys, mounds
and stream-beds, wander in and out of one another, criss-

crossing and combining, until the very rabbits must have difficulty in finding their way home.

Furthermore, in the 20 years that have passed since the children were buried there (if, that is, they were, and we have only the word of the murderers to go on), any such landscape, even if every detail as she last saw it was fresh in Miss Hindley's mind, will have changed beyond any chance of recognition. Vegetation alters, trees wither or fall or grow, rocks tumble or sink into the ground, bushes die or are uprooted by trippers and vandals; the murderess and the band of PC Plods who took her to the moor could have been standing on the spot where the bodies were buried without any of them having the least notion that they were doing so.

Nor is that all. Long before the prisoner was brought to the moor, the police had begun digging up bits of it. Possibly they fancied themselves as amateur dowsers, and went horsing around with hazel-twigs, but if not, with what pattern they dug, and what reason they imagined they had to dig *here* rather than *there*, has not so far been explained, and since the police have carried out the operation in impenetrable secrecy, apart from a fortnight spent announcing it in advance and the 40 television cameras, 400 journalists and 14,000 spectators milling around the scene, we are left with nothing but guesswork.

Then there is the legal side of the business. Opinions have been solemnly canvassed as to what would or should follow, as far as the law is concerned, if bodies were to be found. Could the two convicted murderers be charged with further crimes and, if convicted, sentenced to life imprisonment? It seems that the answer to both questions is yes, but nobody has yet explained what purpose would be served by staging a new production of the original trial or by sending to prison people who are already there.

This shoddy Grand Guignol will not find so much as the bone of a little finger unless Plod, gazing up at the fleets of helicopters taking pictures of him, should stumble and fall into a hole that turns out to be a grave. Nor will it contribute in any way to the question of what should be done with Myra

Hindley, let alone suggest any general principles about dealing with such people. The show should never have begun, and the curtain should be rung down upon it, in perpetuity, *now*, except for a one-clause bill, to be pushed through Parliament as soon as possible, making it a serious offence for any policeman ever to appear on television.

But all the foregoing still leaves out the most important – the *only* important – lesson to be learnt from this chilling series of official blunders. What good purpose could have been served even if bodies had been found? Ignore the fact that the bodies by now would be crumbling skeletons; they would still be human remains, and it might be possible for them to be identified. Suppose they were; suppose we could match a name to each pitiful heap of dust so cruelly abused 20 years before. I must yet ask: *cui bono?*

The unassuaged grief of the surviving relatives of the murderers' victims is not to be tampered with; no comment. The desire for revenge which still possesses some of them must be handled with great care by us who have not known a loved life so brutally cut short. I believe, and always shall, that a thirst for vengeance, however justified, is the most tragic and stultifying cul-de-sac that human beings can enter. But then, I have never had such cause, or anything approaching it, to think thoughts of revenge. I have met Jews whose every relative died in the Holocaust, yet who, though they can never expunge the pain from their hearts, have cleansed themselves utterly from hate. But no one can demand that others should rise to such heights of wisdom and charity, and sickening though I found the picture in which a relative of one of the Moors victims was brandishing a knife and longing to use it on Myra Hindley, it would be pointless, as well as intolerably presumptuous, for me to rebuke him for such feelings.

I am emphatically of the opinion that whatever pleas there were, from the relatives, for the moors to be dug over, with or without Miss Hindley in attendance, should have been kindly but firmly denied, and I would remain of that opinion even if the ensuing events had not degenerated into a repulsive peepshow. For is not an unmarked grave in soil troubled only by wind and rain, storm and snow, as good as any plot in a crowded cemetery? 'The trumpet shall sound, and the dead shall be changed.' If that is true, be sure that it is true for those whose last resting place is unknown to mortal man, just as much as for those who lie in marble and the gilded monuments of princes, or beneath the simplest moss-grown slab in a churchyard. 'Are not five sparrows sold for two farthings, and not one of them is forgotten before God?' If *that* is true, is it likely that children done vilely to death will be ignored in the final reckoning, wherever they are buried?

Whatever happens, or should happen, to Myra Hindley and Ian Brady, their victims can gain nothing from it. So much is obvious; less obvious but no less true is that the victims' families cannot gain by it either. The dead need no advice; would that someone could persuade the living that they have amply discharged their duty to the dead, even the missing dead, and can now throw off the chains with which they have hitherto bound themselves to dwell in the tragic past of death, and turn their faces towards life and the future.

The Times December 22nd, 1986

Divided they stand

I HAVE LONG BEEN of the opinion that, in an age of mass-circulation newspapers, the greatest problem facing the Church of England is the fact that 'vicars' rhymes with 'knickers'. Having sat through the whole of yesterday's debate, in the General Synod, on homosexuality and allied matters, I begin to believe that the Church now confronts a greater challenge.

To be met on the front steps of Church House with a placard reading 'Happy Gays are here again' is one thing; but to listen to an array of ordained clergymen and devout laity chatting happily and knowledgeably about perversion, oral intercourse, condoms, genitals, and masturbation, is to wonder where it will all end. The Rev Tony Higton is in no doubt; it will end in a rain of fire upon the modern Cities of the Plain. Others were not so sure.

As I looked down upon the assembled ranks of the Established Church, there was Durham, looking as always as though he was about to break into song, and not only song but dance as well; there was London, in turn giving the impression that he knows exactly what Cranmer felt when he heard the executioner ask if anybody had a light; there was Chester, straight out of the more reflective pages of Trollope; and over there was a glorious figure, the kind of man that England must cherish for ever because when his kind die out England will no longer be England, tabling an amendment urging all Christians – clergy and laity, men and women – to be mindful of the teaching of Tertullian, Jerome, Clement of Alexandria and John Chrysostom, and practice lifelong virginity, on the

ground that these Fathers were unanimously of the opinion
that 'an orderly sex-life is inferior to no sex-life at all'.

At that point, Mr Peter Tatchell materialized behind me like
Banquo's Ghost, and thrust into my hand a leaflet (surely he,
of all people, ought to be able to spell 'harass') condemning
'right-wing Christian fundamentalists' for 'stirring up hatred
against lesbians and gay men'. The Church of England was
now complete, its ranks augmented by its eccentrics and its
enemies, and battle could begin.

And then the wonder grew. The obvious comparison for
this debate was Parliament, but anybody present who has had
any experience of the legislature discussing a contentious
measure will instantly have noticed the difference. Missing
entirely, even from the remarks of the harshest speakers, were
the characteristic stigmata of the House of Commons being
serious: dishonesty, vulgarity and illiteracy. An observer with
any sensibility must have been struck by the pain, care and
charity with which the Church by Law Established went
about deciding whether homosexual acts were or were not in
all circumstances sinful, and if not, or even if so, what should
be done about them.

No less apparent was the dignity of expression with which
the opinions were delivered, and perhaps the most remarkable
difference of all is that the Church spoke clearly, freshly and
with a scrupulous adherence to the belief that words matter,
and matter most when important things are to be said.

But that leaves still to be considered the content of what was
said. The motion before the Synod invited the Church to
declare

> that sexual intercourse should take place only between a
> man and a woman who are married to each other; that
> fornication, adultery and homosexual acts are sinful in
> all circumstances; that Christian leaders are called to be
> exemplary in all spheres of morality, including sexual
> morality, as a condition of being appointed to or remaining
> in office;

and in addition called upon the Church

> to show Christ-like compassion to those who have fallen
> into sexual sin, encouraging them to repent and receive
> absolution, and offering the ministry of healing to all
> who suffer physically or emotionally as a result of such
> sin.

Now that must be as unambiguous as a one-eyed man could
wish. With the Rev Tony Higton you know where you are;
but where is everybody else?

The Synod, to be sure, was in more dilemmas than one, and
the most important could not be discussed. It is the obvious
truth that the country as a whole, homosexual, heterosexual
and total abstainers alike, not excluding the Church, will take
no notice at all of anything the Synod says or does or thinks or
is. Most of the population leads an entirely secular life; most of
the Church has an entirely secular attitude to such matters as
sexual morals; the result was that the debate was taking place
in a balloon, floating free.

Yet as a record of a Church wrestling with its conscience, its
teaching, its founders, its history and its place in Britain today,
the debate could hardly be improved upon. Mr Higton's was
the most extreme voice raised, and his evidence was largely
anecdotal; but he had a shrewd grasp of the relevant theology,
and it was going to take a powerful grip to wrest it from his
hand. The Bishop of London was not a likely candidate for the
attempt, but to everybody's astonishment it was he who,
speaking right at the beginning of the debate, doused Mr
Higton's fire and cooled his brimstone. Dr Leonard resound-
ingly endorsed Mr Higton's view of sexual morality, but he
would have nothing to do with excluding the sinful clergymen
from office, and in knocking that argument down, he bowled
over a good many more as well.

From then on, it was clear that Mr Higton would be heavily
defeated. But that did not rob the debate of its fascination. The
Archbishop of Canterbury tiptoed across the minefield,
clearly thinking that he preferred the ones he had to negotiate

when he was an army officer in the Second World War; the Rev Malcolm Johnson, leading the assault against the motion, gave a most exemplary demonstration of what Christian charity entails; the Bishop of Chester, who put forward the compromise which ultimately, and easily, carried the day, eschewed fine phrases for calm reason; Mr Williams refused to say that homosexual acts in a stable relationship are right, and added that he would not say they are wrong; the Archdeacon of Leicester offered solid wisdom wrapped in the finest irony; the Bishop of Chichester, in the shortest contribution of the day, denounced tabloid witch-hunting with so fiery an eloquence that I instantly thought of his great predecessor in that see, George Bell; the man who was in favour of lifelong virginity withdrew his motion amid relieved applause; and only two speakers said that the eyes and ears of the nation and the world were upon the Synod. In Parliament it would have been fifty.

I emerged with a wondering but intense admiration for this amazing body. The Church of England, facing for once a real problem, predictably and inevitably fudged it. But in the very act of fudging, it spoke with tongues. It will be denounced, from within and without its ranks, for both cowardice and brutality; but the result was a victory for all the best qualities of this country. The Church is as puzzled, worried and uncertain as the rest of us; but in a strange way, it gave us all a lead, if only by telling us that to be puzzled, worried and uncertain is the lot of all thinking people, and it is no shame to confess as much. The Church of England – loving, muddled, holy, generous, wise, humble, well-meaning, daft, forgetful, brave, honest and absurd – is certainly not all right. But it is, emphatically, All Right.

At the next session (I couldn't stay for it, alas) the Synod was to debate the motion:

This Synod expresses its thanks to Mr and Mrs Spagnoli and the staff of the Vitello D'Oro Restaurant for their service to its members and staff over the years and hopes that they are able to continue their services to the Synod in any new location.

I rest my case.

The Times November 12th, 1987

Index

Note: Theatres etc. in London are entered directly; elsewhere they are to be found under location.

n = note